Brendan James Murray is an award-winning author and teacher. He has twice received National Literary Awards from the Fellowship of Australian Writers for his short stories, and his first book, *The Drowned Man*, was joint winner of the Ned Kelly Award for Best True Crime in 2017. His second book, the critically acclaimed *Venom*, was featured on the ABC's *Conversations* program as part of the 'Best of 2018' series. Brendan lives with his wife, Greta, and continues to teach full-time.

Facebook: Brendan James Murray – author
(bjamesmurrayauthor)
Instagram: bjmurrayauthor
Twitter: bjmurrayauthor

Also by Brendan James Murray

The Drowned Man: A True Story of Life, Death and Murder
on *HMAS Australia*

Venom: The Heroic Search for Australia's Deadliest Snake

Brendan James Murray

The
School

The ups and downs
of one year in
the classroom

PICADOR
Pan Macmillan Australia

Pan Macmillan acknowledges the Traditional Custodians of country throughout Australia and their connections to lands, waters and communities. We pay our respect to Elders past and present and extend that respect to all Aboriginal and Torres Strait Islander peoples today. We honour more than sixty thousand years of storytelling, art and culture.

First published 2021 in Picador by Pan Macmillan Australia Pty Ltd
1 Market Street, Sydney, New South Wales, Australia, 2000

 A catalogue record for this
book is available from the
National Library of Australia

Typeset in 11.9/16 pt Adobe Garamond Regular by Post Pre-press Group
Printed by IVE

The opening paragraph of Part One, Chapter 10 (page 64) is taken from the film *Dead Poets Society*, Weir, P (1989). Buena Vista Pictures Distribution.

The closing paragraph of Part Three, Chapter 1 (page 213) is taken from 'The Left Man' by Liam Davison, from *Collected Stories*, Davison, L (2001). University of Queensland Press.

The author and the publisher have made every effort to contact copyright holders for material used in this book. Any person or organisation that may have been overlooked should contact the publisher.

Aboriginal and Torres Strait Islander people should be aware that this book may contain images or names of people now deceased.

For my students

AUTHOR'S NOTE

THIS BOOK IS a true story. However, names and details have been changed to protect identities, and some characters are composites. While the narrative takes the form of a single school year, the characters and situations have been drawn from across time and from a variety of schools.

Prologue

The ghost children

Schools are haunted.

Ghost children flitter and lurk and whisper, banished by neither the tolling of electric bells nor the trembling of fluorescent tubes: no latest initiative, no departmental 'best practice' will exorcise them. They are shades of the living and the dead, of the absent and the present. Some carry warnings, others pleas for wrongs to be made right. Others are simply *there*, wordless and oppressive. Your dreams are occasionally disturbed by their presence.

A few are ghosts in the traditional sense, aligned with the Banquo of my senior Literature class.

I taught Bevan Cowley in Year 10 English some years ago. He had a narrow face and sullen, pencil-lead eyes. At least half the time he was absent, and when he did attend he was usually late, bringing his backpack as though anticipating the need for a sudden escape. Some students have an aura around them like a gas leak waiting for a spark, and that was Bevan: cold silences, muttered expletives, his corner of the room ringed by empty seats nobody dared fill. He had no social connections and no apparent desire to build any. Still, I liked Bevan. He did not work but he listened to me. Once, counselling him after a confrontation with another teacher, I had said in a kind of desperation, *I'm trying to help you*. His vacant, window-gazing stare had shifted to me then, and he'd replied, *I know*. I remember the sympathy in his voice – for me, I thought.

He did not finish Year 10. In fact, he had spent very little time at The School before I taught him, only a few months as a Year 7. Students like Bevan are often itinerant, dragged this way and that by the unpredictable currents of their family situations.

It was years later that I learnt Bevan was dead. He had overdosed in a Melbourne flat at just twenty, surrounded by young men and women too high or too ignorant to notice the silence once filled by his breathing. I never saw any of this, of course, but nonetheless the scene fell upon me: dried sick, charred spoons, the cold. Bevan.

And I was responsible. In part, at least. That's how I felt when I heard the news and how I feel now. I had an opportunity, a fleeting window during which I might have shown him another way of being. But I failed. I didn't see enough, hear enough, say enough. I made too few calls home; I didn't push when the calls I did make went largely unanswered. I wasn't hard enough on him; I was too hard on him. I focused too much on failed attempts to turn him into a reader; I should have tried *harder* to get him reading, should have suggested Bukowski or Burgess or Welsh, something that might have appealed to his own renegade nature.

But I didn't. And he dropped out and wandered off into the dark.

His ghost was not apparent for a long time, but eventually it began to make itself known. There were the initials carved on a table in a woodwork room. Later, somebody happened upon an old detention slip, unsigned, mouldering in a dented filing cabinet. One afternoon, I was scrounging through a stack of used manila folders when I was confronted by his wraith in black Sharpie: *Bevan Cowley, 10F.* The folder was sketched with ill-formed figures – sportspeople, I thought – and breathed with the stink of decaying paper. It smelt of history. Inside was a disorganised scattering of incomplete worksheets. His hand-writing was large and awkward.

In that quiet, late-afternoon room I felt his presence. I said aloud that I was sorry. There was no reply.

So Bevan's ghost persists.

But there are others, including the strange shades of the living departed. These are the students who are now adults somewhere out in the world. Like Bevan, they have left their presence behind in graffiti and forgotten books. A few exist in stories told by teacher and student alike. There's a strong oral tradition when it comes to schoolyard mythology. The stories are good and bad. It might have been a violent fight, or a gesture of kindness so profound that its warmth still lingers in the coldest of winter corridors.

Remember those ones, we often say. It's too easy to focus on the negative.

Some ghosts peer down from honour boards, medal cabinets, framed photographs. Carpe diem, Robin Williams whispered to his students in *Dead Poets Society*, but every real secondary teacher saw through the fiction. In Hollywood, teachers only ever have one class. We have four or five: maybe two Year 7s, a Year 9, a Year 11 and a Year 12. A hundred and twenty students, aged eleven to eighteen. Movie audiences aren't expected to keep track of that many characters, but we have to. You will find these pages cluttered with souls jostling for your attention. That is the reality of teaching.

But of all the ghosts, perhaps the most haunting are the ghosts of the present. Around each student hover spectres of what they have been and what they might still become.

'We've got to keep Dylan here,' I said to my principal recently. Dylan, only fourteen, was on the verge of expulsion. Transgressions too many to list; a child railing against a world that had been betraying him since birth. 'What will happen to the kid otherwise?'

And my principal – one of the good ones – had agreed. She and I could see the path forking before this child, one direction receding into murky gloom and the other to – what? To still more forks further down the road. But if we could keep steering him he might be alright, might grow into that spectral version of himself that hovered as a glinting possibility.

'We need to keep him here until he's old enough for work experience,' my principal said. 'Get him in the workforce. Get him out there. He could thrive.'

After that meeting I walked to my Year 9 class, wondering if Dylan would be there. The School wasn't the only authority deciding if he would attend; even more powerful was his own authority, essentially a total self-governance unfettered by any kind of parental control. I feared that Dylan could become another Bevan Cowley, but knew that Dylan at least had the advantage of academic capability. He was sharp, attentive, a good reader and a fluent writer. His opinions on the novels we studied were insightful, mature – perhaps a by-product of the traumas of his upbringing. And in that way he was a leader. When the Dylans and Bevans of this world participate in class, they bring everybody else along with them.

I stood at the door greeting them by name, a ritual established years ago after a colleague pointed out that it might be the first time they have heard it all day. Dylan was not there. When the rest of the students were inside, I hesitated in the corridor for a moment, looking into the fluorescent half-light of early morning. There was no sign of him. I knew if he didn't show in the next five minutes, he wouldn't come at all.

I skipped Dylan's name on the roll, hoping he might appear before I got to the end. How many lessons since we'd seen him? Two? Three? I wasn't sure, but knew it had been several. If he did come, I would need to work one-to-one with him for at least the first twenty minutes to get him caught up.

'Right. Has anybody seen Dylan?'

A stocky boy with close-cropped hair raised his hand. 'I seen him last night.'

Should I correct that? No. Not now. 'Yeah? Where was this?'

'At the skate park. He'll be there again tonight.'

All eyes in the room were on me. There are these moments in teaching, lingering, electric, where you know that what you say next will mean both nothing and everything. And it's not just the words: it's your body language, facial expression, and – more important than any of these things – your honesty.

'Well, tell him he's missed,' I said. 'I'd love to see him back in here.'

The lesson went on, a kind of absurd, workaday juxtaposition to the real human drama of Dylan's absence. The topic was homophones, of little real-world value to these students but an identified area of weakness in standardised testing that had to be addressed. I wrote the heading on the board and waited. It took less than a second.

'Homo!' First one boy, then another.

'This'll be up your alley, Mitch.'

'Fuck off. Sir, Cooper's the expert on this, can he take the class?'

I put down the whiteboard marker and folded my arms. 'No more of that language, Mitch. And definitely no more bigotry.' They picked up on my tone, sat back, silent but grinning. 'We wouldn't tolerate racism in here and we won't tolerate homophobia, either.'

'I was *joking*.'

'We're not at Clown College.'

I forged on, needing to quiet the boys every now and again. They weren't bad kids, and I'd seen kindness in them, and curiosity, and patience. But they were immature, and more naïve than they would ever admit with their streetwise banter. Their exposure to the world extended little further than our town boundary, and the walls of the local footy club.

The biggest problem was that they drowned out the girls. I looked at Layla, seated neat and silent in the front row. She was the type whose name every teacher learns last. It's a penance such students pay for their compliance.

'I want some more examples of homophones.'

Mitch didn't miss a beat. 'How about –'

'No no no.' I cut him off. 'Hands up.'

When Layla didn't budge, I pointed to her anyway. In a small voice she said, 'Know and no?'

'Exactly. Easy.'

We bounced around the room.

'Ate and eight.'

'Won and one.'

'Missed and mist.'

I wrote it on the whiteboard. *Missed and mist.*

The rest of that day I thought about Dylan. He was missed, but, of course, he was also *mist*, drifting beyond reach in some reality that overlapped only partly with my own. I remembered a fight he had been in recently, only the very end of which I had seen. For all his toughness Dylan had lost, wound up with a bloody lip and a sleeve torn clean from his jumper. Still though, he was not finished. He roared and swore and threatened, completely at the mercy of his inner chaos: feelings as old as the mountains in a body fourteen years new.

Later that day in our staff meeting his ghost hovered. I heard little of what was said, instead pondering absurd possibilities. I could go to the skate park myself – tell him in person that the class missed him. I could tell him about Bevan Cowley, about all the Bevan Cowleys of this world. But I knew that would be overstepping. I knew I couldn't do it.

Walking to my car that evening, I thought about Liam, my teacher of all those years ago. He occurs to me sometimes, and when he does the memory is always accompanied by a gulp of sadness and anger. The weight of that day was too heavy for thoughts of Liam, so I pushed them away, turned around and walked to my office.

The computer was five minutes in booting up. When it was ready I found Dylan's father's number and dialled it.

It rang out. Eventually there was a beep (no recorded message preceded the tone), and I took my chances.

'Hi, this is Brendan Murray from The School. I'm calling to express concern that Dylan has missed quite a few classes lately. It would be fantastic if you could give me a call so we can discuss strategies for keeping him engaged.'

Strategies for keeping him engaged. I hated the sound of

myself. Like a bureaucrat, not like a human being. Not like somebody who actually cared.

I drove home knowing that my message would never be answered. In fact, I never did see Dylan again after that day. He joined the legion of the ghosts.

Term One:
The end of summer

1

Carnival

IN THE HOT darkness of a summer night, a Ferris wheel lifts its gondolas high above the weeping chords of the carnival, so high that its occupants can see over the coastal banksias to the sea. That direction reveals only the white glow of the sand; without a moon the ocean is little more than a sighing void. Still the teenagers crane their necks, waiting. When the dial stops the gondolas swing and creak. Their wooden slats seem thin suddenly, the wire of their cages as insubstantial as spider webs. There is a sense of danger here, of risk. The air hums with an indefinable energy, something born of the juxtaposition of light and dark, frivolity and threat.

The carnival is less than a kilometre from The School. It opens for the duration of the Christmas holidays, and has done since the 1950s. All of us locals spent many summer nights there growing up.

In mid-December the first hints of that freedom come to Seadale in the form of deconstructed rides in huge trailers. We watch as they are unpacked, strange assortments of parasols, fibreglass characters and incomprehensible mechanisms. Before their arrival it is just the year-long loneliness of the

Ferris wheel, its steel supports howling with sea wind that goes unheard by all but those using the lot as a shortcut.

To us children in December, that carnival seemed as though it would last for eternity. Everything was infused with a strange magic, from the cheap prizes to the plastic clown heads whose gaping mouths gulped air thick with cigarette smoke. And though that magic may have been somewhat dispelled as we became teenagers, it nonetheless lingered in some altered form. Perhaps it was the danger: there were city kids at the carnival, we knew, kids who looked for fights, who carried knives; there were the ride operators with their hard stares and stained smiles; there was the thump of illegal fireworks on the beach nearby.

More than anything, though, that place and time was an antithesis to school. Those multi-coloured lights (all the brighter for the blackness of the surrounding night), the sickly sweet food, the ocean waiting in the hot morning – all of it contrasted so sharply with the cold rigidity of the classroom that the very existence of The School seemed impossible. Class was like the memory of a vaguely unpleasant dream. Tomorrow would be summer, and the day after that more summer, and the day after that still more. The only clock that mattered was the sun in the sky. If for an instant we disbelieved, we needed look no further than the exuberant spectacle of the carnival.

But gradually, inexorably, it came. The holidays ended. Driving past the carnival with our parents on some mundane errand, we would gape in horror at the deconstruction of the rides, and think, *No! Just one more week.* We felt even then that we hadn't known what we had until it was over.

And later, months later, we might glance for a moment at one of the cheap prizes we'd won, something dumped half-forgotten on a chest of drawers or beneath a bed. We might look at that relic, feel just a hint of its magic, and wonder if the summer past was the final time we would visit the carnival. We might wonder if, at last, we had grown too old.

2

What Jude was

A VIOLENT BULLY almost killed me when I was twelve years old. As a teacher, there are moments from your own childhood that stand out, that you remind yourself of again and again in your working life. For me, one such moment occurred in the charcoal-skied wind of a late afternoon, long after all the teachers had gone home for the day.

As a Year 7 I was meek, scrawny, bookish. All I wanted was to be a writer. On the holidays before beginning high school, one of my mother's friends had gifted me an old Remington typewriter, and I spent almost all of those six weeks sealed in my room, relentlessly snapping away at the keys. With each word I was emulating my heroes, striving to become Stephen King, Paul Jennings, RL Stine. It was not a lonely time, but one alive with possibility. I have distinct memories of that holiday: late nights, summer storms, the smell of old books and the ocean. More than anything though, I remember that typewriter. My parents were saints to endure its incessant rattling.

When I walked into class on the first day of school, my fingers were hard with calluses, and I proudly handed my teacher a stack of pages almost an inch thick.

Despite this enthusiasm, I was not naïve to the dangers of high school. In the closing days of the holidays – while we watched glumly as the carnies packed away their rides – my friends and I concocted nightmare fates awaiting us at The School.

'The older kids flush your head down the toilet,' Nick assured us.

'It would be hard to put a kid's head down a toilet,' somebody said. 'I mean, you could grab onto the edges. Thrash around.'

'You *have* to let them. If you don't they'll bash you. It's best to just let them do it and get it over with.'

Luke had an even darker imagination. 'Some of the seniors are drug dealers. To get you addicted they drag you behind the sheds and inject you with heroin. After that you come back for more.'

'Yeah,' Nick added. 'And you can get AIDS from it. They don't care as long as they're selling drugs.'

We never doubted these stories. Sometimes we invented them and forgot that we had; we believed our own lies and imagined school as a world of omnipresent violence. In those early days we skulked warily through the labyrinth of 1970s brickwork, uneven asphalt and dented plaster. Disadvantage was written into the very timber of the walls, and I found some of those walls unchanged when I returned to The School as a teacher almost twenty years later.

Exactly when the bully first noticed me, I couldn't say. I thought later that it might have started after a school assembly when I was presented with a writing award. He would have seen a slim, pale boy on stage, small for his age and refusing to look out into the crowd.

15

Jude was several years above me, so we shared no classes and had never spoken. I was aware of him, though – all my friends were, and many of the other Year 7s. He towered over all of us (and even many of the teachers) with a strange, broomstick-backed alertness as he loitered around the younger children. Today, it's common for students across year levels to congregate together, play sport, socialise, but at The School in the 1990s that was unusual. It marked Jude as odd, an outsider. He had few friends his own age, just a couple of other boys who mirrored his strangeness. Where they were awkward and guffawing, however, Jude was cold, silent. Shadows skulked perpetually beneath his eyes. I knew even then that these were born of something other than late-night video gaming or part-time work.

Despite the coastal beauty of our surroundings, the urban hinterland scabbing the coast was often a place of darkness. My own family struggled; our home was loving, but our car was pocked with rust holes, some big enough for my fist, and one year the Salvation Army delivered our Christmas gifts. I was lulled to sleep at night not by the sighing of waves but by the sighing of cars on the freeway. They passed barely fifteen metres from where my head rested on the pillow.

That was Seadale: a juxtaposition of beauty and poverty, foaming waves and housing commission accommodation. I understood that there were secrets hidden behind all that brick and weatherboard, behind the unmown lawns and cheap swing sets. Growing up, a friend's father had suicided, though my friend knew only that his dad had passed away. Often he told classmates that he did not know the details, and that his mother had promised to tell him 'when he was old enough'. I knew what had happened, even in primary school, because I'd overheard my parents discussing the tragedy late one night. Every time my friend raised the topic I would sit in a sick, miserable silence, struck by the sadness of it all and the adult gravity of my own knowledge.

Worse, a local toddler was one day beaten to death by his stepfather in a murder that gave rise to the mandatory reporting laws teachers follow today. My sister had been the same age as the victim's brother, and I had never understood why the kindergarten had blacked out his surname in their class photograph. I asked my mother at the time, but she would not tell me.

So I had a sense of what Jude's reality might have been like.

We all knew about bullies. That was kids' stuff. Namecalling, dackings, maybe the odd push or shove. Jude's two offsiders were bullies; Jude was something else. He prowled the school grounds, leading his friends by violent example. Always he targeted the most vulnerable Year 7s, the small, the quiet, the unathletic. I remember him lurching from a bush one recess and pouncing on my friend Ash, throwing him to the ground and then leaping astride him. Remarkably, a man walking past on the street witnessed this, jumped the fence and dragged Jude off.

'*What do you think you're doing?*' the man had cried, while Jude – almost a head-height taller than him – had laughed icily, turned and walked away.

So we avoided Jude as best we could, spending our time drawing cartoons in the library or sheltering in the relative safety of the so-called Year 7 Area. But we could not stay there forever, and when we ventured further we always kept an eye out for Jude.

One lunchtime, Jude saw us in the yard and said something to his offsider. That boy loped over, seized me around the neck, angled me headfirst towards the brick wall of a boiler room and took off at a gallop. I was dragged along with him, remarkably unafraid. I knew he would not drive my head into the bricks. If it had been Jude I would have been terrified, thrashing and screaming.

We stopped just before the wall. The boy's face was huge and leering. 'You realise I just saved your arse?' he asked.

Jude watched on, as bolt-upright as a colossal meerkat, dark-eyed and smiling.

I did not then know the word 'sadist', do not know even now if a child can be one. I think perhaps that they can't, but that the sadism of their parents can manifest in frightening schoolyard rituals.

Some time after that, my friends and I rounded a corner to be confronted by a bloody spectacle.

Three people were approaching us. In the centre was a teacher. To his right was Jude, vaguely smiling as the teacher gripped him by the arm; to his left was Beau, a Year 7 who always wore cheap jeans and had an awkward bowl haircut.

Beau's nose was destroyed. I remember it as a split, bloody fissure, a smear of black-red chaos that for a moment I could make no sense of. Jude must have attacked him only moments before, because blood cascaded down Beau's face, over his slack jaw, into his mouth and in horrible clotting comets down the front of his white school shirt. Behind the three of them was a trail of droplets as large and round as dollar coins.

It was then that we understood – *properly* under-stood – what Jude was.

I was engulfed by a sick, black fear. This wasn't the fear I felt when reading Stephen King novels, which was exciting and fun. This was something cold, heavy and primal, something that stole your appetite, distracted you in class, made the hair on your neck prickle at too sudden a noise behind you in the yard. Schools can be places of fear. It can hang in the classrooms and the yards, at the bus stops and in the throng of assemblies. As a teacher, I try to remember that.

Jude was not expelled. Expulsions – then and now – are rare. When a student is expelled from a government school, that school is expected to take on an expelled student from *another* school. Principals often decide, for better or worse, that it is better to keep a student they know, and for whom they have developed at least a few management strategies.

In Year 7, I would stay at The School later than most students because I caught the last bus, which left about an hour after the final bell. I would often wait in the library with a book, or proofread my own typewritten stories in some quiet corner.

That afternoon, I remember, was dim and cold. I was alone. It might have been a schoolyard in Chernobyl for all its grey, whispering menace. A stone wall ringed our hockey oval, and I was sitting there reading. I think it was about ten minutes before my bus was due to arrive when I saw Jude, far away on the other side of the schoolyard on his BMX, staring.

By the time I stood, he was already halfway towards me, legs pumping, head down. I remember his face being utterly expressionless. I hauled my schoolbag onto my back, picked up my book and braced for impact. At the last moment he pulled out of his charge, skidding the rear wheel so I was sprayed with clods of earth and grass.

I almost giggled with relief as he pedalled away and disappeared around the corner of a portable classroom. I had got off lightly – exceptionally lightly. I sat back down and resumed reading.

At some point in the next few minutes, I realised something was not right. I looked around the schoolyard. It was cold and wet and empty, a tapestry of brown leaves and litter. Some instinct, perhaps millennia old, told me I was in imminent danger, that Jude would return. I needed to hide until my bus arrived.

I packed my book, stood up and refitted my schoolbag. I started to walk back into the school itself, fearing that Jude might be waiting at the bus stop.

Then I saw him, far away in the late afternoon murk. His bike was gone, and he was marching towards me with his strange, straight-backed, dark-eyed malevolence.

He was adult-tall, probably twice my weight, athletic. I knew there was no point running.

3

New classes

TWENTY YEARS LATER and The School was much as I remembered it. Some parts had been rearranged, some buildings bulldozed, but at its core it was the same. Looking at it gave me the strange sense of having stepped into a historical photograph.

I was on yard duty near the Year 8 lockers, where a series of portables loosely surrounded an asphalt courtyard of hopscotch and handball. In the heat of mid-February there were few students to be supervised. Most had retreated for morning break to the air-conditioned haven of the library (non-readers included), or to the shade of the willows flanking the hockey oval. It was not yet eleven o'clock and already close to thirty-five degrees.

Standing in the shade of a portable's doorway, I strained to hear what two nearby girls were saying. Tessa and Lonnie were sitting on the edge of a banksia garden with their backs to me, seemingly unbothered by the heat and unaware of my presence.

Class, I thought I heard, and then *Tomorrow*. Perhaps *Liar*. I strained.

The conversation sounded civil. Tessa's voice was a low murmur, Lonnie's louder, occasionally breaking into a cough of dry, abrupt laughter.

We were only two weeks into the school year and already there were problems. Tessa's parents had telephoned to tell me they were worried their daughter was being bullied by somebody in 8G. Tessa had been reluctant to give a name, they said, but eventually confessed that it was a girl named Lonnie. There had been issues in Year 7. It had all been sorted out at the time, they had thought, but seemingly it had started up again. They wondered why the girls had been placed in the same class.

Tessa was, in some ways, the quintessential bullying target. Small and slim with short hair the colour of rust, she was yet to establish herself in a social group. Each lesson she was sitting with somebody different, and her hand shot up whenever I asked a question. After class she always lingered to chat about her passion – beagles – and had even visited the staffroom at lunchtime to show me a photograph of her dog. These were sure signs of a student who had not yet found her feet in the complex social system of high school.

The bell went, a nerve-shredding electronic pealing that reverberated off the hot brick, asphalt and steel edges of The School. Students slouched their way into the courtyard, removing books from their lockers and lining up outside their respective portables.

I was 8G's Home Group teacher that year. This meant I saw them each morning for ten minutes, and also taught them English and Personal Development. Every junior class was assigned a teacher of this kind, the idea being to give them a 'significant adult' to whom they could turn for advice or support. Home Group teachers, more than any other, were expected to take on a nurturing, protective role with the juniors. I took pride in being selected for the job. It also meant carrying a greater weight of responsibility. We were a first port of call for the students and their parents. Problems we couldn't manage would involve the coordinators, and beyond that, the assistant principals.

8G had twenty-five students – the maximum class size allowed. I knew already that their abilities ranged from significantly advanced to early primary school.

That day I watched as they filed into the room, sweat-streaked and puppy-panting over carpet worn threadbare by decades of children's feet, including my own. I tried to cast my mind back to when I was that age, tried to conjure up some of the horrible magic of that time. Perhaps for a moment I could hear the snapping of my typewriter, see Jude's dull eyes peering down at me, but that was all. It felt too long ago.

'Mr Murray,' somebody said. 'What are those things stuck in the roof?'

I looked up. The ceiling was porcupined with the ink-cylinders of pens. I reached up on tiptoes and plucked one out, tossing it to the student. 'There you go. Did your dad go to The School? Maybe he shot it up there. Might even still work.'

I spent the beginning of that lesson watching Lonnie. She was a fast-talking girl with darting eyes and drumming fingers. Her hair was long, black, piano-wire straight, perhaps not cut in years. Dirt made crescents beneath her fingernails.

What I noticed was that, when she spoke, everybody listened. No, not everybody – every *girl*. The boys joked and tried their luck with miniature skateboards while Lonnie held court with the rest of the room. And once – just once –

I caught a flicker of an eye-roll after Tessa spoke. It wasn't much, perhaps nothing at all, but I registered it. Bully or not, Lonnie was Queen Bee.

'Mr Murray?' The boy with his hand up was Kelvin. He was tall and sandy-haired, with shoulders broad for his age. 'Can I ask a question that has nothing to do with the work?'

'Sure.'

'Did you see that thing on TV last night about sharks?'

'No.' He and his desk partner, Heath, looked up at me in earnest. I knelt. 'Tell me about it.'

Kelvin's reputation preceded him. I like to believe – all us teachers like to believe – that for every Jude there is a Kelvin. He was kind, hard-working, by equal measures an academic and a sportsman.

'Can I get my phone out of my locker? To show you a picture? It's of a shark.'

When they're passionate about something – anything – bend the rules for them. I let him go.

'Can Heath come?'

'Seems like a one-man job.'

'Fair enough.'

I watched as he sprinted out the door, across the shimmering courtyard to his locker. I knew I was lucky to have him in 8G. Kelvin had thrived in Year 7, and had even impressed his primary teachers before that. Once, in Grade 4, he had stood up for a boy who wanted to play football when others would not let him; a courageous move for any ten-year-old, but it worked. That boy was taken into the fold, and Kelvin was never challenged over his kindness. His teachers had soon put him in a leadership program, and we could see that he would be a future leader at The School as well.

The picture on his phone proved to be of a great white shark launched completely out of the water, teeth aglow and streaming.

Heath shook his shaggy, labrador head. 'Imagine *that*. Imagine seeing *that* while you were surfing.'

Kelvin and Heath's mothers had been friends since their children were babies, and now the boys were almost insepa-rable. This would be their second year together in the same class. On weekends they rode BMX and played basketball, and they were in the process of creating their own team.

Tessa and Lonnie shared a briefer history; they had come from different primary schools and were now in a class together for the first time. I did not know the details of the bullying allegations from Year 7, but it struck me as odd that they were in 8G together. Perhaps, like Tessa's parents, decision-makers in The School thought the situation had been resolved.

It soon became clear that putting them together had been a significant mistake that would have extremely destructive consequences for one of them.

4

Say it to my face

ONE THING I remember in particular about that afternoon was how heavy my schoolbag was. That was true throughout Year 7; I was forever leaning forward to counterbalance the weight of my books. Often my shoulders ached.

'Hey faggot.'

Jude was not fifteen centimetres away, filling my universe. I had to crane my neck to look into his face. The lower hollows of his eye sockets were sunken, and so dark they looked almost bruised. His face was slack: completely without expression. He might have been a mannequin.

Where boys are concerned, the hallmark of the 'normal' bully (reluctant as I am to use that term) is humour. It's the guffaw, the mocking tone, the name-calling. Inflicting pain and humiliation is not his true motive, just a quick and easy way to get a laugh from his audience. And he acts almost exclusively for an audience. Away from his friends he is different, someone you can reason with, perhaps relate to. For teachers, this is common wisdom. Get them away from their friends and you'll see who they really are.

But Jude was no normal bully. That day there was neither

humour nor audience, just he and I in that lonesome school-yard. The wind eddied around us. Traffic moaned far away.

'You called me a fuckwit.'

I stood paralysed, not sure what to say. For a moment I was overcome with horrified guilt, something that later struck me as the worst part of the experience. Something terrible was about to happen, true – but was it also *my fault*? Had I muttered 'fuckwit' when he charged me on his bike? I did not remember doing so. Perhaps, though, I had called him a fuckwit at some other forgotten time. Word got around at The School. Had I brought this on myself?

Jude towered over me in steely, violent righteousness. His eyes were small, tired-looking. His spine seemed unnaturally straight. 'Say it to my face.'

Terrified as I was, aware that this was happening far from adult eyes, perhaps *any* eyes, I nonetheless considered the problem rationally. I was academic. I studied hard, read books, played dice-throwing fantasy games with my brother on week-ends. The world, I felt, was a place of logic and reason. Any problem could be worked out rationally, and this should be no different.

'You called me a fuckwit.' His tone did not change. There was no yelling, no real hostility. It was the voice of an auto-maton. 'Say it to my face.'

I remember with absolute clarity what I intended to say to Jude. I pondered, weighed up, then formed the sentence in my mind. It was as if I was sitting at my typewriter. In that moment of careful reasoning, I had remembered Beau's bloody wreck of a nose. I would simply say to Jude, *No, I will not say anything to your face, because I won't give you the opportunity to do to me what you did to Beau.*

My naivety was colossal. I actually believed I would be protected from this damaged, angry boy-man by simply refusing to insult him directly. Either way, it was immaterial. I never got to speak those words.

What I didn't realise in that moment – and what I'm sure Jude was acutely aware of – was that immediately behind me was a flight of concrete steps leading down from our elevated position on the hockey oval. At the bottom of those steps were stone pavers and a drainage gutter running with water from the day's downpour.

Jude shoved me in the chest with sudden, explosive might.

As I flew, no part of me was in contact with the ground. I remember that something, perhaps the weight of my schoolbag, caused me almost to flip. I saw my cheap school shoes in the air against the overcast sky and knew I was going backwards headfirst into the concrete.

I did not know then about one-punch kills, that falls from standing height can be fatal on such surfaces. All I knew was that this impact, when it came, would hurt me badly. I was so puny in relation to Jude's strength and aggression that the arc of my flight down those steps had to have been four metres, perhaps more. Had I landed, I have no doubt that I would have come away with a fractured skull, at best.

But I did not land. The physics of my earthward journey turned chaotic; I felt my jumper wrenched, my body right itself, then all at once I was hanging from the hand of an older boy who had caught me by the collar. Calmly, undramatically, he put me back on my feet.

I remember, too, that boy's words: *'Don't push him!'* He spoke not with defiance or threat but with utter shock.

Jude stood high above me at the top of those steps. His face remained flat, his eyes dead circuits betraying nothing. 'If you call me a fuckwit, say it to my face,' he said, then turned and walked away.

*

As a teacher, one of my most sobering reflections on that afternoon is that I never told an adult. The assault to which I was subjected was serious, and certainly the kind that could have resulted in catastrophic injury. Nonetheless, I went home that night and spoke not one word to my parents, nor to any of my teachers when I returned to school the following day.

The reasons for my silence are complex, and I do not fully understand them, even today. Certainly there was a vague sense that dobbing was simply not the right thing to do. In primary school our teachers, probably exhausted by ceaseless trivialities, had encouraged us to solve our own problems. Later, as teenagers, those who dobbed were seen as traitorous or weak – a viewpoint happily promulgated by students like Jude. More than that, though, I was afraid. I felt that dobbing would lead to even more violent repercussions. The teachers would deal with Jude, probably give him detentions, suspension, maybe even a complete expulsion, but what was stopping him from returning to The School, loitering at the gate some unexpected wintery afternoon when all the teachers had gone home for the day?

Some parents may think that *their* child would tell them of such an attack, that the relationship they share prevents the keeping of ugly secrets. But I had that relationship with my parents, who were caring, patient and available. There were many other things I opened up to them about.

Later, when I got a job at The School, I would walk past those concrete steps and remember. They reminded me that children won't always speak up, and that it's therefore our job as adults – whether teachers or parents – to *notice*. We won't succeed every time, but we must dedicate ourselves to attentiveness, to noticing the subtle changes in the behaviour of the young people for whom we care.

I don't bear Jude any ill will, wherever he is today. I know now as a teacher that he would have been carrying extraordinary pain to behave in the way he did. The chance that he himself was a victim of abuse is virtually one hundred per cent.

At some point after that incident, Jude disappeared from my childhood. I do not remember him leaving; there was no great moment of relief or celebration amongst the vulnerable students. When I look back he simply drifts ghostlike from my memories of childhood. I thought I saw him years later in a shopping centre, less upright, but with the same darkness beneath his eyes. I don't know for sure that it was him.

What, as teachers, do we do when we encounter young people without empathy? When we search for kindness in them – give them every opportunity to demonstrate it – but human warmth simply does not appear? I've encountered perhaps two such students in the last decade. There are myriad referrals available (counsellors, psychologists, social workers), but what do we do as teachers when we see the dangers ahead for these young people but feel powerless to help them?

Some years ago, a Year 9 boy from a nearby school entered the grounds of the local primary late one night, where a pet goat was kept. Using a box cutter, he popped the coarse skin at its throat, so when the children arrived the following morning they found the carcass amid bloodied and trampled straw.

Recently, I tracked down and sent a message to the older boy who had caught me when Jude pushed me down the stairs.

I asked him if he remembered, which he did, then I thanked him, saying that I thought it possible he had saved my life.

All of this was on my mind when that first call came from Tessa's parents saying that a girl in my own Year 8 class was tormenting their daughter.

5

Androcles and the lion

A TEENAGE BOY might punch another boy in the face, threaten to put his skull through a brick wall, toss him down a stairway; he might trip him and jostle him and manhandle him, hurl projectiles, trample the first green shoots of his victim's manhood.

For all this, though, his actions are visible. The male bully is a blunt object. The female bully works from a much subtler and more complex playbook.

After Tessa's parents contacted me about the possibility that Lonnie was bullying their daughter, I had asked all teachers of 8G to keep an eye on both girls. It quickly became clear that something *was* going on. The signs were subtle and difficult to challenge, but they were there. There were the eye-rolls, the whispers, the sideways remarks rich with connotation and plausible deniability. What made this even more concerning was the sway Lonnie held over the other students.

One hot afternoon, as the ceiling fan hacked the air and a rusty light slumped through the shadeless windows, I caught Lonnie whispering something to another girl right after Tessa answered a question.

'Lonnie.' I stopped mid-sentence and turned to her. 'Could you say that a little louder so the rest of us can hear?'

Her black hair was immaculately combed, a contrast to her dirty nails. 'Say what?'

'Whatever you just said to Bethany.'

'It was just about what we're doing on the weekend.'

I looked at Bethany. She dropped her gaze.

'Save weekend conversations for after school, girls.'

At the end of the day I kept Bethany back, but when I asked her what Lonnie had said she told me that she couldn't remember. I pried, goaded, encouraged, but got nowhere.

Back in the office (a cluttered shoebox of a space adjoining the classroom), I phoned Lonnie's mother. She did not answer, but I left a message asking that she call me as soon as possible about an important matter relating to her daughter. When she hadn't been in touch by the following evening, I left a second message. At the end of the week that, too, was unreturned. This was to become a pattern that would stretch over the entire course of the year.

Schools are easy to criticise, and such critiques are frequently levelled in opinion columns and carpark conversations. To a point, this is fair. Education is a vital institution, and the decisions made in schools every day are pivotal to the lives and futures of children. What's more, teachers are responsible for the most precious things in other adults' lives. We stand *in loco parentis*. Schools should be rigorously questioned, examined and challenged where necessary.

What is rarely raised in such conversations, however, is the reality that almost all school problems are not school problems at all, but social problems. Schools are simply the sites of manifestation. Take Jude: had my parents learnt of the fear and trauma he was causing, they could easily have said The School was not doing enough. Why wasn't every square metre of the playground supervised until the last student had left? Why wasn't Jude expelled? Why wasn't he *fixed*?

The reality is infinitely more complex. It's a reality of parents who don't return calls, and for reasons not so easily criticised, reasons hidden in dark and unknowable caves echoing with love, uncertainty, suspicion of authority. But it's more than that: it's a reality of generational poverty, of abuse, of alienation, of depleted cultural capital. In classrooms all over the world children emerge blinking from that darkness at nine o'clock each school morning. And why do they lash out? The thirsty seek water, the hungry seek food and the powerless seek power.

Of course, I don't suggest for a moment that schools are therefore absolved of responsibility. Teachers have the highest responsibility to address bullying. Frustrated as I was, the situation with Tessa and Lonnie offered an opportunity, a moral and professional challenge. I could help both students, victim and bully alike.

Next lesson, I lined up the Year 8s and brought them into the classroom, but stopped them before they opened their books.

'First, we're going to hear a story. Primary school style. But this is an ancient story. It's about violence, danger and empathy. Who has heard of Androcles and the lion?'

None had, so I was able to tell them the tale. Androcles, slave to a Roman stationed in Africa, escapes from his master and seeks shelter in a cave. Immediately he is confronted by a ferocious Barbary lion, enraged by a thorn in its paw and ready to flay this intruder against the rocky walls. Instead of running, however, Androcles – at great personal risk – gently removes the thorn, empathising with the animal's fear and pain. Years later Androcles is recaptured and sent to Rome, where Caligula orders he be torn apart by wild beasts in the Circus Maximus. However, the lion that emerges is *his* Barbary lion, which immediately nuzzles him like a house cat. Both are pardoned and live out the rest of their days in peaceful friendship.

'So today,' I finished, 'each of us is going to write a memoir. The word "memoir" connects to *memory*. You are going to write about your memory of the kindest thing anybody has ever done for you. Think of a time when somebody showed you empathy, just like Androcles did for the Barbary lion.'

Storytelling is a powerful teaching tool, even with high school students. Though they are loath to admit it, many teenagers are only too happy to sit cross-legged on the floor and be transported to a fictional world.

'Lonnie.' I turned to her. She was sitting in the back row, safely centred within a garrison of girls. 'Can you think of a time somebody showed you empathy?'

I could not tell if she considered the question or not, but she shook her head.

'Think for a bit. You'll have time. How about you, Tessa? What kindness have you been shown?'

'Well, there was the time my parents got me Gonzo, my beagle.'

'Good, but I'm going to make this tough. You're not allowed to write about a time you were given a gift. No Xboxes, no skateboards, no birthdays. I want you to tell me about a time somebody treated you with kindness for no other reason than because they *could*. Start with a plan. For the next fifteen minutes we'll brainstorm. Not a brain light shower. I want to see lots on the page.'

I walked up and down the rows, peering over students' shoulders, encouraging, questioning. Every one of Tessa's pencils had a sliver of paint shaved off with a razor near the end, where her mother had written her name on the bare wood.

I thought, then, about the story Liam had encouraged me to write all those years ago – the story I never had written. *Put it down on paper*, he'd said, eyes smiling beneath the prematurely white hair another student insisted was dyed. *If I had that story, I'd definitely write it.*

If I had been sitting alongside my students, I would have written about Liam. But the roles had reversed. Now, I was the teacher.

'Right, you all have enough in your brainstorm to get started. This will be short. No pressure. I'm not even grading you. Write.'

And write they did – Lonnie included.

When the period ended, Tessa lingered. After the last student had left she came to the front of the class, smiling from behind large glasses that I suppose her parents thought she would grow into.

'Mr Murray, can I work on this tonight? I know you said it was classwork, but I'm enjoying writing it.'

'Of course. I can't wait to read it when you're done. What's it about?'

She wagged a finger. 'You'll just have to wait and see.'

I laughed, raised my hands in surrender. 'Fair enough. Now, you better run off to your next class, or both of us will be late.'

'There is one other thing.' She was so small she needed to wrap both her arms around her stack of books and laptop.

I thought, fleetingly, of myself all those years ago. 'I've finished the book I'm reading. Do you have something to recommend?'

In my classroom I had a bookshelf I tried to keep as stocked as possible. I often spent weekends loading up at op shops, and that weekend I *had* found something – an old edition of *Alice's Adventures in Wonderland*, fully illustrated on glossy plates.

I lifted it from the shelf and held it out. 'Not sure if I should add this to your pile of books. Might be the straw that broke the Tessa's back.'

'I'll manage. Thanks, Mr Murray.'

6

Facades

I WENT BACK to the office feeling that I had won a small battle. Empathy, I believed – still believe – can be taught. All that's needed is an ember in the student, something to be fanned, piled with kindling, ignited. Writing can do that. Androcles and his lion, I hoped, had worked.

'How'd it go, Murray?' The desk opposite mine belonged to Ana, by far the best teacher I know. We'd both started at The School at the same time, straight out of university. Together we would weather the storms of our graduate years and the countless triumphs and tragedies that followed. Without the mutual debriefing, we may not have lasted.

'Good. They did a lot of writing.'

'Are you teaching this period? I'm off.'

I was rushing, scooping up folders and booklets. 'Yeah. My Year 9s.'

'Ugh. You're boring, Murray.'

'I know.'

Ana radiated empathy. It was in everything she did: the way she prepared and delivered her lessons, the way she spoke to her students, the way she listened when I unloaded my frustrations upon her. I'm yet to meet a teacher as generous with their time. I've seen her spend hundreds of hours working one-to-one with students, often at her cramped desk outside of hours and even on weekends.

She swivelled her chair away from a pile of marking. 'How are your new Year 9s?'

'They're okay. There's one clown already, but I kind of like him.'

'Remember, don't smile until Easter.'

The remark was tongue-in-cheek. Both Ana and I resisted the accepted wisdom of behaviour management, which dictated you should begin the year as an unyielding wall. For better or worse, we were smiling on the first day of Term One.

'Sure. Toughest teacher in town.'

'Very alliterative, Murray. Well done.'

Ana had come to Australia from Serbia as a five-year-old, head still ringing with the wail of air-raid sirens. The Yugoslav Wars had been raging for a year, and though as a child she did not fully understand what was happening, she nonetheless felt the unease, heard the sirens, and later saw the masticated buildings and streets choked with debris. Once she had sat up late into the night waiting for an uncle who might never come home. Along with her father and pregnant mother, she was granted temporary refugee status by the Australian government in 1992. At that time she did not speak one word of English; Ana could not have guessed she would eventually be teaching the subject.

'*Hey, Mr Mur-ray!*'

The voice as I approached my Year 9 classroom was unmistakable: Connor. He stepped out of the queue and swaggered towards me, a lopsided grin ringed by a corona of hair that was almost cellophane red. 'Thought you were gonna leave us waiting all day!'

'I wouldn't do that to you, Connor.'

'Good man, good man.' And with that he raised his palm for a high five.

I heard the distant voices of my lecturers at university. Begin firm. After Easter, we could allow ourselves to be resurrected in the form of human beings.

I ignored those voices and put my own hand out, flat. He slapped it, grinned, then went inside.

Year 9s are infamously disengaged. There's no other cohort quite like them. This is recognised by almost all schools, public and private, where administrators experiment with various programs to get the kids through the year. These programs range from a day away from normal classes each week (our approach at The School when I taught Connor) to entire terms in alternative settings. Year 7s can be silly, Year 8s ratty, but Year 9s can drift away, sometimes so far they can't ever be pulled back.

'Mr Murray, my dog shat inside.'

Laughter rose, glittered in the morning light, cascaded around us. I hadn't even taken the roll.

'Connor.' I looked at him hard. 'Inappropriate. Inappropriate and poorly timed.'

'That's what I said to my dog.'

He would have been easy to dislike if he wasn't so funny. 'Okay. Zip it. You're getting off to a poor start, mate.'

'But seriously, sir, I'm worried about her. She's old. She's started shitting inside. I think she might be giving up.'

Just then, two girls – Teagan and Jada – erupted from the back row.

'Shut up, Connor!'

'Yeah, shut up! Nobody cares about your stupid fucking dog.'

'*Teagan!*'

She turned to me. Like Jada, her face was not her own; it was a simulacrum of make-up. They must have spent hours applying it in the pre-dawn fluorescence of their lonesome bathrooms. Foundation, lipstick, eyeliner, brows as stark and sharp as angling blades. 'It's alright for you, sir. We have to put up with him *all day.*'

Always in these situations it was the quiet students I noticed, the ones sitting patiently, often expressionlessly, portraits of muted despair.

'We're hitting reset on this class,' I said. 'But Connor, you're shifting. Close your book, collect your things and move to the front row.'

His gasp was part pantomime, part genuine. 'But sir! I'm genuinely worried! I want your advice!'

'Connor, close your book, collect your things and move to the front row.'

'I'll stop. Fair enough. I'll be good.'

'Connor, close your book, collect your things and move to the front row.'

He groaned, rolled his eyes, complied.

Behaviour management 101: When you ask a student to do something and they argue, repeat the instruction without rephrasing it. The moment you rephrase, it's not an instruction, it's a debate, and kids like Connor will love every moment of it.

I got on with the lesson, but there was a tone now, an ominousness. Connor moped, while Teagan and Jada gave off bolts of hostility: to Connor, to me, to their world. For tourists,

41

Seadale was 'the beach', but we locals knew that was only the make-up, the thin facade. Jada and Teagan's world was one of underemployed parents, relentless bells, concrete freeway overpasses casting heavy shadows across the long walk home. It was a place haunted by non-places. None of my students were waking to beachfront views. I knew the anxiety and ennui from my own childhood.

I felt for Teagan in particular, who I knew had spent the preceding years being shuffled between homes following her parents' marriage breakdown. She carried the burden of a domestic instability that spilled into every area of her life: social, developmental, educational. She had a reputation for defiance, even hostility. All this had culminated in her near-death the previous year.

I had not known Teagan then, but had heard the story. While wagging school as a Year 8, she had climbed into a car with a group of friends and a much older boy. Within fifteen minutes she was trapped inside the destroyed vehicle, slick with her own blood, while another girl screamed down the phone to Teagan's mother that her daughter was dead, dead, dead.

I needed to ask her about that day at some point, I knew. It was vital to really knowing her, understanding her as an individual student and a human being. But I would need to wait for the right time.

Then there was Connor. Though he struggled with the basics of spelling and grammar, the first weeks of Term One had revealed that he had something even the most studious of his classmates lacked. His words were slingshots to the forehead, funny and earnest and original. He SCREAMED in capitals, underlined, wrote the way he spoke. It was the kind of writing most formal assessment would condemn, but that readers in the real world would love. I would come to look forward to Connor's essays as I corrected late into the evenings. For a tired teacher with a stack of marking to get through, his writing was alive, refreshing, ice against glass on the hottest of days.

At the end of that period I kept Connor in, told him to tone it down, pointed out that Jada and Teagan may not have been the only ones a little tired of him hijacking their lessons. He smiled, shrugged.

'I feel bad for Teagan,' he said. 'She was in a bad car wreck.'

'I know.'

He seemed to ponder, serious suddenly, looking out the window. 'Reckon I might go and apologise to her at recess.'

'I'm sure she'd appreciate it.'

He turned to go. 'Seeya, sir.'

'One more thing,' I said. '*Shat* isn't a word.'

He grinned. 'Pooped?'

'That's better.'

'You know, that story was true,' he added. 'I am kinda worried about her.'

'Dogs are like people. They can go a bit funny as they get older. I wouldn't worry about it too much.'

He nodded. 'Thanks, Mr Murray.'

If Connor encountered a lion with a thorn in its paw, I felt, he would devise some ingenious means of extracting it.

7

Elders

WAMBUI DID NOT know what time it was when the knock came at the door, only that it was night. The darkness was dense, still, impatient. Daytime realities – the bustle of the village, mules dragging trailers, maize crops shimmering green in the benevolent light – had the flavour of imagination. She considered for a moment that she had been dreaming, that there had been no knock, but then the sound came again, firm and insistent, the pounding of a policeman's knuckles.

This was it. She would be cured.

Wambui climbed out of bed right as she heard the murmuring voice of her mother through the wall. She dressed, slipped on her shoes and went out.

'It's the middle of the night,' her mother was saying, those words – *ni usiku* – at a low whisper. 'The girl needs sleep.'

'She asked me to come.'

'It would have been better if it had been during the day.'

'Nature works to her own timetable.'

Right then Wambui came to her mother's side, eyes bleary but smiling. 'I'm here, Grandfather.'

For years he had been a Kenyan policeman and a brutal

44

disciplinarian, but his granddaughter's arrival had transformed him. The old man smiled, laid a hand on Wambui's hair. 'It's time. She's ready.'

They went out into the darkness. Wambui could just detect the shapes and tones of Kaandiki, the bougainvillea, the unsealed roads, the pale pastel houses with ornate balconies contrasting the rusted iron of their patchwork roofs. Kaandiki was a place of contrasts. Everywhere was red soil and verdant growth. Wambui's home was of stone and wood, not like the simpler houses elsewhere in the village.

Wambui's grandfather led her to a small yard separating his home from her own. On the stubbly grass the cow lay with her legs out straight, her flanks rising and falling like a bellows as she laboured. The tiny face appeared, black and slick with mucous, tongue protruding.

'It won't be long,' he said, holding her close. Out there it was cool, stars perforating the cloudless night.

But it did seem like a long time. Eventually, though, the calf fell free in a shimmering slick of afterbirth. Its mother climbed to her feet, turned and instantly began cleaning her child. Mothers, somehow, always knew what to do.

'Alright, Wambui.' Her grandfather pushed her forward. 'You be quick.'

She did not hesitate. Kneeling in that hard, stubbled grass alongside the calf, with the great tongue of the cow working tirelessly at her ear, Wambui, too, began to lick the mucus from the newborn.

*

When I got back to the office after speaking with Connor, I found a student sitting alone on the frayed couch Ana and

I had manoeuvred into our little space. As I walked in, he stood with an almost militaristic formality.

'Good morning, sir.' The boy – short and thick-necked with a dark goatee – offered a handshake. 'Ms Nikolic said I could wait in here. I hope that's not a problem.'

We shook hands. 'Of course not, Charlie. Make yourself comfortable.'

In teaching, the students you meet affect you in countless ways. Some frustrate, irritate, even enrage, while others motivate and challenge; some amuse, some perplex, some unsettle. You'll find students like this in every one of your classes, every year. There is also another type of student, much rarer, encountered perhaps a handful of times in a career. This is the student who changes you. Such students teach you more than you ever teach them (as much of an educational cliché as that has become). Something about them – their kindness, their positivity, their resilience in the face of buckling hardship – guides you to reflections well beyond the classroom. These are the children who are inspiring and humbling. Their impact never goes away. Walking years later on a cold Parisian street, where thoughts of The School could not be more distant, the explosive ruffle of alighting doves and the grey glint of light on your wedding band might make you stop for a moment and say unexpectedly to yourself: I wonder how Charlie is going these days.

He sat on the couch, craning his neck to study my left hand. 'Hang on. What's going on, Mr Murray? I don't see a ring.'

As with the introductory handshake, we went through this ritual every time we spoke. 'No ring.'

'So you still haven't popped the question.' He frowned, shaking his head with exaggerated disappointment. 'How does Greta put up with you? How long have you been together?'

'You know how long we've been together.'

'Sir, sir, sir.' He had small, kind eyes set close together, and spoke with the bouncing timbre of the Spanish-Australian. 'What are we going to do about you?'

I dumped my books on my desk, slumped into the chair opposite. 'You've gotta learn some patience, mate.'

'Well, you've kept me waiting long enough today, sir. I need some advice.'

That was often the way with Charlie. He was direct, confident, mature beyond his seventeen years. I had taught him only once, three years earlier, but since that time he often stopped me in the yard, or visited the office for a chat. This year was his last at The School and I knew that I would miss him when he was gone.

'Now, you may not like this, Mr Murray, but I want honest advice. Me and a couple of other kids are thinking about moving out together. Pooling our funds and renting a place.'

'At the end of the year?'

'No. Right away.'

'I think it's a bad idea during your last year of high school, Charlie.'

He winced, nodded. 'Yeah, I figured. But we're all in bad situations we need to get out of. It's not just for fun.'

I knew Charlie's story. He had told it to me gradually, over many months, when I taught him in Year 9. His mother had managed her bipolar disorder and schizophrenia by retreating into pills and marijuana; as a little boy, Charlie had lost count of the number of times police and paramedics had been to their house, alongside stern-faced bureaucrats from the Department of Health and Human Services. Amidst it all, Charlie shielded his younger brother Xavier as best he could, while their older sister Rachel looked out for them. Charlie described his father as a violent man who had been repeatedly incarcerated, and who he had seen only on weekends as a little boy. Eventually, it became clear that Charlie's mother was not able to look after her boys. Charlie was eight then, Xavier only six. Rachel was in her teens and insisted on staying, but for the younger children there was no choice. They needed stable parenting. In the end, their aunty – an elderly, traditional Spaniard – took them in.

I still remember meeting Charlie's aunty. It was on parent–teacher interview night, and she approached me beaming, hand outstretched in the manner she had clearly imparted on her nephews. She was small and grey-haired with a knitted shawl covering her rounded shoulders; she was, I supposed, about seventy. Her brother – Charlie's father – had to have been twenty years her junior. Indeed, they seemed to come from different worlds.

'Good evening, Mrs Blanco,' I had said, standing from behind my desk.

She closed her eyes and shook her head. 'Please. Call me *Tia*.'

And I did, from that day on. It was not her name but the Spanish word for *aunty*.

Even as a Year 9, Charlie understood the sacrifice his aunty had made. 'She is the best,' he told me one day, 'in every single thing she does.'

A few years after Tia took the boys in, Charlie's mother died. He needed somewhere to retreat, and he found that safety within the pages of books.

In my English classes, Charlie had read. And read. And read. He had read when he was supposed to be reading, he had read when he was supposed to be writing, he had read when the bell had tolled and he was supposed to be leaving. His special passion was fantasy.

'This pains me as an English teacher,' I said to him once as he chuckled up at me, 'but I have to tell you to put that book away. You need to put pen to paper.'

Eventually I learnt that reading was his escape. He admitted to me that it was hard to make friends when you were angry all the time, when you felt you had been dealt a bad hand in life. If he wasn't reading in the yard, he was hanging out with his little brother, who was then in Year 7.

That day, with Charlie sitting in my office, I asked him what situation he needed to get out of.

'It's my father,' he said, lowering his voice as though somebody might hear. 'He's spending more and more time at the house. Some of his old issues are coming up and obviously Tia wants to take care of him.'

I thought of my own father, a quiet country boy who drove a truck and made cups of tea for my mother. What did I know – what could I *ever* know – of what it meant to be Charlie Blanco?

For me, one of the greatest challenges of the job is trying to teach students – trying to *help* students – whose life experiences lie an immeasurable distance from my own. I felt that way about Wambui, too, and thought of her then as I continued chatting with Charlie. The two were nothing alike, and yet both were bound in my mind by shared childhood traumas experienced along the sharpened blades of machetes.

8

The banality of kindness

THEY WERE ALL there, Wambui included, though really they weren't – really they were in the brick belly of a government classroom, years-old posters over greying walls, kiln-light pulsing murderous through the windows in an irresistible haze. The ocean nearby smelt of dried seaweed. Gulls cried. It was the final period of the day, but this meant little to these seventeen- and eighteen-year-olds, many of whom would go straight from school to part-time jobs upon which their households depended.

But the illusion held. I saw it in their furrowed brows, their slightly squinting eyes. They were enveloped in the darkness of an enormous pavilion, its sawtooth roof pulled tight in a snarl. The floor was dusty, uneven, dangerous. In the centre was a steep-sided pool, its surface humped with the carcasses of horses. Still more horses galloped and cantered on the rim, while a lone shepherd, arms outstretched, tried to prevent them from falling.

'So tell me,' I said, aware suddenly that the electric clock uttered a faint, continuous whine. 'Does this story make no sense whatsoever? Or is there a hidden logic? Something a good Literature student can find?'

Tim put up his hand. He was a tall, lanky surfer who – by sheer chance – I had taught continuously for the past five years. 'I'm not sure.' His voice was all sea breeze and glinting horizons. Waves broke behind his eyes. 'But I like it, Doc.'

Years before, when Tim was in the junior school, my class had been discussing the controversy surrounding vaccines. After a barrage of questions, I felt the need to remind them that I wasn't a doctor. 'I'm pretty sure you are,' Tim had replied, and so I remained, all the way through to his graduation, and even today.

'What about everybody else? Forget about meaning. We've all chosen Lit for a reason. Do we *like* this story?'

Twenty-five heads nodded. I've taught a lot of books, but Peter Carey's *Collected Stories* is perhaps the only one that has enchanted every student, without exception.

'I totally agree. I *love* Peter Carey. Like, *really* love him. Who's the teen heart-throb these days?'

'Bieber!'

'Well, Peter Carey's my Bieber.'

Laughter. It's easy with Literature kids. They're studious, interested, in the class by choice. They're often high performers who want to achieve and expect you to provide. For them, the teacher isn't the enemy. Working with them is a joy.

(And all at once – as sometimes happens in teaching – my consciousness was waylaid. Should I telephone Charlie's aunty immediately after class, tell her what he told me today in the office? It seemed like a good idea, but of course it was laden with complications. Would Charlie feel betrayed by this disclosure? He never told me that I *couldn't* speak to Tia, but that certainly wasn't the same as giving permission. And what if his father – a man I had never met – answered the phone?

Would I hang up? What could I possibly have to say to *him*? And how might Tia react to criticisms of a man who was, ultimately, her brother?

Then there was Tessa and Lonnie to think about. I still hadn't managed to reach Lonnie's mother, and nor had the coordinator. Should I try again? Did I have time for any of these things, with the 3.30 pm staff meeting, the drive home, the shopping, the twenty-five Literature essays I needed to mark? Of course I had the time, it was my *responsibility*, I *had* to have the time.)

'I promise that analysing "Life and Death in the South Side Pavilion" won't make us hate it,' I told my Year 12s. 'The opposite will be true. So let's stick some pins in this butterfly. We like it, but does it make sense?'

'It makes sense, but not in the normal way,' somebody said. 'It's like a dream – or a nightmare, maybe. It tells you something about yourself, but you're not sure what.'

'Good. So what *might* it be telling us about ourselves?'

I scanned the room, one face to the next: Wambui and Tim and Mya and all the rest, too many to name, each fighting for what intellectual and emotional real estate I had to offer, their eyes greedy for answers, and I struggled not to relent and just write an explanation on the board and then settle at my desk, open a newspaper like the teachers of my childhood.

The clock whined. Wambui, large-eyed and thoughtful, tapped a pencil on her chin, paused, wrote something down.

At last Mya raised her hand, and something inside me softened. I knew she'd had the answer from the beginning, had hesitated only to give the others an opportunity. You saw it so often in children: the banality of kindness. A gesture subtle, easy to miss, but more genuine than all the self-conscious benevolence the adult world has to offer.

'The shepherd is trapped in the pavilion, and it seems like it's The Company trapping him. But it isn't.' Mya: platinum braids, ruled lines, work submitted days early. 'He's trapping himself.'

'What makes you say that?'

In the junior school Mya's voice had been a barely audible whistle, but now she spoke with surety, confidence. 'It's the pavilion. The whole point about a pavilion is that it has no walls. He's carrying on like The Company is responsible for this terrible situation he's in, but there's nothing stopping him walking straight out. Nothing except himself. He says he has to stay to protect the horses from drowning, but that isn't really his responsibility. That's The Company's stupidity. It isn't the shepherd's fault.'

'I could not agree more, Mya. And maybe Carey is warning us that we're all trapped, and each of us is our own jailer.'

But Mya would not be trapped – not by anything, and all her teachers loved her for it. She was on the verge of breaking a generational poverty cycle. Her ruled lines and meticulous braids were not superficialities, they were weapons of defence in an arena whose dangers she had come to understand years before.

When she was ten her parents divorced, and Mya was uprooted from Queensland to Victoria, leaving her with little more than one half of a love heart necklace tearily gifted from her best friend. Soon her mother had a part-time job in a bakery, and Mya was walking home from school and cooking dinner for her little brother, making sure he did his homework, putting him to bed. They could afford little. When she began high school, Mya's uniform hung off her like a clown suit, her mother knowing she would be unable to afford larger sizes as the years progressed. In Year 10 Mya first felt the desire to break free. Life, she understood, could be different, and education was the key. She wanted to leave Seadale to study archaeology at university, and knew the score she needed to the digit.

And I carried that weight – in Literature, at least. It was my job to make sure I did everything possible to get Mya the score she deserved.

*

It's called the ATAR score: the Australian Tertiary Admission Rank.

If that term is instilled with a tepid, bureaucratic dullness, don't be fooled; beneath the surface lies the reality of a system that is at best problematic, and at worst inextricably linked with power, privilege, class and the perpetuation of the social status quo.

The obvious and well-trodden path is to decry issues of funding. While The School is still armoured in places with the 1970s brickwork of my childhood, many private institutions are handed public money to spend on the most privileged young people in the country. I'm not for a moment arguing that children in private schools don't deserve the best start to life – only that, to a degree, the educational privileges they enjoy come at the cost of the less fortunate. Where I've been forced to hang my own curtains in classrooms and buy books for students, a prestigious nearby college recently unveiled a 550-seat auditorium, complete with orchestra lift. For public school teachers dealing with flickering lights and asbestos warning signs, contrasts like this are difficult to take.

But where this becomes especially problematic – and of major importance to ATAR scores, and therefore the economic futures of young people – is with regard to class sizes. I'm aware of private schools running Literature classes with as few as five pupils, a luxury far beyond the financial reach of almost any government school.

Class sizes are controversial, with some arguing they are of little significance and others adamant that they are profoundly important. The reason most classroom teachers fall into the latter category is because we are aware of the power of rapid feedback in helping our students learn. Class size slows feedback just as surely as four flat tyres slow a car.

Consider the maths. It takes fifteen minutes to read, and provide feedback on, a Literature essay, and that is going at full tilt. In a class of twenty-five, that's a little over six hours work. In a class of five, a teacher can have that work done in just an hour and a quarter. Multiply that over four writing tasks, and the government school teacher has worked for over twenty-four hours to the private school teacher's five.

What this means is that the public-school teacher is more tired and, significantly, *gets the work back more slowly*. A class of five might get their feedback the day after writing the essay, then immediately begin a new one, their errors and feedback fresh in their minds. The students in the class of twenty-five need to wait far, far longer.

What must be remembered, too – and what is poorly understood by many – is that the ATAR is not an assessment of competence in the traditional sense. It's a *rank*. Each student is placed in a great, snaking line, the front of which often meanders through suburbs like Toorak and Darling Point while the tail recedes into a murky hinterland of housing commission blocks, barren yards, poorly tuned radios hissing footy scores in bulbless rooms. And in such gloom, students like Mya await their Literature feedback without complaint.

All this, of course, is assuming such classes even *run* in government schools. Let's take as an example a traditionally challenging subject like Chemistry. If only five students enrol, a government school may simply be unable to afford to proceed with the class. This leaves the students with two options: go to a different school or pick a different subject. Most opt for the latter. As Chemistry is a prerequisite for some university courses, those students have had doors to their futures closed for no other reason than their socioeconomic background.

Other examples are more specific and, arguably, insidious. At the time of writing, students are not permitted to use a dictionary in the Literature examination in Victoria, despite repeated studies showing a clear relationship between poverty and reduced vocabulary. Every child carries with them the invisible dictionary of their socio-economic status – and that's to say nothing of students for whom English is not their first language.

The ATAR measures student ability, but it also measures so much more: privilege, wealth, position. This can create an illusion of competence in private schools, where results are touted in well-funded marketing campaigns with no acknowledgement of the underlying social realities from which they emerge.

While students from wealthy, stable homes studied – perhaps with the support of tertiary-educated parents – Mya cooked dinner for her little brother. Likewise, Charlie (one terrible night) cowered under the bed with his little brother to escape the glint of a hacking blade. And Wambui, on the other side of the world, wrestled with the superstitions of her village, which dictated that a cure for bedwetting involved licking the mucus from a newborn calf.

9

Growth

A DAY PASSED, a week; half a dozen horrendous nights, dragon-breath hot. Power outages, the smell of distant fires, paramedics calling for checks on the elderly – then all at once a window-rattling twilight storm, shimmering cold, electric ice sluicing over the rim of a daguerreotype horizon. Rain streamed down the Ferris wheel at the abandoned carnival ground.

I lived alone then in a little rented shack by the beach. There was no air conditioning, and when it was hot the fan in the wall furnace would whir to life, fooled by its own thermostat. The night of that storm I walked to the beach and watched clouds flicker and grumble over the sea. Often I sat on the sand thinking of my classes: the strategies I might employ to engage them, the stories, the subterfuge.

The following day I found The School glittering, bright. The storm had left in its wake a sky blue and clear. Even my students seemed to feel it, responding to my questions with an unusual clarity. The world had come into sharp focus.

For me, that focus came with a shocking realisation. In my Year 8 class was by far the weakest student I had ever taught.

Grace was quiet, kind, not the renegade personality often attached to low levels of literacy. This, coupled with some untimely absences (and the fact that she had been at a different school in Year 7), had allowed her to escape my notice in the early weeks of Term One. Now, though, it was abundantly clear.

I wrote some instructions on the board then stood back, watching. Where the rest of the class scratched away in their notebooks, Grace formed the letters with the slow deliberation of a calligraphist. Those letters, though, were no calligraphy. They were large, overlapping, awkward. In the time it took the others to take down four sentences, Grace had finished just one word. Hers was the writing of a five-year-old.

When the rest of the class was getting on with the lesson, I pulled up a chair opposite. 'How are you today, Grace?'

'Good thank you.' Her words were like heavy things dragged through water.

'Any ideas on what you might write your poem about?' Already I knew that even a simple poem would be challenging.

'No.'

'Well, what are some of your favourite things?'

She was smiling, thinking, *trying*. Thirty seconds passed, a minute.

'What's your favourite place to go?'

'I'm not sure.'

'How about the beach?'

She flashed a nervous laugh of small, crowded teeth. 'I'm not very good at swimming.'

'Never mind. I only doggy paddle.' I looked at her page. It was blank but for that single word copied erroneously from the board. 'How about I give you five minutes to think of your favourite place? Don't worry about copying down everything else on the board. Just think of that.'

I checked on the other students. When I returned to Grace she had made no progress.

'Couldn't think of anything?'

'The beach.'

What this student needed, I knew, was an integration aide, somebody to work one-to-one with her regularly, and not just in English. It is perhaps telling that we refer to such students as 'funded' – assuming they are, of course. One-to-one support means money.

I wrote a note to myself: *Check if Grace is funded. No evidence of an aide yet.*

It was a juggling act, as teaching always is. Grace needed one-to-one support, but the rest of the students in the class were just as deserving of my time. I would not let any of them become invisible. I would not let them drift into the land of ghosts.

I walked across the room to Kelvin and Heath. They were into their poems, lines and stanzas already dropping down their pages like rope ladders. They would need extension. People often talk about students being a year or two behind, but the gap between Grace and Kelvin was probably more than ten years of literacy development.

'What'd you think of that storm last night, boys?'

Kelvin slapped his pen down, eyes wide. 'Wow.' His sharp, angular features would not have been out of place in an Art Deco painting. 'What a cracker.'

He was kind; it was just that simple. As with Mya, it mani-fested subtly, in a million little gestures, often banal, day after day. I knew if I asked Kelvin to help Grace – to show her his poem, perhaps read it to her – he would do so, without self-consciousness. Perhaps it was because he had felt the need for help in his own life.

A year after he had so famously challenged a mob of young footballers over their cruelty at only eleven, he told his mother he had a lump in his groin. It was, he had said, the size and hardness of a golf ball.

'How long has it been there?' Kelvin had seen the panic in her face, a fear primal, sharp, unknown perhaps to all but mothers.

'A long time, I think. Like, almost as long as I can remember.'

There was a tense car trip – lingering red lights and ticking indicators – then the GP palpating the lump. He was an ageing doctor with a walrus moustache and an inclination towards humour, but that day he was businesslike. Kelvin was sent for more tests and the diagnosis was Non-Hodgkin Lymphoma.

Aside from Heath, few of his schoolfriends knew, and Kelvin worked to keep it that way. Though he understood that he was ill, he did not at that age grasp the full implications of his condition, could have no real awareness of his mortality – if, indeed, any adult ever does.

Relief came for Kelvin and his family: the cancer had not spread. The lump was removed, along with some of the lymph nodes on his left side. Not long afterwards he was sitting on the drizzling sidelines of a lunchtime football match, his lower stomach swollen, his eyes heavy with tears. He felt lost and alone. The other kids knew that he had been through surgery, but were too young for the empathetic concern that would have told them to comfort him. So he sat and watched them play, disconnected, distant. Their happiness was unreachable. That day he felt like he was watching a film of a film.

But he was strong. As the months passed and he developed a better understanding of what he had been through, he felt that he could overcome anything. It was as though he had aged five years in just a few months. He doubled his application in both school and sport.

'My poem's about basketball,' Kelvin told me. 'It's not done, but I'm getting there. Reckon I have some good poetic techniques happening.'

I continued around the room, faces appearing and disappearing like flashcards. I hadn't learnt all the names yet. There was Kelvin and Heath, Grace, Lonnie with her mysterious mother – and Tessa.

She had situated herself at the far end of the front row, alone. In contrast, Lonnie floated in a shining butterfly-glade of female reverence. Kelvin was a leader of one kind, Lonnie – for the time being – was another.

'Let me guess?' I spun Tessa's book around. 'A poem about Gonzo the beagle?'

As we chatted, I became dimly aware that the period was almost over. I asked why she was sitting by herself.

'No reason.' But no eye contact, either. 'Just felt like working alone.'

The bell went and the rest of the class drifted out. Tessa packed up slowly, hauled her books into her arms, headed for the door.

'Tessa – how's *Alice's Adventures in Wonderland*?'

She gasped, turned, dumped her books on the desk. 'I almost forgot!' Some shuffling, and the book appeared. 'Here, hold this so I can prove I'm not cheating.'

I took the book from her and she closed her eyes, began to recite:

'Alice! A childish story take,
And with a gentle hand
Lay it where Childhood's dreams are twined
In Memory's mystic band,
Like pilgrim's withered wreath of flowers
Plucked in a far-off land.'

I applauded.

'It's not the first part. But it's the part I like the most.'

'Have you finished the book?'

She shook her head. 'Not even close. But I love it.'

I had the next period free, so retreated to the office. Tessa had huge potential, but I was deeply worried about her. I told Ana what was going on.

'Do what you can with the girl exhibiting bullying behaviour,' she suggested. 'But work on Tessa as well. Help her build a social group. Help her find her people. Sounds like this other girl is turning her into a bit of an outsider, and you don't want that to gather momentum.'

'No. And we need to get Lonnie on the right track for her own sake, too.'

'She probably isn't a bad girl,' Ana finished. 'With a bit of luck her mum will get in touch soon, anyway.'

10

Scales

SEIZE THE DAY. Gather ye rosebuds while ye may. Why does the writer use these lines? Because we are food for worms, lads. Because, believe it or not, each and every one of us in this room is one day going to stop breathing, turn cold and die. Carpe diem.

In the prologue of this book, I dismissed Hollywood classrooms as unrealistic (including Mr Keating's in *Dead Poets Society*, no matter how much I adore the film). The problem is one of character numbers. Audiences – perhaps critics – are only expected to track a handful. I want you to know that it isn't like that in real life. I want to *show* you. And yet here I sit on a bright winter morning, years removed from these children, and I think: Can I afford one more? Is there room for Claire, the poet? And there must be room. She's one of the most important of all, a student with all the kaleidoscopic fragility of a leadlight window, something complex and wonderful that I could never quite see into.

She's the last, so even I am fraudulent. Really, this book should be volumes long. A hundred and twenty students, a hundred and twenty biographies with footnotes and addendums and hidden chapters whose presence is sensed but never confirmed. I know I'm mixing metaphors, but that's how it needs to be. Any single analogy is reductive, a dishonest simplification. So let them come. School, like society, is a mosaic, light and dark. The more you learn about your students the more it grows. It's a fractal, glittering, expanding, infinite.

But I will stop at Claire.

She was sitting outside our office the evening after the storm. Ana and I had been in a meeting in another part of the school, but nonetheless Claire had waited. It was well after five. She was out of uniform: outsized jacket, laceless skate shoes, backpack rattling with charms. In her hands was a copy of Peter Carey's *Collected Stories*.

'Hey.' She held up the book, speaking as though even that small effort was an inconvenience. 'Thought you might want to chat about your boyfriend.'

Ana laughed. 'Of course he does. But be patient if he gets tongue-tied.'

'Working after hours to help students, and this is the thanks I get.' I unlocked the office, feigning irritation. 'Also, if that's your idea of an insult then you're a heterosexist.'

I lost sleep over Claire, but knew she had the potential to soar in adult life. If depression is a black dog, for her – a fiercely intelligent poet, reader and Literature student – it was something worse, Tolkien's Smaug perhaps, thumping its great scaled head against classroom windows by day, rasping its claws against bedroom carpet by night. She was in the care of a psychiatrist, but even that was only taking her so far. Plus, for teachers, such students are always *ours* once we come to care for them, and perhaps remain so forever, in a way.

Two years earlier I had taught her in a challenging Year 10 English class. The group was mostly boys, and a footy club raucousness often dominated the room, in spite of my efforts. But one day a sudden silence had descended upon the room, as surely as if I had been struck deaf. I turned, knowing something was wrong, and there was Claire, standing before me with her pale arms outstretched and running with blood. She had slashed herself with a plastic ruler. The visible wound was superficial, at least.

Afterwards while we were chatting, she admitted to me that she would never call the Children's Helpline. I was stunned. How, I had asked, could somebody as intelligent as her, as self-aware as her, be unwilling to make use of a service like that?

'Fear.' There wasn't a moment's hesitation. She looked at me with eyes that seemed too large for her narrow, ghost gum face. 'Every time you call those people they want details of your planned suicide, the exact self-harm, and if it's not severe you're not important. How do you talk to or trust those people when you don't know them from a bar of soap?'

I tried to persuade her otherwise, point out the flaws in her perspective, probably failed. But I was grateful, for she had illuminated something previously unseen. For some children, getting help isn't just about picking up a phone and punching a keypad; it's a terrifying leap across a dark and bridgeless void that may not even have another side. We can't wait for them to ask for help. We need to offer. And if that means extending an unneeded hand to a thousand kids who look at us awkwardly, roll their eyes and tell us that we need to relax, then that's a small price to pay.

Claire and I talked about Peter Carey's stories that afternoon, then went through one of her essays. All the while she took notes, agreed, knitted her brows, challenged. That, often, is the mark of a great Literature student: I think you're wrong, Mr Murray. And maybe the study guide's wrong, too.

Eventually the books went away and she sat back on the couch. Ana had gone home, and I began to pack up. I chose my moment, trying to sound as unworried as possible – and as *unfatherly*. I knew she had no dad at home and did not want to give the impression I was trying to take on that role. 'And how are you going? How are you managing Year 12, overall?'

'It's okay.' Her lips narrowed, whitened. 'It's shit though. All anybody ever talks about are ATAR scores. And not just at The School. Online. Everywhere.'

'ATARs aren't the be-all-end-all of life.'

'That's what everyone says. But they never shut up about them. And *pathways*. God, if I hear another adult use that word. You can go to uni. You can go to TAFE. You can get an apprenticeship. What if I don't want to do any of those things? What if I just want to *be*?'

I wanted to say that just *being* doesn't pay the bills, but refrained, not least of all because I thought she had a point. 'Look at it as us old people pushing our anxieties onto you.'

'Pfft. What are you doing calling yourself old?'

We walked out together. It was a glassy, cloudless twilight, warm and still. Parts of the asphalt were streaked with sandy dirt where the stormwater had washed it out of the garden beds. 'That's another thing,' she added as we neared the carpark. 'Except for Lit, all my subjects scale down.'

I moaned. 'God, Claire. Don't worry about bloody scaling.'

'Easy for you to say, Teacher Man.' She waved with her copy of *Collected Stories*. 'Seeya.'

*

The final year of high school is a difficult one, regardless of what the certificate awarded may be called. There is often a sense that those twelve months will dictate the entirety of a young person's future. Some of the subtler aspects of educational systems exacerbate these stresses, particularly for those already carrying the burden of depression, anxiety and fragile self-esteem. One of the most problematic and poorly understood of these aspects is scaling.

At a glance it's simple. A student's ATAR score is generated using their results from several subjects, and in Victoria, each student can achieve a maximum score of fifty per subject. However, these individual results may be scaled up or down. Why? Because different study areas pose different challenges. Let's consider the imaginary 'Arithmetic for Beginners' and 'Quantum Field Theory'. Common sense dictates that a forty in the former is very different from a forty in the latter. We would expect the first to scale down and the second to scale up.

A real example: in 2018 a score of thirty in Business Management scaled down to twenty-six, while a score of thirty in Specialist Mathematics scaled up to forty-one.

Ostensibly, scaling helps ensure consistency and fairness. It protects students from being punished for selecting challenging subjects. However, it has some extraordinarily toxic side effects, some known, others rarely acknowledged.

A well-understood problem is that some young people will select classes based purely on scaling. Their subsequent disinterest often results in extremely low grades for which no amount of scaling will compensate. Another poorly understood facet of scaling is that it is non-linear; low scores stay low, high scores stay high and the big shifts occur in the middle.

Schools have become adept at helping students and their parents overcome the two-dimensional logic of selecting subjects based on scaling. We are less adept, however, at combating the social and emotional fallout the scaling system can have on young people.

Most innocuous are conversations about 'hard' and 'easy' subjects. Specialist Mathematics, students will tell you, is hard; Art, they will smugly insist (often those without a glimmer of artistic ability), is easy. The problem is that naïve young people do not recognise that scaling applies only in the very narrow bureaucratic realm of ATAR calculation. Some will broaden this value judgement to the world at large, strolling galleries years later while unconsciously scaling down the achievements of Magritte, Gentileschi, Rembrandt. In their most impressionable years, they have been fooled into seeing false depths in the shallow pond of their high school experience.

We need to be far clearer with children about this.

More disturbing, though, is the minority of individuals who come to view scaling not only as a value judgement of subjects, but also of the people within those subjects. Dozens of interviews across dozens of schools reveal that this is a widespread problem. Some Specialist Mathematics students may come to view Art students as inferior, incapable, lazy. If we as teachers don't sufficiently explain this aspect of the system and its implications, perceptions of scaling can breed condescension and arrogance. Currently, I think we're failing.

I have even spoken with past students who remember some teachers perpetuating the problem. One claimed that a science teacher declared that 'Psychology is not a real science,' and even once asked the Psychology kids to sort coloured counters, suggesting this was no job for Physics and Chemistry students.

Such remarks are no doubt tongue-in-cheek, but how might they sound to young people like Claire?

The ranking system only makes matters worse. Students' awareness that their ATAR score ranks them against the rest of the state is a small part of the problem. Far worse is that they also know they are being ranked against their classmates, their friends. Each Year 12 teacher is required to rank the students in their class, and there is massive pressure on teachers to 'get their ranking right'.

Learning is at its richest when children work cooperatively. They share, compare, correct. Put two children together and each will cast light into the gloom of the other's misunderstandings. There is, then, an absurd tension between the power of collaboration and the anti-collaborative paradigms of a competitive system. Countless students have admitted to me that they withhold information in class discussions and avoid helping friends with work. For aspirational learners, the goal often shifts from passion for the subject to their final ranking.

'Dean and I loved History,' an extremely successful past student told me recently. 'But in Year 12 all we talked about was marks. If he got a point higher than me on an assessment, I'd say, well, I need to get a point higher than you on the next one. It was a ranking thing. When we should have been having conversations about History we were actually having conversations about marks. It's ironic, because if we'd been talking about the work instead, we *both* would have done better.'

Why are Year 12 teachers required to rank their students? It's connected with the complex mathematical processes the government uses to generate each student's final score and to compensate for inconsistent marking across schools.

Officials assess the exams and combine the results with the marks awarded by the school to generate a final, overall score for the subject. However, *the government strives to maintain the teacher's rank*. In other words, when we send in our rankings (before the exams have even occurred), we all but lock in the students who will get the highest overall scores in our subject.

If you're confused, you're not alone. Few understand these processes well. There are, though, some important and troubling ramifications that need to be more widely discussed. The main one is that, due to the ranking system, *students' marks are entangled*. What I mean is that students can affect one another's results.

To put it in plain English: in some instances, your son or daughter's score in a subject could actually be pushed down (or up) by the exam performance of a classmate due to the mathematical complexities of the ranking system. External assessment seems to carry more weight than that conducted by teachers within schools.

Needless to say, this exacerbates teacher anxiety around rankings, and also impacts students. I have had multiple empathetic Year 12s express to me their fears that their exam performance could negatively impact their friends' results. Most commonly, highly ranked students can convince themselves that if they underperform, the ranking system (and prioritisation of exam results over school-assessed results) will push their friends' scores down.

When I recently asked an expert on the system if such students' concerns were true, he replied with a somewhat perplexing, 'Not necessarily.'

In the face of such systems, a renegade teacher may be tempted not to rank their students at all. This, of course, would create even more issues, and would essentially require each student to be given identical marks. The Victorian Curriculum and Assessment Authority (VCAA) warns that failure to separate learners can result in disadvantage.

If there was one thing every expert I spoke to agreed upon, it was the fact that very few teachers and even fewer students fully comprehend how the system works. Clearly, this is extremely problematic.

All this weighed on me as I sat in my car that evening, watching Claire march away into the twilight. She held the straps of her backpack like a girl embarking on a journey into some great wilderness. I thought of her bloodied arms two years ago, of the endless tweaking of her medication, of the quiet desperation in her mother's eyes. I thought, too, of her words: 'All my subjects scale down.' I sensed that on some level, she felt that she scaled down, too.

11

Great teacher you are

I HAD SOON arranged a meeting to request an integration aide for Grace. The person to speak with was Helen, a tall, grandmotherly woman with large hands coarsened by years of rock gardening. She worked with our integration department three days a week, and had an endearing habit of breaking into fits of giggling at the most vaguely humorous of observations.

I liked her; she cared deeply about the students with whom she worked. Nonetheless, our conversation soon descended into Kafkaesque absurdity.

'Grace in 8G needs an integration aide,' I told her. 'And pretty urgently.'

She smiled, her face folding with the reassuring warmth of fresh linen. 'Yes. But she doesn't qualify.'

'What do you mean?'

'There aren't aides for everyone. There are certain thresholds . . . benchmarks . . . and she doesn't qualify.'

'I do not see how that could be the case.'

'I'll show you.'

We were in a small spare office at the front of The School. Countless cardboard boxes – each containing reams of A4 paper – filled much of the space. Helen spread Grace's documentation across the table like an arcade fortune-teller dealing cards behind impassable glass.

'See? It's her testing scores. She *just* misses out.'

'But she *can't read*. She can barely write. I've never met a student as low as her.'

'And you probably won't again. But look.' She tapped one large, cracked finger on a bureaucratic tarot card. 'This is it. Her visual processing is too high.'

'What sort of tests determine visual processing scores?'

'Rearranging shapes. That type of thing.'

'But when is she rearranging shapes in English? Or any other subject, for that matter?'

Helen giggled, as aware of the absurdity as I was. 'Oh, never, I imagine. Maybe sometimes in Mathematics. But she'll need to read the instructions and express her ideas in writing, which she won't be able to do. Somebody will need to help her.'

'Like an integration aide.'

'Exactly. But she doesn't qualify.'

I leaned against the boxes, fearing that perhaps I hadn't outlined the situation clearly enough. 'I've sat with her and asked her to read to me, Helen. She cannot do it. She might know one in every ten words, and that's from the simplest primary texts we have. And her writing is restricted to the narrowest, *narrowest* vocab. It takes fifteen minutes for a ten-word sentence, and even then –'

'I know, darling.' I saw Helen in her rock garden then, stooped and smilingly patient in the appalling summer heat, gloveless and indefatigable. 'I've been doing this since before you were born and Grace is one of the weakest I've seen who isn't funded.' She allowed a moment for that to sink in. 'Probably *the* weakest.'

'She'll be spending her days *not learning anything*,' I said. 'She can't read the textbooks. She can't read the board. She can't read the worksheets. The teacher can't sit one-to-one with her every session. It's bloody ridiculous.'

'It is. She *needs* an integration aide. But she doesn't qualify.'

'Because she's too good at rearranging shapes. Never mind that she can't read or write.'

'If you want to put it like that.'

'Well, I think that's bullshit.'

She giggled. 'So do I. But it's a money thing. And a lot of the work our aides do, they never get paid for.'

I felt a twinge of guilt. I knew the aides were paid about half of what I was, despite spending their days working one-to-one with the most challenging students. One of our aides had even learnt Braille in her spare time to support a student.

'So what do we do?'

'I'll have some university students doing their placement with me this year. We can get them working with Grace as much as possible.' Another giggle. 'Free labour.'

'But that isn't a long-term solution.'

'No, it isn't. But we'll do the best we can. It doesn't matter if Grace can barely read and write. She simply doesn't qualify for funding.'

*

These worries – Claire and Grace, Tessa and Lonnie – were punctuated by the ordinary, workaday reality of teaching life. Not long after the meeting with Helen came an oasis: a Year 9 silent reading session. Each student would bring their own book and so would I, modelling for the kids that you can be a reader, and an adult, and a man. Without doubt it is mostly the boys who drift from reading during adolescence.

They came in, sat down, pulled out their books. A few had none, so I let them choose from my shelf. Five minutes later and we were in silence.

Then there was a sound, high, sharp, penetrating. I looked up and it stopped. My eyes fell straight on Connor.

He peered from above his graphic novel, faint red stubble darkening his upper lip. 'What?'

'What do you mean, What?'

'What do you mean, What do you mean, What?'

Teagan snapped her book shut and looked over. Her make-up was so thick her scowl almost fractured it. '*Shut up, Connor!*'

'I didn't do anything.'

'Okay, okay, okay.' I stood, palms spread. 'Everyone be quiet. Back to reading.'

I rarely raise my voice to students. There's a simple reason: when we do, we teach them that aggression is a valid means of resolving conflict. Occasionally teachers have no choice, usually when students are doing something dangerous, but each time I do, I'm afflicted with guilt that sometimes lingers for days.

A little more reading and that sound came again, wheedling, like a nail over glass.

'Connor, I know that's you. You're blowing through a pen lid. Cut it out.'

'Sir,' he said, the biro lid clamped between his lips making his words indistinct, 'do you know why all pen lids have holes?'

'This isn't the time to –'

'It's to stop kids choking. My uncle told me. If you breathe in the lid and it gets stuck in your throat, some air will still get through.'

Instantly, every student in the room put their books down and began studying their pens.

'Everyone, put your pens away.'

'That wouldn't work,' somebody said. 'The hole's too small. You'd still suffocate.'

Connor stood. 'Not necessarily. Time me!' He pinched his nose, sealed the lid like a straw between his lips and began breathing through that whistling aperture. His face reddened.

'Connor, *sit down now.*'

He nodded, waved, sat down – and continued breathing through the lid.

Now Jada stood up. 'Connor, *shut up*!'

Teagan was right there with her. 'Yeah, stop being such an attention-seeker!'

I walked across the room and snatched the lid from Connor's mouth. He fell back, taking great gulps of air. 'Sir,' he said. 'You saved me.'

Everyone laughed – except for me, Teagan and Jada.

'Front of the class, now. Don't argue. Bring your books.'

Connor had already achieved his desired reaction. He complied, marching as a stand-up comedian from his stage.

Five minutes, ten, and the tension eased. They were silent again. I read, keeping one eye on the class, then there was a knock on the door.

'Keep reading.' I crossed the room. 'We still have twenty minutes.'

The glass of the classroom door was frosted, and for a moment the student on the other side was blurred, an indistinct phantom. When I opened it, though, I saw Tessa, small and pale and slack-faced, a stack of papers in her hand.

'Tessa.' I kept my voice low, stepped out into the corridor. 'How's things down the Rabbit Hole?'

She was so white she looked almost on the point of fainting. 'I'm helping in the office today. These are permission slips for your class.'

'Thanks.' I took them. 'And how are *you* going? How's Gonzo?'

The moment lingered while she looked up at me, then her face contorted and she was crying.

I knelt. 'What is it, Tessa?'

'Nobody will talk to me.'

'What do you mean?'

'Lonnie told everybody to stop talking to me.'

'Why would she say a thing like that?'

But all she could do was sob, and they were the cries of an even younger child, unhidden, unashamed, a convulsive affair of the entire body. Right then I heard a girl's voice behind me in the classroom: *'Shut up, Connor!'*

I stood, half turned, saw with relief that Bill – a no-nonsense Mathematics teacher – was approaching. 'Bill, Tessa's a bit upset. Can you take her down to the Year 8 coordinator's office?'

When they had gone I returned to the room. As I entered there was a moment of trembling silence – I could sense that something had just been said, something incendiary – then Connor laughed, knelt on his chair to gain more height and turned to Teagan and Jada. He flicked the words at them like darts: 'Whatever, Cake-Faces.'

'*Connor!*' Now I was yelling – almost. 'Outside. You can read in the corridor. We'll talk when the bell goes.'

Again he was on his feet, smiling, strolling. It was more than Teagan could handle.

'Watch your mouth, you fuckwit.'

'Alright, Teagan. You can come and sit up the front where Connor was.'

'*What the fuck? This was all his fault!*'

'Stop swearing at me, Teagan.'

'I didn't swear *at* you!'

Teagan's life: her parents' divorce, the chaos, the instability, the near-fatal car wreck from which she had been cut, bloodied and broken – I sensed it all in the room then, felt its immense weight.

'Come to the front and we'll have a chat.'

'This is *fucked.*' She swept her pencil case across the room in a clattering rainbow of textas and sharpenings then walked out, overtaking Connor and slamming the door so hard the frosted glass bulged and stretched with an almost impossible elasticity. Somehow, it did not break.

I followed to see her disappearing up the corridor.

'Teagan, you need to come back.'

She turned for a moment. 'Go back to your class. You're leaving them unsupervised. Great teacher you are.'

Then she was gone.

12

Fight

You're a parent; your child is being bullied. This is not a matter of interpretation or misunderstanding. It's clear-cut. There are multiple witnesses. The bullying could be emotional, physical or a combination of the two. You know who's doing it.

And it's *affecting* your child. Maybe they've claimed to be sick some mornings when you weren't quite sure. Maybe they've told you not to worry about paying for the upcoming camp, that they don't want to go anyway. Maybe they cry out in their sleep, or insist they're not hungry when you cook breakfast.

You don't expect your child's school to do something. You expect them to do *everything*. And, in instances like these, they should.

After Tessa's breakdown in the corridor, myself and the Year 8 coordinator – a hulking PE teacher named Paul – spoke to almost every student in 8G. At last, a clear picture emerged. The previous day, Lonnie had explicitly told a group of girls to ignore Tessa when she approached them. Tessa was, Lonnie said, a bitch and an attention-seeker who thought she was better than everybody else; in Year 7 she had wronged Lonnie in some vague, indeterminate way that could never be forgiven. To befriend Tessa was to challenge Lonnie, and there wasn't a girl in the year level prepared to take the social risk.

'I did manage to speak to her mother,' Paul said, as a call over the PA system summoned Lonnie to his office.

'You've done better than I have.'

'It wasn't easy. We're trying to sort out a time for her to come in for a meeting.'

Like the rest of the class, Lonnie had submitted her memoir inspired by Androcles and the Lion. The moment of great kindness shown to her, she said, was when her grandfather lifted her onto his shoulders at the football. He was, she said, skinny and stooped and his arms trembled, but he wanted her to see the game.

How did that make you feel?

Loved.

When Lonnie arrived she was in the company of perhaps eight other girls. It was lunchtime. Paul clapped his huge hands together, eyes smiling behind a grey beard. 'You can run off, girls. We only need Lonnie at the moment. She'll catch up with you afterwards.'

Her power in the group was palpable. They looked to her, and she almost nodded her permission. They ambled away.

'Hi, Lonnie.' I gestured towards a seat. 'We wanted to have a chat with you about something that's been going on recently. Have you got any idea what that might be?'

She looked at each of us. 'No.'

'Yesterday Tessa was very upset,' Paul said. 'She claims you had been telling other girls not to talk to her.'

Lonnie's face contorted in a mask of defiance. 'I never said that.'

Paul's voice remained level, kind. 'We've spoken to a few other girls who agreed with Tessa.'

'Who?'

'It doesn't matter who.'

She had bright green eyes and wore hoop earrings – technically not uniform. 'Well, if people are talking shit I should be allowed to know who they are.'

'Don't use that language, please, Lonnie.' Paul wrote something in his diary and I saw Lonnie straining to read it upside-down. 'Did you say anything *like* that about Tessa?'

'Well, she came over when I was talking to Bethany, and she interrupted. So I said not to talk to her until I'd finished because she was being rude. I didn't say *never* to talk to her.'

I tried to sound unbiased, formal. 'That sounds quite different from what we've been hearing.'

'People are lying then. That's all I said.'

'So you don't have any problem with Tessa?'

'No. As long as she doesn't interrupt me.'

I let Paul take the lead, and he and Lonnie talked for some time. Her explanations were nebulous, imprecise. Every allegation against her was a misunderstanding or overreaction. Worse, her rebuttals would require both of us to go back and speak to dozens of students all over again.

By the end of the meeting Lonnie had at least warmed a little. She would not, however, apologise to Tessa; she remained insistent that she had done nothing wrong. Before he let her go, Paul spoke seriously and earnestly about the importance of kindness, the need to think carefully before we speak, and the fact that we don't need to be friends with *everyone* but should nonetheless treat them the way we expect to be treated ourselves.

'What's your feeling?' I asked Paul, once she had gone.

'She is bullying Tessa, I think,' he said. 'And some of the other girls are probably quite intimidated by her. You saw how she spoke to me, and I'm her coordinator.'

He was right. But she was only twelve, too, with dirt under her nails and a mother who did not return phone calls from The School. What if Tessa had been born to Lonnie's parents, and the reverse? Would it be Lonnie sobbing behind that frosted glass door, nails clean, hand shooting upwards when the teacher posed a question?

But our responsibility first and foremost was protecting the real Tessa, and not allowing ourselves to be distracted by the shade of a different, imaginary Lonnie.

*

Lonnie's world beyond school was a closed one, an indistinct landscape whose topography I could only guess at; it might remain forever unseen and unmapped. Whatever took place in that dim shadow country was, I felt, the cause of both girls' problems. Tessa was paying a price for the darkness of Lonnie's world, just as my friends and I paid a price for the darkness of Jude's world all those years ago. The only way to understand the problem was through Lonnie's mother, and – for the time being at least – I had to rely on Paul for that. He told me not to worry about calling her again.

A dark world into which I *had* been invited was the one inhabited by Charlie Blanco. That invitation had been gradual, but by the time he was in his final year at The School he spoke with me freely and openly.

'You don't need to worry, sir,' he said not long after my meeting with Paul and Lonnie. 'I'm not moving out this year.'

It was the end of an unseasonably hot March day. I was on yard duty near the carpark, which slashed at us with the aching glare of chrome, mirrors and glass. Insects screamed, and homebound students shambled like biblical pariahs.

'What happened?'

'Nothing. It just fell through. We can't scrape the money together.'

'But what about your dad?'

He squinted into that scalding light. Sweat beaded on his forehead. 'He's not staying with us right now. But I'm scared he'll come back. I'm not going to lie to you, sir.'

'You just let me know the moment you feel that you're not safe.'

He laughed, though it was mechanical, humourless. 'Sometimes I'm more worried about what I could do to *him*.'

At seventeen, Charlie was already an accomplished kick-boxer. After our ritual handshake that day (and the usual interrogation on why I still had not proposed to my partner), he had been telling me about the upcoming fight for which he was preparing. He was single-minded, training every day of the week and even jogging while wrapped in plastic garbage bags to keep his weight down. His aim that year was to win an Australian title, and there would be numerous fights to get through before he would have the opportunity.

It had all started years before, when I first taught him. A few boys had begun bullying Charlie and Xavier at the bus stop. One of them even leapt into Tia's car, repeatedly punching Charlie until Tia managed to drag him out. But it was far more than that.

'I have this image in my head of my dad as a tough guy,' he told me once. 'I want to know that I can beat him.'

The irony was that Charlie hated violence. In many ways, it was fear that had driven him into the ring. But the kickboxing helped; he took it up seriously not long after the incident at the bus stop, and soon found that he was not as angry as he had once been, not as bitter towards the universe that had tossed and tumbled him through his early childhood years. He had an outlet, he could channel his feelings, and his coach (a retired cattleman with a dirty ponytail and a nose as flat as the palm of his hand) was a good mentor.

With this came a newfound desire to protect his little brother, and not just in a physical sense. Charlie would often visit Xavier's teachers in their offices, enquiring about how he was going. Did he pay attention in class? Was he doing his homework? In the absence of an available father, Charlie had unconsciously assumed the role. As noble a gesture as this undoubtedly was, it worried some teachers. A few even phoned Tia and warned that he was taking on too much.

'I'm glad you're staying with Tia this year,' I told Charlie. 'But I meant what I said, too. I want to know you're safe. Talk to me if you need to.'

'I'll always talk your ear off, sir.'

Regardless of how tough Charlie was, I worried about him. I was aware again of that *other* Seadale, the one beyond the glowing boathouses and seaside restaurants. It was the Seadale of graffiti, broken concrete, shuttered rental properties smelling coldly of dust and cigarettes smoked long ago. As kids walking those streets, my friends and I had joked that the shoes dangling from the power lines were secret codes. One pair above a lot choked with blackberries indicated a boy had died there; another near a derelict shed was an advertisement for heroin.

'I know you will, Charlie. And don't overdo the training.'

He cocked his head to the side and gave me a look of mock reproach. 'I won't. And propose to Greta, for God's sake.'

I thought then of a day when Charlie had spied a boy roughing up his brother in the schoolyard. This was after his kickboxing had taken off, and Charlie didn't hesitate. It all happened very quickly: torn shirts, bloodied noses, the breath-stealing thud of asphalt, a gathering crowd – and then the teachers, pulling the boys apart. That day, the bully had been lucky.

A Year 9 coordinator sat Charlie down afterwards. 'This is because of your kickboxing,' she had said. 'They did it on purpose. You're a target now because you like to fight.'

Charlie had walked out of there sad and seething. The coordinator didn't understand who he was or where he was from. He hated fighting, violence, conflict. The memories were lodged in him like shards from a shattered mirror: the machete, the blood on his sister's neck, the police crowded into that little room.

This was Australia in the twenty-first century, but every bit as horrifying was the experience of another child around the same time on a different continent, a girl who had hidden behind her bedroom door and waited, knowing that she had two options: either come out, or let those men come for her.

13

When the boys lose

Licking the afterbirth from the calf did not cure Wambui of bedwetting. Nor did any of the other suggestions of the village women, which she diligently tried, including drinking tea made from salt each night before bed. In the end it was time that fixed the problem.

Kaandiki was a place of rusted corrugated iron, red soil, laughing crowds. Verdant growth thrived everywhere, unintimidated by the labours of humankind. Fences and even the wires from electricity poles were lost beneath creepers, and the ground in places was a lush green blanket onto which a girl could fall, arms spread.

Wambui saw herself as a tomboy, and she loved to be outside, especially with her grandfather. From a very young age he would take her out to work with the chickens, cows and goats, some of which he even named after her. In the evenings she would see the women setting up rickety stalls by the roadside, where they would sell kale, spinach, tomato, onions, potatoes. There was a sense of belonging, of being just one small part in something larger. The place often thronged with people. One of the first things to strike her when she came to

Australia was just how lonely it was. You could walk outside and find yourself in an empty street, everybody shut away in their cars and houses.

Like everywhere else, though, Kaandiki was not a utopia. Jobs were difficult to come by, and pay was low. At the local shopping centre were several bars where men milled about in caps and loose shirts. Many of these men, Wambui knew, were alcoholics, and she never saw a woman go in there. Sexism was coded into the routines and rituals of the town, its origins seeming to lie in the religious legacy of the European missionaries. Before dinner every evening, Wambui's grandmother would wash her grandfather's hands.

Worse, though, was the very real danger. Wambui and her little sister were allowed to walk together to the bus stop to go to school, but otherwise were discouraged from going out alone. As she got older, she became aware of reports of rapes.

Sometimes, late in the night, she would hear a certain type of scream – high, keening, resonant – and know that something terrible was happening. That scream was a call to arms for the villagers, who could not rely on the local police for protection. If it wasn't that scream it would be a house alarm. When one sounded, the neighbourhood men (including Wambui's father, a pastry chef) would answer the call, gathering together to confront whatever robbers or rapists might be waiting in that lightless void beyond the safety of their own homes.

One night, Wambui sat in her bed trembling as a nearby house alarm ruptured the darkness with its ceaseless cry. She heard the urgent, confused fumbling of her father rising from deep sleep, and immediately afterwards her mother's voice: '*Usiende! Usiende!*'

But he had to go. And, oftentimes, he would return with stories of home invasion and horror. It was not unusual for Wambui to learn through eavesdropped conversations that axe-wielding robbers – perhaps from Nairobi, perhaps from within the village itself – had marched into sleeping homes and threatened to kill parents in front of their children.

After almost eight years of planning, Wambui flew with her family to Australia at fourteen. She stepped off the plane at Melbourne airport, stunned by the brightness of the place, not least of all everybody's skin, and a month later was sitting in a classroom at The School. I met her in the yard on her first day, not knowing that in a few years she would sit in one of my classes and produce perhaps the most powerful piece of student writing I have read.

*

Do aborted babies have souls?

I had written this question in large black lettering on the board before my Year 12 Literature class entered. As they did – Wambui, Claire the poet, Mya the aspiring archaeologist and Tim the surfer – they eyed it with a range of expressions. Some frowned, puzzled, while others nodded knowingly, revealing to me that they had done their homework: they had read 'Peeling', the latest Peter Carey story in the unit plan.

I was about to learn something about the subculture of The School, perhaps of all schools, though it was not a revelation I had anticipated.

'Well?' I asked the room. '*Do* they?'

Tim, sunburnt and smiling, raised his hand. 'Does anyone?'

'Depends if you're religious or not,' Claire said.

'Doesn't matter if you're religious or not. Souls either exist or they don't.'

The conversation flew about the room in streamers, multi-coloured things that swirled, wove and intersected without ever becoming entangled. Some believed in souls and some did not; some thought yes, if souls exist then the smallest foetus surely has one; others disagreed. We came back to the story.

'Nile is an abortionist's assistant,' I said. 'What are some of the things she says about her job?'

Mya now, squinting over the pages: 'She says she has killed more people than live in their street.'

Tim: 'She doesn't know why they don't get named in the births, deaths and marriages.'

Claire, wincing: 'Gross. She reckons the abortions sound to her like a pear being sliced.'

'Mr Murray, does it really sound like that?'

I doubted it and told them so.

'The big question,' I asked, wondering not for the first time while teaching this story if anyone in the room had aborted a pregnancy, 'is what's the deal with the dolls?'

In the story, Nile passes the hours by stripping dolls of their hair and eyes and painting them white. In the bizarre climax, her unnamed male companion is undressing her and discovers – after peeling off layers of her skin – that at Nile's own core is one of her dolls, small and featureless.

'We're focusing too much on the abortions.' Mya's hair was unbraided today, but still her books were stacked with archi-tectural exactitude, her margins ruled. 'This story is about how disgustingly sexist men can be.'

I thought of her parents' marriage break-up, her relocation

from Queensland to Victoria, the parenting role she had taken on for her younger brother. I waited, gave her time.

'The story is not from Nile's perspective. It's from this creepy guy who is maybe her boyfriend and maybe isn't. And she wants to talk with him about her feelings – about the little lost souls she feels responsible for – but he doesn't care. He basically tells her to shut up. When she doesn't he *actually* says . . .' She paused, flipping through pages. '. . . He says that Nile might as well have kicked him in the stomach. *That's* the metaphor he chooses.'

'Oh my God,' somebody breathed. 'He *does*.'

And, as so often happens, the students learnt more from one another than they ever did from me.

'He just wants her to be quiet and submissive,' Mya finished. 'He wants her to be a doll, and that's exactly what he gets. When he's stripping her clothes off and she becomes the doll, Carey describes some strange noise like glass breaking. The boyfriend doesn't listen to her and he destroys her. That's what the smashing sound represents. I think Carey is showing us the damage men do when they objectify women. Actually, Nile's boyfriend would fit in with some of our boys.'

'What do you mean?' I asked.

There was a collective, sympathetic groan that I knew well. I heard it whenever I didn't know the name of a band, or misunderstood some pop-culture reference.

'Not *all* the boys.' Mya patted Tim's arm. 'But a lot of boys our age are absolutely disgusting, Mr Murray.'

A murmur of agreement. Hands raising, palms spread like blooming flowers.

'I won't name names,' Mya continued, 'but somebody used the word "fag" in the Year 12 Study Centre yesterday. I picked him up on it, and he said, "Oh, sorry, I meant *faggot*." I don't think I've got through a single day of my schooling without hearing that word.'

I was naïve. Teachers in the schoolyard are often surrounded by a radius of respectful behaviour; you will see trouble-making students fall silent on your approach. When you pass, you know their conversation – their behaviour – will resume. The teacher's presence is like the glow from some shifting fire that sends antisocial behaviours retreating momentarily into the dark. This was something I had understood dimly, but only during this conversation did its true significance become apparent. I heard the word 'faggot' perhaps a couple of times a semester, and challenged it on every occasion, even outlining its horrifically violent origins. Since my own childhood, I had somehow forgotten the degree to which unsupervised children can be exposed to cruelty, bigotry and judgement.

Just then I had a memory triggered, the way a chord of music might remind you suddenly of a forgotten song. It had been a Friday afternoon (hot, bright, sweat-smelling) and I was in my final months before graduating from The School. Standing at my locker and packing the books I would need for the weekend, a boy had roared into the back of my head, *Hurry up, you stringbean faggot!* He was popular, athletic, the perfect cliché. Before I could respond, a girl who I only remember for her long, pale face and tumbling red hair began to berate him. In reply, the boy just repeated, over and over and in laughing exasperation, *He knows I'm joking*.

How, I wondered, had I forgotten about that until just now? I had become uncoupled from what was perhaps a vital aspect of childhood, certainly one vital for a teacher to understand. Something of that distant time – the vulgarity, the sexism, in some instances the explicit desire to harm the marginal-ised – had simply faded away.

'You have no idea, Mr Murray.' Claire's eyes were dark unblinking pools, glittering with intensity. 'The boys have taken over most of the Year 12 Study Centre. They create a massive ruckus, and nobody challenges them, especially not the girls. And they sit around on their phones looking for bikini pictures of local girls on social media, and if the girls don't go to The School they message their friends up the road at Beachview High to get their names. The boys there are just as bad. It's *everywhere*.'

It was the same study space where, all those years ago, that boy had reduced me to a 'stringbean faggot'. And that, I knew, was nothing. What of the students who actually were homo-sexual? Or the ones who were treated in this manner day after day? I do not for a moment feel that I was bullied after Jude disappeared, and this was perhaps part of the reason I was able to forget that experience in the Year 12 Study Centre.

'I was at a party with a heap of Beachview High kids recently,' somebody said. 'A boy verbally abused his girlfriend in front of everyone. It was all, "You used to be fun" and "You never used to be such a bitch". Nobody pulled him up on it.'

Tim was staring down at Carey's *Collected Stories* like it was suddenly infused with a strange power. 'Maybe that's why Nile's boyfriend in "Peeling" doesn't have a name. Maybe it's Carey's way of saying that he's sort of *all* men. Or lots of them.'

Mya was emphatic. Her cheeks were flushed, and I could see the anger now. 'Freya, do you remember the Year 8 Swimming Carnival?'

Everyone turned to Freya. She didn't falter. 'At the Year 8 Swimming Carnival a boy groped me under the water. I won't say who, but he's since graduated. He got in trouble, obviously. But recently – only, like, a few months ago – I asked my mum why she didn't push to have the boy expelled. And you know what she said?'

We waited. The electric clock whined.

'She said, "You begged me not to push for that. Begged me."'

Right then another girl put up her hand. She was dating the captain of the local footy team, and for that reason enjoyed a kind of regal status in The School's social landscape.

'The boys at the footy club.' She said it with a kind of tired resignation that could have meant everything or nothing. '*Some* of the boys at the footy club. You don't want to be around them when they lose.'

The bell tolled. It was not yet lunchtime, so they all hurried off to their following lessons. I was left pondering those words, which seemed to be infused with a terrible significance that lay somewhere beyond the shifting glow of my adult awareness.

14

Peeling

THE FIRST THING I did was send everything the girls had told me to the Year 12 coordinator in an email flagged as highly important. I spent almost no time in the Study Centre, but the coordinator's office was there. It was his role not only to monitor and supervise the space, but to follow up all the allegations my students had made.

The next thing was to speak with Teagan and Jada about the events of our last Year 9 English session. I still hadn't addressed what had happened. Some deeper, more complex social machinery was grinding away beneath the superficiality of these classroom irritations. I wondered in particular about the make-up our coordinators so ruthlessly policed. More than once I had seen them stand, arms folded, as students scrubbed their faces pink with coarse wipes.

I decided, too, that I needed to talk to Teagan about her car accident. It was a huge part of her biography. If I could understand it then maybe I could begin to understand her.

I eventually found them sitting alone below a weeping willow near the back of The School. It was a lonely spot that I rarely visited, and which was technically off-limits to students.

Behind them was the tumbledown back fence of an adjoining housing-commission home, and nearby a pile of mulch was half-visible above clotted tussocks of unmown grass.

I saw the eye-rolling on my approach and cut it off. 'It's okay, I'm not here to tell you off. I just wanted to have a chat.'

'You should be talking to Connor.'

'I will. But I wanted to talk to you first.'

They were on a rickety picnic table I had never noticed before, its warped planks and rusted bolts hidden by the shade of the willow. The graffiti on the table had all the hieroglyphic detail of an Egyptian tomb.

'Connor has no right to disrupt the class the way he does,' I said, sitting down. 'And he *definitely* doesn't have the right to call you names. And I take responsibility for all that. I'm the teacher and it's my job to get him to do the right thing.'

Both peered back at me from behind their masks of foundation and concealer. The thickness of it gave their skin a coarse look, almost like sandpaper. I saw now, though, how different each girl was. Teagan was stern, self-assured, ready to tackle the world, while Jada was quieter, deferential. She often looked to her friend as we talked.

'It's not the first time we've heard "cake-face", sir.' I smelt cigarettes on Teagan's breath as she spoke. Now, though, was not the time to challenge her.

'That doesn't make it okay. If anybody says that to you again I want you to let me know.'

'Why?' Jada's voice was high, sharp. A subtly upturned nose and a sceptical half-smile gave her an elfin quality. 'The coordinators will just tell us to take our make-up off. They care more about uniform than they do about our education.'

'I don't think that's fair.'

'Yeah?'

I sighed. 'I don't know anything about make-up, except that my partner likes to wear it. It seems a bit unfair when we're getting ready to go out to dinner or something. She always say to me, "Men have it easy."'

'They do,' Teagan said.

I told the girls some of the stories my Year 12s had shared and asked what they thought about it. They shrug noncommittal. Teagan had never noticed any sexism from boys her age.

'I mean, it's not like any boys *tell* us we need to wear make up,' Jada said. 'If they did we'd tell them where to go.'

By then the girls' hostility had evaporated. The willow made a sound like fire as it shifted in the hot breeze.

'Do you find it annoying putting your make-up on each morning?'

'Yeah.'

'Why don't you just skip it then? Sleep in? I'm not saying this because of the uniform policy.'

'We can't.'

'How come?'

'It's just not a *thing* to go out in public without make-up.' Teagan was answering all the questions now. 'And I don't look good unless I have it on.'

'Don't be ridiculous.'

'I'm *not* being ridiculous. You don't get it. There's a lot of pressure. It's just what girls have to do.'

I thought absurdly of the painted dolls in 'Peeling', stripped of identity, reduced to objects. I thought, too, of Mya's analysis. I had been ready to guide the class into a discussion of the ethics of abortion, but she had redirected me. This was really about gender and power. And who was *I* to be talking to Teagan and Jada – however indirectly – about the patriarchal pressures on teenage girls? What did I know about it? It should have been Mya sitting there, not me.

I asked, 'Have the coordinators tried to get you to take it off?'

Teagan scoffed. 'Yeah. But I always say no. I'll just sit in the chair and refuse. And if they keep going I'll walk out and go home. One day that happened because I wouldn't take off a coloured headband.' She looked at me in a kind of desperate appeal. 'A *headband*. And Mr Dodson followed me all the way home.'

Spread amongst the ratty, unmown grass around us was a universe of dandelion seed heads. As kids, I remembered, my friends and I would blow on those fragile orbs after making wishes, few of which ever came true: Nick wanted to captain Australia in the Ashes, Luke wanted Kate in our class to fall in love with him, I wanted to be the next Stephen King. Something about the silent neglect of that corner of The School gave me a sense that the past was pressing down upon us. I felt that if I glanced across the aching glare of the schoolyard I might glimpse Jude, or my younger self, or *my* old teachers, but I did not. It was decades later and I had grown up.

'Teagan,' I began. 'Don't feel pressured to answer, but I wanted to ask about your accident. How you're recovering.'

She swung around and hoisted her leg onto the bench. An inflamed, triangular scar covered almost the entirety of her left calf.

'My gosh, Teagan.' Unsure where to go, I added absurdly: 'That looks painful.'

'It's not so bad. That crash in some ways was the best thing that's happened to me.'

'How?'

'Because it woke me up.' She looked off across the glare of the yard. 'The drinking, the partying, all that. I had to get out of it. You look at things different when you're only fourteen and you think you're dead.'

*

Just before the crash, Teagan had moved out of her mother's home to live with her fourteen-year-old stepsister, Belle. Teagan was honest with me about her reasoning: at her home the boundaries were too strict, at Belle's she had more freedom. It was easier to get away with smoking and drinking, and soon the girls had settled into a life of dangerous freedom. They often skipped school, and began associating with older boys and even men. Disaster was inevitable.

One of those men was Lance. He was eighteen, whip-slender, and carried with him a hinted darkness with origins perhaps as distant as his infancy – or older. They could have stirred even further back, before his birth, maybe even before the birth of his parents. He had been cast into this world on the dark rush of an ancestral wave, its awesome momentum unfelt because it had always been there: in lonesome cradle-nights of unanswered howls, in skipped meals, in adult voices made of gravel and glass, in opportunities missed or never even considered.

When Lance arrived at the house that morning there were already two other girls in the car. It was a weekday and Teagan and Belle should have been at school, but they made the decision to climb in.

Teagan, sleepy, took the front seat. When Lance looked at her, his pupils were wells sinking into an impenetrable blackness. 'Just gonna go to a friend's place first.'

They drove a short distance and pulled up at a small weatherboard house shadow-smeared by gum trees. The windows offered damp reflections of the girls' own pale faces peering out of the car. The freeway rumbled with trucks nearby and the sound system thudded. Lance went inside.

The girls chatted for a while, and at some point Lance's friend's mother came out. They had met her before. She was a kindly woman with tired eyes and a slight rasp to her voice. As soon as she appeared, Teagan could see that she was worried.

'Going out with Lance today, hon?'

'Yeah. Going to Beachview. Just waiting for him to come back.'

The woman pursed her lips, looked back at the house. The screen door whined and Lance appeared, talking loudly now, quickly, his movements jerky.

'Listen.' She lowered her voice. 'Be really careful.'

Teagan knew there were implications in those words, some warning she could and probably should examine. Still, she put her head back and closed her eyes as the car roared up the street, moving with the surge of Lance's ancient wave, which was just about to break.

The car was carried from Seadale into an adjoining suburb. Aside from a few morning commuters the traffic was light. Teagan dozed. The tyres murmuring on the road sounded like the deadened rushing of water. Going fast, they went down a hill, into a depression, began to climb, the engine labouring as they accelerated. The road levelled and they sped up once more: sixty, seventy, eighty kilometres per hour.

Lance veered off the road, into a ditch and slammed head-on into a power pole.

The impact was such that Teagan did not wake up, but transitioned directly from sleep to unconsciousness. There was a wheel-lifting concussion, roaring glass, the hot stink of petrol and coolant as the vehicle disgorged its entrails. The car was no longer a car but something else now, a terrible symbol that belonged for the children not in reality but in half-glimpsed news bulletins and cautionary schoolroom posters. There were screams. One of the girls wet herself. The power pole fractured, but remained upright.

Lance punched out his driver's side window and climbed free. Belle and the other girls also managed to escape. Only Teagan remained inside.

When she did wake up a fire truck had arrived. A man was at her window. He smiled at Teagan from beneath his huge yellow helmet, gentle, sympathetic eyes hovering mesmeric over a whiskered jaw.

'You're alright, sweetheart.' His words and mouth seemed a fraction out of sync. Teagan's head buzzed. 'You're fourteen, right? My daughter's that age. Try not to move too much.'

She saw in the side mirror that she was covered in blood. It felt like the great jaws of a steel shark had closed over her lower body. Looking down, she realised her legs were pinned by the dashboard, which had been forced backwards by the engine block. The entire front of the car seemed to be bearing down on her like a knee to the chest, all that steel and grease and petrol and heat. The power pole they had hit loomed crookedly overhead.

'Don't worry, sweetheart. It's not half as bad as it looks.'

Teagan looked over to the road and saw other firefighters

shouting; they were trying to get their friend back, telling him that the car could catch fire. He just grimaced and waved them off.

Then the pain hit. Teagan rocked her head back, screaming, wanting to wrench at her leg to deaden the pain but unable to do so because the fractured windscreen had collapsed onto her lap.

'*Give me scissors!*' As she wailed, the fireman perhaps heard his own daughter. '*I need to cut my leg off.*'

'You're doing great, Teagan. We'll have you out of there soon. And the ambos will be here for pain relief.'

She looked at her bleary, bloodied world and it was nothing but pain: the fractured glass, the razor-edges of tortured steel, the tottering pole – all of it seemed part of her, part of her *leg*, so that there was no division between her shredded nerve endings and the surrounding destruction. With a moan she bit down on her tongue so hard that her mouth filled with blood. For a moment at least, the agony was somewhere else.

What came next was a blur of pain and shock and near-delirium. Her mother arrived, Belle having telephoned her to say that Teagan was dead; later, Teagan could only imagine how that drive to the site of the accident must have felt. A little while afterwards, the power pole caught fire. Teagan could have burnt to death in minutes were it not for the rapid efforts of the emergency services. Still trapped inside, she watched as water from the hoses streamed down the pole and formed dirty, steaming puddles in the footwell of the car. Her fireman stayed with her the entire time, but the problems compounded. Somebody decided that the pole was in imminent danger of falling onto the car, and that the only option was to drag the wreck clear.

After dosing her with morphine, they secured a winch to the back of the car and started to pull. Teagan drifted in and out of consciousness, the agony spiking occasionally despite the drugs. She felt herself lurch, jolt, heard a sharp crunching as the ruined bonnet came away from the pole. As the vehicle levelled there was a new sound as projections of steel cut sparking gouges in the road. Finally, the scene was safe enough that they could begin the process of cutting Teagan free and saving her life.

'I can't even tell you what it was like,' she said to Jada and me as we sat, a year later, on that old picnic table at the back of The School. 'The sound when they cut the roof off. It was *so* loud. And they had to unscrew my seat because they were scared I'd broken my back. And I had. Five vertebrae. But like I said, it was a good thing. I'm different now. I'm back at home. And I want a good life.'

We sat in silence for a while. I thought of what Teagan had seen, what she had experienced, and imagined her storming home (an assistant principal in pursuit) because she wouldn't remove her headband. She existed in two entirely different worlds, each absurd in its own way. Did it *really* matter if Teagan wanted to wear a coloured headband? For her, couldn't something like that – small as it was – help to stave off the dark memories of that other world, the world of danger, reck-lessness, the risk of death? And that world did linger: years later, a different Teagan with a child on her arm would admit to me that she had still been having flashbacks and nightmares the year I taught her.

'Hey, sir,' she said to me that day on the old picnic table. 'I'm sorry for swearing at you. I actually really like your class.'

'Yeah.' Jada smiled. 'English is the best.'

Each year, teachers are required to complete performance and development plans that are ultimately assessed by a senior colleague. Nothing they ever say, however, compares to the validation of a kind, appreciative student.

'Thanks,' I told Teagan. 'Honestly, that means . . . heaps.'

The bell tolled, we went to class, and a week later it was holidays.

15

Night visit

THE THING THAT woke her was not one of the nightmares of early childhood, the nightmares that sometimes visited thirteen-year-old Tessa still. It was something more real, more modern and no less monstrous. In fact, the sound was momentarily like a snarl in the darkness, or perhaps the gnashing of teeth. She sat up and waited.

It came again, from across the room. It was her silent phone vibrating across the wooden top of her dresser. She kept it face-down, so the glow now came as only a sliver of light.

She lay back. Whatever that was, she could check in the morning. Minutes ticked by. Then it rattled and buzzed again. And again.

When I climbed onto the school bus as a twelve-year-old at the end of the day, Jude was finished with, at least until the following morning. For students today, the bully's reach extends much further. And we can't think of phones and computers as mere devices; somehow, through some insidious combination of marketing and adaptation and naïve social sleepwalking, we have allowed them to become extensions of our children's selves. The idea that we can simply confiscate the devices or ban them from bedrooms shows an ignorance of how far the problem has developed. That invisible world – pulsing all around us in wi-fi and Bluetooth signals – has grown into a sinister peripheral nervous system, with each child's thumbs acting as a synaptic bridge to the core of the self. For a victim of bullying, other students' cruel remarks online are as uncontrollable and intimate as their own thoughts. The words of today's bully can come in the still of night, whispering through sleep-suppressing blue light to write themselves directly into their victim's psyche.

Those vibrations kept coming, one after another after another.

Eventually Tessa got out of bed and picked up her phone. Her small face shone an icy blue in the darkness as she began to read.

Term Two:
Autumn

1

Datum

WHAT WOULD EVENTUALLY develop into one of the most challenging periods of my career began with a call to the Year 8 coordinator's office on the first day of term. I wandered over at recess and found Paul waiting for me with a series of printouts. Immediately I saw that they were screenshots.

'We had a nasty incident in the holidays, Brendan.' He motioned for me to shut the door. 'It's Tessa. You might've noticed that she isn't here today?'

'I don't have my Year 8s until after lunch.'

He slid the printouts across the desk. 'Have a look. Almost the entire class is involved – the girls, anyhow.'

It appeared to be a Year 8 Science project. Tessa's name was at the top.

'Ross gave them this assignment to complete over the break,' Paul said. 'They were all working with online documents that the whole class could access and comment on – Ross is big on peer feedback and support. But look at *these* comments.'

Running down the right margin of Tessa's work were dozens of electronic speech bubbles. Each one identified who had made the comment, and Paul was right; they came from about a dozen girls, all members of 8G.

'See the date and time stamps?' He pointed. 'All late on that middle Saturday night of the school holidays. It's not a coincidence. They ganged up on her. And poor Tessa, being such a studious kid, had it set up so the alerts went to her phone.'

Any one of the comments could be interpreted as meaning-less, but together they combined into a cacophony of cruelty: *good work tessa*, *A++++*, *wow amazing tess*, *awesome <3* – and so on it went. I scanned the page.

'And no other students found comments like this on their work?'

'Nope. Just Tessa.'

'And of course Lonnie's name is there.'

'Of course. Date and time stamped. She was the first.'

It was a simple, capitalised *AMAZING*, all sharp edges and sarcasm.

'You won't have to worry about Lonnie.' Paul under-lined something in his diary. 'We'll talk to her, and try her mum again. What I will ask you to do, though, is talk with the entire group about bullying tomorrow. Don't pull any punches. We'll have Tessa and Lonnie out of the class, so you'll just be dealing with the rest of them.' He passed me what looked like a photocopy from a newspaper. 'And read this to them – it's an opinion piece a guy wrote a while back about his own experiences of being bullied as a kid. We've used it before. Happy with that?'

'Sure.' I slumped into the chair. 'She's just such a great kid. I don't get it.'

'May not be anything to get. If Tessa wasn't the target it

would be someone else. It can be a way for some kids to assert their power. Build a mob, then turn it loose. Our job is to show Lonnie that's not a good way to be.'

'And what about Tessa today?'

'Her parents couldn't get her to come in.'

I was 8G's pastoral care teacher, as responsible for their wellbeing as I was for their learning. I felt that I was failing. 'What should I do today?'

Paul smiled. 'Business as usual.'

When I got back to my office, there was just enough time before the bell to call Tessa's parents. I dialled the number and her mother, Debra, answered almost immediately.

'Thanks so much for getting in touch, Mr Murray.'

I insisted that she call me Brendan and asked how Tessa was going.

'The last week's been tough. She'd improved a little and we thought we may have been able to get her to school, but this morning was just awful. She couldn't eat her breakfast. My husband almost took the day off work.'

We talked for several minutes about what Debra could do to support Tessa at home. Eventually the bell went, its ear-splitting caw swooping down like some terrible electronic bird.

Debra must have heard it, for she spoke quickly now: 'Would you take a minute to speak with Tessa? She'd love to talk with you. Only if you have the time.'

'Of course.'

There was silence, then Tessa's voice came down the line, quiet, almost guilty. 'Hi, Mr Murray.'

'Hi, Tessa. You taking good care of Gonzo?'

'Me and Mum took him for a walk this morning.'

Something in my chest shifted. 'He would have loved it.

111

He'll be loving having you at home, but we don't want him getting too used to it.'

'Yeah.' I could almost hear Tessa thinking. 'That's another thing. I don't want to fall behind.'

'We'll get this all sorted out and have you back in here in no time. I think a lot of the girls didn't even want to write those comments. They just felt pressured.'

'By Lonnie.'

'Seems that way.'

I looked out the office window. Students were streaming into the Year 8 locker area. I thought then that what was happening to Tessa wasn't just a schoolyard triviality to be remedied; for her, it was – and would continue to be – so much more. These events were writing their way into her personal mythology, just as Jude was a part of my own. In twenty years she would remember it all, would think of it as her own children walked alone through squealing school gates for the first time; when at such moments her muscles stiffened with worry, it would be under the clamping grip of a fist reaching up from her own childhood, reminding her that the world was not always a place of safety and that sometimes the dangers were unpredictable, mindless, indiscriminate.

'I *want* to come back,' Tessa finished. 'I don't want to miss out on anything important.'

'Don't worry,' I told her. 'I want you to just find a sunny spot and read *Alice's Adventures in Wonderland*. That'll teach you more about good reading and writing than I can.'

*

In addition to my growing concerns about my Year 8 class, I had the added pressure of the approaching NAPLAN test.

And so that afternoon, after teaching my Year 8s (with Tessa's ghost so oppressive that in her absence she was almost more present than she had ever been before), I began preparing my Year 9s for the annual standardised tests.

The National Assessment Program – Literacy and Numeracy is the standardised testing regime the Australian government uses to get an annual snapshot of student ability. All children in Years 3, 5, 7 and 9 sit a series of tests over the course of a few days in Term Two. The results of these tests are used for a range of purposes, from identifying student weaknesses at a school level to helping parents make decisions about school selection via the MySchool website.

It isn't necessary to point out that standardised testing is controversial. Questions posed by students, teachers, administrators and the general public are myriad, though there's really only one that matters: Does testing of this kind benefit the individual child?

In the last decade, I have seen state education move gradually but inexorably towards an almost pathological fixation on data. Everything must be measured, perhaps in some cases even the immeasurable; if something can't be represented in a graph, plot or chart, that *something* takes on an ethereal quality that puts it in danger of dismissal. The current problem, then, is not the data fixation itself, but the prioritisation of quantitative over qualitative data. Anybody could compare Teagan's Year 9 NAPLAN results with her Year 7 results to get an estimation of growth – it really is primary school mathematics. But how do you measure what lies between? What numerical value can be placed on the experience of watching flames writhe up a power pole as you sit, bloodied and trapped, in a destroyed car? And that's an example we can see. What about the silent struggles of a student coming to terms with their sexuality in a culture where words like 'faggot' are normalised?

We need to be honest about what NAPLAN achieves, and how the data it generates differs from data generated by teachers over the course of a school year. The best way to understand it is in terms of a familiar competition: *How many jellybeans do you think are in the jar?*

The jar is the student, and the jellybeans are what the student can *do*, what they *understand*; in short, their capabilities. What the NAPLAN test does is make a one-off estimate of these abilities with a very limited amount of information (a single test), just like a person at a carnival glancing at a jar of jellybeans and estimating its contents. In some cases, that person's guess may be quite good. They know the size of the jar and the size of a jellybean. Perhaps they count some of the visible jellybeans and do a simple multiplication. Maybe they've played this game before.

That, in essence, is NAPLAN. It can't be dismissed summarily, but nor can it be embraced as a precise measuring tool of student, teacher or school capability.

Now let's consider the teacher's assessments. Teachers aren't forced to make a one-off estimate of student ability, but spend a year making such estimates over and over again. Take writing, for example (one of the core focuses of NAPLAN). Over twelve months, English teachers will assess a student's writing hundreds of times, both formally and informally. It could be as 'high-stakes' as a lengthy essay, or as 'low-stakes' as a glance at handwriting and spelling on a note requesting a trip to the toilet.

It is not open to debate: the assessments of competent teachers are far, far more accurate than NAPLAN – and that's making no mention of the fact that we're the ones who put many of the jellybeans in the jar to begin with.

Why, then, does the government seem to prioritise NAPLAN data over teacher data? At best it's for consistency, at worst it's for ideological reasons that imply a paranoid mistrust of teachers. As with the calculation of Year 12 scores, bureaucrats seem to value external assessment over that which is conducted in schools by professionals in the best position to make such judgements accurately.

None of this, of course, answers our core question: Is the NAPLAN test good for the individual child?

Like competitive ATAR scores and subject scaling, NAPLAN carries with it a bevy of unintended consequences, and there lies the risk to the individual child. An oft-cited danger is that schools will teach to the test. Some people, naïve to the complexity of the issue, will simply say, 'That isn't a problem, because the test assesses what they need to know anyhow.' However, part of teaching to a test means teaching test-taking skills or, worse, teaching NAPLAN test-taking skills. Any school that falls into this trap will find itself teaching children an extraordinarily narrow band of skills with little application beyond the test itself. What does this look like in the classroom? Often, it looks like drilling students on past NAPLAN tests, and issuing mind-numbing warnings about how certain *kinds* of questions can trip up the unwary. I would advise any parent of a child being taught in this way to challenge the school. Be wary, too, when selecting a school, because some insist they do not teach to NAPLAN when in fact they do precisely that in a focused, almost militaristic way.

But the biggest concern of all is a simple one that is rarely acknowledged. Tests are boring. Preparing for tests is boring.

Building lifelong learners is about sparking passion and curiosity, not anaesthetising teenagers by outlining the pitfalls of 'all of the above' questions on multiple-choice tests.

Imagine two fourteen-year-old boys the day before NAPLAN, Student A and Student B. Neither likes reading much, but we know they're still at an age where we can sell it to them, convince them that sitting down with a book is a worthwhile endeavour. We have an hour with each.

With Student A, let's spend half an hour teaching test-taking skills and half an hour doing a practice NAPLAN paper. We'll explain words as we go, prompt his thinking. We'll help him eliminate incorrect answers in multiple-choice questions.

With Student B, let's do something a little different. Let's give him half an hour to read Stephen King's short story 'The Monkey', about a wind-up toy with an eerie connection to several violent deaths. Let's spend the second half of his hour talking about the story, then finish by tipping him off on a few other great stories by Stephen King.

The following day, Student A will do better on the NAPLAN test. But the following *week*, Student B will be reading Stephen King while Student A reminisces about how much he hates English. Perhaps by the following month Student B will have finished a King novel and be in search of another. And by the following year? We can't know, but we can hope.

A while back, I started hearing the phrase *value adding* used around schools, especially in reference to student data. As best I can tell, the term has its origins in manufacturing and marketing. Around the same time, people who once would have been called *wonderful teachers* started being described as *good operators*. *Good operators*, it seems, apply *best practice* to *value add* for students – or perhaps I should anticipate this linguistic trajectory and start calling the children *stakeholders*.

Data has its place, and so does standardised testing. We need to measure student achievement where we can, and devise methods of determining when our teaching strategies have worked and when they can be improved. Not for a moment would I suggest a total abandonment of quantitative data.

So what do I fear? I fear the heart going out of the teaching of English. I fear the day when student learning – especially that measured in standardised tests – begins being referred to as *profits*.

2

Lockdown

I STOOD IN the yard the next day at recess, waiting for my session with 8G to begin. It was cold, but the sunlight was hard, golden. The wind picked up, and a girl's white hijab flapped and whipped furiously, a dazzling contrast with the blue sky beyond.

I did my best, tried to sound tough but caring, frustrated but patient. Focus on the behaviour (we had been taught), not the individual. Neither Tessa nor Lonnie was there, at least, both of them off somewhere with Paul, talking the whole thing through. The remaining girls looked guilty, the boys confused. I talked about Fairness, Responsibility, Respect, did my best to sound like a human being. I reminded them of Androcles and the Lion, and of their own memories of the kindness they had been shown. It's our job to be kind when we can, I said. Yesterday, Tessa didn't feel that she could come to school – didn't feel welcome – and we should all feel terrible about that.

I finished by reading aloud the article Paul had given me. It was hard-hitting, gritty, the visceral reflections of a man bullied almost to the point of suicide in the 1980s. His victimisation had been so ruthless that he missed entire terms of his education.

I thought back to my experiences with Jude. Had I ever been too intimidated to come to school? I tried to recall, and all at once another memory leapt upon me, one I hadn't thought of in years. One weekend, a prank call had come to our house. I answered the phone and heard the voice of an older boy, level, robotic. *You're fucked*, he had said, repeating the incantation several times before hanging up. *You're fucked. You're fucked.* There had been no laughter, no background voices. *You're fucked.*

Initially I had been unbothered, but as the weekend progressed a mounting sense of dread had overcome me. That time I *did* tell my parents, who had been in the kitchen when the call came in. They insisted that it was nothing, just a prank, that the caller probably didn't even know who he was speaking to. I felt that they didn't understand my world. Thinking back, the only voice I can hear coming down that line is Jude's.

What I could not remember was if I missed school that Monday, or any other day because of Jude – including after he pushed me down the stairs. Possibly I had. Possibly there was still more that I could not remember. Whatever the case, I was going to do everything in my power to make sure Tessa didn't feel the way I had back then. At the same time, though, I needed to remember that Tessa wasn't me – and, more importantly, Lonnie wasn't Jude. I needed to remain emotionally distanced, something I've always found difficult, in every area of my life.

Walking to my next class in the throng, I overheard Kelvin and Heath chatting ahead of me.

'I reckon blue,' Kelvin said. 'Like a navy.'

'Yeah. With red trim.'

'Or white?'

'Maybe both.'

I caught up and asked them what they were talking about.

'We're designing the uniform for our basketball team, sir.' Kelvin grinned, his pale face flushing slightly. 'Guess what it's called?'

'Tell me.'

'The Spuds. We're going to have a flaming spud on our uniforms.'

I could still hear their laughter as they moved off into the crowd. I tried to hold on to that little glinting moment, tried to carry it with me like an ember to my Year 9 session. What good was I to my students preoccupied? On my first ever job interview, I had said, starry-eyed, *In a room full of learners, the least important person is the teacher.* I could be morose on my own time. And what right did I have to feel that way, anyhow? Tessa was the one being bullied; Teagan had been cut from a car wreck; Kelvin had survived cancer; and Wambui –

Five minutes into my Year 9 lesson, the PA – a dusty wood-panelled thing certainly older than I was – spoke.

'Attention all students.' It was the principal, his voice brisk but cheerful. *'We will now be commencing a lockdown drill. Please follow your teachers' instructions.'* A short siren followed, then was replaced by the excited chattering of the class.

'Alright, alright.' I flicked the lights off and locked the door, then began rolling down the blinds. 'Under the tables, away from the windows.'

All schools are required to complete at least one lockdown drill each year. In reality, such a lockdown could be triggered by anything from a serious crime in the local area to a student producing a weapon. As far as I knew there had never been a real lockdown at Seadale, though I was aware of them taking place in the high school at nearby Beachview.

I sat with my back to the door, waiting.

'Hey, sir!' It was Teagan. She was crammed in along with the rest of the students beneath the tables. Her face was brown with make-up and she was in hysterics. 'You're my hero!'

'Keep it down. If there's ever a real emergency we'll all be doomed.'

'Mr Murray, would you use one of us as a human shield and make a dash for your car?'

'Are you offering?'

Right then the doorhandle rattled as one of the assistant principals moved down the corridor, checking that we'd locked our classrooms.

In reply, Connor erupted with a comical cry of horror, part scream, part yelp. He threw himself out from beneath the tables and began crawling on his stomach and elbows like a commando, whimpering.

'Connor!' I was battling laughter – always fatal for a teacher giving a directive. 'Back under the table!'

'Help me! Help me! Help me!'

'Give it a rest.'

It was a circuit-breaker, a relief. The drill ended and we somehow managed to get back to work.

*

That night, I dreamt of a School that wasn't quite The School. It was darker, ashen almost, with grey fields of ocean receding into impossible distances beyond the windows. And there was a lockdown, I knew (though there had been neither instructions nor siren); some presence lurked beyond the door, which despite my efforts I could not lock, and when I looked to the haunted faces of my students I realised they were all there: Kelvin, Wambui, Charlie, Grace, Claire – and Tessa, clutching her shivering beagle. She was crammed in with the rest of them beneath a table. At those lightless windows the ocean was rising up, threatening to swamp us, swamp *her*, and I felt the pressure then of something on the other side of the door, something far stronger than I felt I could ever be.

I woke well before dawn feeling tired, incompetent, powerless. The red digits of the alarm clock hovered in the blackness, and I could hear the ocean nearby, cold and thunderous. In four hours I would be at work and I had no idea if Tessa would attend. Maybe she was lying awake right now, counting down the minutes until morning would bare its cold, pragmatic teeth. Breakfast, bus, squealing locker doors. The day.

Teachers dream: of being students again, of sitting exams, of the children about whom we most worry. We talk about this only amongst ourselves because to a broader audience it might seem strange, but people (especially parents) *should* know this. We care about your children enough that they keep us awake at night.

Lying there listening to the waves and waiting for my alarm, I thought of all manner of things. I thought of the times as a teenager when perhaps *I* had been a bully. No Jude, sure, but not always kind. I could say I wasn't the leader, that I just followed others. I could toss out all the excuses in the world, but in that pre-dawn dark they fell flat. I could have been like Kelvin, could have exhibited courage and kindness, but I had not.

I got up, turned on the light and retreated into Peter Carey's *Collected Stories*. They helped, just as books always have in difficult times, for as long as I can remember. I tried to remember how fortunate I was that, each day, I had the opportunity to lead students to that same wondrous discovery.

3

Five-year survival rate

WHEN MY FATHER went to technical school in the 1960s, he
had a teacher who was too kind-hearted to give students the
strap. Well, not exactly; he *gave* them the strap, but so gently
the punishments soon became a game to the boys. They would
deliberately break the rules. One day they waited until the
teacher had left the room, then drew a swastika on the chalk-
board, agreeing to all raise their hands, Spartacus-style, when
asked who was responsible.

'He would just let the strap fall,' my father laughed. 'It
didn't even hurt a little bit.'

It was a recurrent story of my childhood, but one that
took on new meaning when I became a teacher. That man, I
thought, was not the feeble jester of my father's memory. He
was likely protesting what he saw as the cruelty of corporal
punishment, no doubt delivering his painless blows only to
fulfil the demands of his superiors. It did not work in the classroom but perhaps it worked in his heart. *That* was the type of
teacher I wanted to be, not ineffectual in the realm of behaviour management, but courageous, compassionate. My father
and his friends had not understood that it would have been far

easier for that teacher to just beat them like all the rest. He had chosen the difficult road, and paid a price for it.

I had been lucky enough to have teachers like that. Liam, for one. But wondering what he would do about all these growing problems was futile, not least because he had by then already been murdered. They were my classes, my responsibility. Those children were my burden to carry and I would do so, refusing to buckle under their weight.

*

Although figures vary, it's estimated that forty to fifty per cent of teachers in Australia leave the profession within their first five years. I did not, and still love the job. But I have seen far too many exceptional educators turn away from their careers before they've really begun.

Workload is an issue, but a more significant problem is behaviour management. Interpersonal conflict is a part of the job, especially in government schools where middle- and working-class values collide on a daily basis. This is compounded when empathetic young teachers are exposed repeatedly to the heart-rending reality of disadvantage, abuse and mental illness – all factors that make a class difficult to manage.

Much has been said about this teacher attrition, with some dismissing it as an inevitable consequence of a challenging profession. However, little attention has been given to the role schools themselves play in crushing some of our most inexperienced educators.

Each year, high school teachers are given what we call an 'allotment', a series of classes to teach. Some classes are popular (the more academic Year 11 and 12 electives, for instance) while others are less desirable, particularly Year 8 and 9 groups, where behaviour management issues are the norm. Experienced teachers are adept at arguing for their desired allotments. In some cases their arguments are fair and based on the needs of the students, but in others they are not. With all the absurdity of paramedics listing the types of calls they refuse to attend, some teachers will, without a glimmer of shame, declare that they 'don't teach juniors'. I heard a story of a teacher at another school who once raged during allotment time: 'If they give me Year 9s, I'll walk.'

The consequence of this is that allotments become entangled within the ugly world of office politics, personalities and allegiances. In some schools the problem is partly solved by loading up graduates with the classes nobody else wants because they will not complain.

I am aware of a first-year graduate in a challenging school who was given nothing but Year 8 Science classes, a completely imbalanced allotment no experienced teacher would accept passively.

Schools concoct all sorts of justifications for such decisions. The most common is that the graduate teachers are 'late appointments', and are thus given the leftover classes that have not already been allotted. This is nonsense. Allotments can always be shifted, particularly if more experienced teachers are willing to trade classes with graduates to help make their early years more manageable.

If all of us experienced teachers were less selfish in this way, the attrition rate would drop swiftly and considerably.

While the problem of short-term contracts for graduate teachers has been widely acknowledged, what has been overlooked is the impact this has on a graduate teacher's ability to appropriately manage student behaviour.

One of the best ways to deal with serious defiance is to seek support, usually from year level coordinators. Experienced teachers do this every day. The problem for graduates is that they often fear that repeated appeals to coordinators will be seen as incompetence, and will therefore harm their chances of being offered ongoing contracts. This is not helped by schools that openly cite poor behaviour management as a reason for not extending graduates' contracts. I am aware of multiple schools where this has occurred. When word of this gets around (which it inevitably does), new teachers are disincentivised from seeking support. Soon, they are bearing the full burden of responsibility for students exhibiting extraordinarily challenging behaviours. Combine this with an unreasonable allotment and you have a recipe for burnout, all completely the fault of the school itself.

The idea that the five-year attrition rate is intrinsic to the job is simply untrue. It's something *we* are contributing to at a school level.

Universities, too, need to carry some of the responsibility. At the end of my Bachelor of Education, a lecturer asked a room of soon-to-be teachers for feedback. Every one of us said that while we enjoyed the course it was too theoretical, and that we needed more practical skills in behaviour management. That lecturer spent the next ten minutes explaining why we were all wrong. In researching this book I spoke with graduate teachers from a range of institutions, and they all felt that their university studies had not equipped them to deal with the behaviour management challenges of the job. Their courses were, they said, too theoretical.

Academics have challenged me on this point, insisting that it is impossible for people to teach effectively without a firm theoretical base and that behaviour management skills should be developed during teaching rounds. This is a dangerous assumption, as undergraduate experiences of placement are inconsistent. I have met graduates who spent almost all of their practicum rounds in private schools where little or no high-level behaviour management was required.

Behaviour management must be explicitly and practically taught in universities. We have seen graduates who are not even equipped with the most basic techniques – how to construct seating plans, for instance. Worse, some leave university convinced that behavioural issues are the result of insufficiently engaging teaching, and therefore blame themselves for behaviours that are really societal problems manifesting in the classroom.

I was lucky in my early years as a teacher. I had Ana to bounce off, as well as significant support from The School. I also had my own stress management strategies, even if they were as simple as distracting myself by reading Peter Carey when I could not sleep. Each and every year, though, other graduate teachers are less fortunate.

However, there is absolutely no doubt that those first few years were far, far more challenging than I ever could have anticipated. This was due not only to what happened in and out of the classroom, but to the worries I held for my own students, too.

And nothing affected me more profoundly than the story Charlie told me one afternoon as I sat, wordless and shocked, in an otherwise empty Year 9 English classroom. I knew I needed to listen, to be strong and sympathetic. I could shed my tears later.

4

Mother and non-mother

CHARLIE NEVER BLAMED his mother for what happened that night. It wasn't really *her*, whatever that meant; the woman with the machete was some version of her so distorted as to be almost unrecognisable. He had grown used to these shifts, even at only nine years old. Pearl Blanco loved him, but she was a kaleidoscope whose identity could splinter into a million dark fragments as she was tipped this way and that by drugs and disease. Tip the kaleidoscope in the other direction and she would be herself again, a glittering, ever-expanding landscape of warmth and light.

As much as Charlie had settled into life with his aunty, he looked forward to these weekend visits. He loved his mother, and to him she was the most beautiful woman on earth. Her brown face on its slender neck had the lonely look of a mask on some carved stand. Like her children, she was black-haired, true black, and her eyes seemed to hold ancestral reflections of Madrid, the patios of Cordoba, coppery sunsets rusting to darkness over the Balearic Sea. There were always men in her life.

Charlie loved seeing his sister, too. Rachel was fifteen by this time, but to Charlie she might as well have been fifty.

She was an adult, kind and confident and self-assured – all the things Charlie would become in the ensuing years.

Tia dropped the boys off early that Saturday. Pearl took them shopping for Lego, and Charlie and Xavier chose matching trucks that they played with on the smoke-smelling carpet for the rest of the day. Pizza was delivered for dinner. They lounged and watched TV, and for a fleeting moment they were an ordinary family. When the boys were put to bed, they waited until the lights were out then got a torch and resumed playing with their trucks beneath the covers.

They were still awake after midnight when Rachel began to scream.

There was often fighting in the house, and for the past hour or so Charlie had heard his mother and sister going backwards and forwards, mostly in English, sometimes in Spanish. But he had never heard Rachel scream like that before. It was high and relentless and had the power of air escaping from some ruptured thing. Thinking that perhaps somebody had slipped and broken an arm, Charlie jumped from his bed and ran to the lounge room with Xavier close behind.

As they came out into the light they saw their mother brandishing a machete.

Rachel, it seemed, was prepared. Through all the shouting and the chaos Charlie saw that she had a baseball bat. She glanced at the boys and put herself between them and their mother.

'Mum, put it down, for fuck's sake!'

'Don't you speak to me like that!'

'Put it down!'

'This is my house!'

Pearl advanced on her daughter with the machete, the loose

130

awkwardness of her grip only making it more terrifying. The blade rose and then fell in a wobbling arc that Rachel barely avoided.

By then the screams were so loud that Charlie wasn't quite sure which were his and which were everybody else's. Xavier was crying, and on instinct Charlie took him by the arm and dragged him back to their bedroom, dropping to his knees and tumbling his brother beneath the bed. He followed straight after. The smell of dust burnt his nostrils, and the steel springs of the bed pinched and pulled at his hair.

The shouts coming from the passageway were now throat-tearing in volume. There were thuds, the sounds of stumbling and crashing. Charlie shrank from the hard yellow light of the hallway, pressing his body hard against Xavier's. It was useless, he knew. She would come for them, this woman who was both his mother and not his mother.

Time passed, measured not in minutes but in anticipation of a silence that would signify tragedy.

Now both boys were crying. Charlie could still hear two voices, which meant Rachel was alive – for the time being, at least. The thunderstorm cracking and booming through the house would not blow itself out. Rachel needed to be rescued and there was nobody there to do it – no Tia, no Mrs Dellaware (his primary teacher), no cartoon heroes with their perfect timing and bold declarations of justice.

He rolled towards Xavier, their streaming faces scarcely a centimetre apart.

'We've got to go out there,' he said. 'We've got to help Rachel.'

Once he had made the decision, his body moved of its own accord. Charlie's consciousness floated with it like a passenger.

He felt the burn of the threadbare carpet against his palms and then he was on his feet, Xavier close behind. He came out into the passageway and moved through to the lounge room.

His mother who was not his mother stood with the machete trembling in her hands. Her face was locked in a carnival rictus, her eyes bulging. Rachel was on the floor now, sprawled like Andrew Wyeth's Christina; the baseball bat had skittled away, and blood trickled from beneath the fingers she had pressed to her neck. Charlie screamed then, knowing the next slash of the machete could take his sister's head off.

'*No!*' It was not a word, but an animal sound of despair. He roared it through his tears, feeling Xavier close at his back.

His non-mother turned but did not see him. What she did see was the icy blue light flickering across the curtains. Before she could process what was happening, the front door had belted open and two police came thudding in, appearing to Charlie incongruously as an old man and an old woman.

There were bellows, frantic movements, radio hisses like tearing paper. The machete clunked to the floor. Two more police came in, teen-faced, a constable Charlie would come to think of as the cowboy and a pretty girl with her hair in a dark braid.

'C'mon, sweethearts.' The grandmother policewoman – short with a round face and librarian spectacles – ushered the boys to the bedroom and closed the door. 'You just come and talk to me for a tick.'

But there would be no talking. Both boys howled. The policewoman did the best she could, sitting with them on the bed and rubbing Charlie's back, telling him that it would be alright, that he needed to be strong.

Exactly what happened beyond that door Charlie would never quite know. So much of his childhood had been like this: truths half-glimpsed, half-heard, things from which he was shielded, for right or for wrong. There was no firing, at least. As warm as this uniformed grandmother was, he couldn't help but notice her gun, black-handled and malicious.

'You're brave fellas,' she said. 'Real brave fellas. I've got boys. A lot older than you two, but I'd be proud if they were *this* brave.'

The grandfather policeman opened the bedroom door and leaned in, smiling. 'There's me boys.' He winked, a gesture at once crude and kind. 'Let's all come out and have a bit of a chinwag.'

As they returned to the lounge room Charlie saw with a wash of relief that Rachel was alright. There was blood on her neck but not much, and he could see the cut now, no worse than scratches he had suffered himself while playing with Xavier in Tia's garden.

Rachel came to them, calm and efficient, and as she moved the cowboy put a hand on her arm. She twisted, shrugged him off.

'Oi. We need to speak to you –'

'*I* need to look after my *brothers*.'

Charlie's upset turned to something cold and sharp as he looked at that policeman. The officer was half-smiling, nonchalant, playing a role he had perhaps seen in a thousand Hollywood fantasies growing up. The cowboy wanted to show Rachel, his partner and perhaps himself that all this was nothing to him, a bit of fun, a sideshow spectacle he would soon share with his mates at the pub.

As Rachel moved the boys to the kitchen Charlie saw his mother. She was on the couch, with the young female officer standing over her.

'Rachel!' Charlie felt that he was about to cry again, and gripped his sister's shoulders, studying her cut.

'It's alright, Charlie.' She touched her neck, then looked at her fingertips. A little blood was smeared on the pale skin. 'Nothing. Nearly stopped bleeding. Did you tell them anything?'

'No.'

'Good.' She lowered her voice and looked over her shoulder. For the moment, the police seemed preoccupied with their mother. 'This is what you're going to say . . .'

Years later, Charlie came to believe that the story she concocted – designed to protect their mother – was inspired by fear. They had all been raised not to trust police and certainly never to tell them anything. So the boys listened, and nodded, and tried to memorise the narrative that Rachel dictated. It was really all a misunderstanding, things weren't how they had sounded to the neighbours, and certainly weren't how they had looked to the officers who first came in and saw a woman waving a machete.

Rachel went out and spoke with the police. Xavier and Charlie stood behind her, listening. The grandfather officer listened, stern-faced and unmoved, while the cowboy slouched, arms folded. His pretty partner, Charlie noticed, was red-faced and teary.

'I'm staying here,' Rachel told them. 'You lot have the wrong idea about everything.'

'Maybe.' The old policeman scratched his grey head, shrugged. 'But these two are coming with us.' He pointed to the boys. 'Pearl doesn't have custody. They're going back to their aunt's tonight.'

Immediately Xavier began howling again. He was terrified of leaving Rachel behind. Charlie put an arm around him.

'It'll be okay, Xave. Rachel will be okay. She knows what to do.'

There would be no debate. The older two officers took the boys outside and put them in the back of their car. Just before they took off, the old man turned and raised a huge plastic evidence bag sagging with their mother's machete.

'It's me lucky night.' He smiled with big straight teeth that might have been false. 'Got meself a new steak knife.'

Driving into the night, Charlie felt somehow that he and his brother were in trouble. The idea chewed at his guts, made him sweat and squirm in his seat. He peered through the steel-grilled window as the night smeared by, black and blue and orange.

The police pulled up at Tia's house and knocked on the door. There was no answer. When they came back to the car the policeman smiled under the dim internal lights.

'Nobody home, boys. Where's your aunty at?'

'We don't live with her here,' Charlie said. 'We live with her at the other house. The holiday house at the beach.'

'What's the address?'

'I don't know.'

And he didn't, no matter how hard he tried to think. They went back to the station, but no amount of searching on the computer managed to solve the mystery. It seemed like hours before Charlie's mother turned up with a man in black jeans and singlet who neither of the boys had seen before.

This was not the first time the boys had been to a police station, and their mother had taught them exactly what to do.

If ever the police took them away, she said, she would send somebody to come and rescue them; what the boys needed to do was pretend to know the person (no matter who it was), run up and wrap their arms around them. This is exactly what Xavier and Charlie did, Xavier embracing his mother while Charlie buried his face in the sweat-smelling singlet of this strange man.

'It's all good, buddy,' the man had croaked, ruffling his hair. 'We're here now, ay?'

What happened next is difficult for Charlie to understand, even today. The police spoke with this man while their mother went and bought them McDonald's. By the time she returned, the officers were satisfied the boys could go home with their mother, despite everything that had happened only a few hours earlier.

They drove back to the house through empty streets. The first thing Charlie looked for when they arrived was his sister.

'It's okay,' his mother said. 'She's gone to her boyfriend's.'

When Charlie climbed into bed he felt something hard and sharp pressing into his leg. He recoiled, gasping, then realised it was only the shattered remains of his crushed truck.

The light clicked out, revealing a pale rectangle of dawn on the curtains. Pearl's lips were cool on their foreheads.

'Sleep tight, my angels. You done good tonight.'

And Charlie did sleep, not only from exhaustion but also in the knowledge that the woman with the machete was gone. The kaleidoscope had tilted back in the opposite direction and his real mother had returned.

5

Explain this to me

THE MORNING AFTER the lockdown drill I was drained, distracted. The glary overcast of nine o'clock felt wrong, as though I had wandered into a lighted Nordic midnight. As a teacher there is no 'quiet day to yourself', no extended breaks or early finishes. Your students are there and you owe it to them to be ready.

But if there was one thing Charlie had taught me, it was perspective. I imagined him training for his title in spite of the horrors of his childhood. If he could go on, then so could anyone.

When I arrived for Year 12 Literature I found Tim standing at the front of the class holding an awkwardly wrapped present.

'How you going, Doc?'

'Loving life, Tim. What's this?'

The class was laughing when he offered me the gift. I looked down at the flat, rectangular object in his hands – a book, I thought. Its plain white paper made a stark contrast with Tim's suntanned fingers. 'Just a pressie from me and the class.'

It couldn't have been better timed, joke or not. 'Shall I open it now?'

'Up to you, Doc.'

'I'll do it at the end of the lesson.'

I set it on my desk, handed out their essays and gave them twenty minutes to read my feedback and self-correct. While they worked, I sat and half-listened to Mya and another girl talking. I was wondering about the boys' behaviour in the Year 12 Study Centre, but the topic was, unsurprisingly, ATAR scores, scaling and rankings.

'I'm ranked second in Chem,' this girl was telling Mya. 'For now, anyway.'

'How do you know?'

'Mr Ballard tells us our rankings on the tests.'

I pretended not to hear. That was, I thought, a toxic way for a teacher to deliver results. It was bad enough that we had to rank students. *Telling* them their rank was an almost guaranteed way to divert attention from learning to competing. Claire was listening, looking as washed-out and tired as I felt.

'Hey, Mr Murray?' Mya turned to me. 'Will you tell us our ranking?' Her tone was of humorous pleading.

'No way. You don't need to worry about that.' I pointed to my scribbled handwriting on her essay. 'Just focus on how you can improve.'

'Okay. But we pretty much know anyway. In all our classes. Not that it matters. The whole system's corrupt. It favours private schools.'

'Not necessarily.'

'Yeah? Well, explain this to me.' She put down her essay. 'A little while ago Pinewood Grammar taught *the wrong curriculum* for Year 12 Visual Communications Design. They only found out just before the exam.' She took out her phone. 'It was in the news. I'll show you.'

'It's okay. I read about it when it happened.'

'Yeah. Well, I went and checked what results those students got.' She spoke with the unrelenting confidence of a prosecutor. 'One of them was straight A-pluses – that kid was in the top eight per cent of the state. How can you be taught the wrong stuff and still be in the top eight per cent when it's a *ranking*?'

'There was an error at the school,' I said. 'You can't punish the kids for that.'

'It still makes no sense to me.' Her face was flushed.

Right or wrong, the most important part of Mya's critique was that these events made no sense to her. The machinations of high-stakes assessment at Year 12 are the domain of a largely opaque, bureaucratic cabal that allows only fleeting glimpses of its inner workings.

One of the starkest examples reveals itself when a student wishes to look back over their exams after receiving their ATAR score. Following twelve months of hard work, many passionate, engaged learners want to do this. Any teacher or parent should celebrate such a desire; it shows their commitment, that they care.

In Victoria, this is how it works. To view just *one* exam, a student must pay a little over twenty-five dollars, and lodge a written application by a set deadline. From there, a photocopy is sent to the school, and the student has just *fifteen minutes*, supervised, to view the copy. No assessors' comments are included. At the end of the fifteen minutes, the student may pay another twenty-five dollars for another fifteen minutes, otherwise the exam is immediately destroyed. It may never leave the room or be reproduced in any way.

It is self-evident that this is hugely problematic, and returns – once again – to the socio-economic capabilities of young people and their families. Most students complete five or six subjects in Year 12, which means the cost of inspecting all exams will be at least $125. Anybody who thinks that is an insignificant sum has never taught in a disadvantaged school or, indeed, lived under economic hardship themselves. This is to say nothing of the fact that some subjects have multiple exams. Most importantly, it is impossible to adequately inspect a full examination in fifteen minutes (on the Literature paper, for example, many students write upwards of 2000 words). This means that whatever the final cost, you need to at least double it, or the entire process becomes futile anyway. Realistically, a committed student wanting to carefully check over all their exams would be paying over $250 for the privilege, and probably closer to $300 given how common it is to undertake a sixth subject.

And how can a student possibly *understand* their result when they have no assessor feedback? I have inspected Literature exams with students, and they are utterly blank. No ticks. No crosses. No question marks.

Cynically, one might wonder if the issue here is not a fear of students understanding their results, but a fear of students *challenging* their results. I empathise completely with this concern, as waves of students questioning their scores would be a significant problem. However, we have a responsibility to our children, who work so hard, and sacrifice so much, in pursuit of their futures.

To have fewer students feeling the way Mya did, bodies like the VCAA need to be courageous. Assessing work thoroughly – with comments and feedback – takes time, and they should dedicate that time to the task. Once, a friend of mine volunteered to be an examiner for a science subject, and while correcting one section of the paper smilingly told me, 'I'll have done 2500 of these questions by next Sunday.' Clearly, this is an absurd workload under which mistakes become inevitable, even with cross-marking and checking.

If departments are insufficiently funded to take their time and provide feedback, they should demand the funds. Students desiring their examinations should pay the necessary administrative and postage fees only, and should be allowed to take their work home and keep it indefinitely. It is, after all, the fruit of *their* labour. Assessors should have the courage to stand by their comments and criteria. Teachers in classrooms do this every single day, including when assessing major tasks that also contribute to ATAR scores.

'Well,' Mya said, 'I think the system is corrupt.'

By that stage, none of the students in the front row were looking at their essays.

'Listen, Doc – maybe you should just unwrap your gift.'

'Fine. But only if you'll work quietly for the rest of the session afterwards.'

'Yes, sir. Of course we will.'

I stood, feeling like the good-natured fool in a carnival dunking chair. As I tore away the paper, scarcely muted giggles fractured into laughter so loud I feared the teacher next door would complain. Beneath the wrapping was a framed portrait of Peter Carey.

It was glorious, heartwarming. 'I love it.'

'Where are you going to put it?'

I looked around. 'It needs to be in here, I think. So he can help me keep an eye on you guys while you're working.'

Eventually Tim suggested it go on top of the PA speaker, and there it resided for the rest of the year.

When the period ended, I asked Claire if the Year 12 coordinator had done much about the boys in the Study Centre. She shrugged, rolled her eyes.

'He's trying, Mr Murray.' I noticed a thin stripe of purple running through her hair. 'And it's improved. But I kinda think they just drive it underground. The boys won't *change*.'

'Well, keep me in the loop.'

I returned to the office and hadn't even sat down when Ana spoke. 'The principal rang for you.'

'Really?'

'Yeah. Not pranking. And he said you needed to call back as soon as you got in.'

I groaned. 'Did he say what it was about?'

'No. But he didn't crack any jokes or anything. It might be serious.'

I dialled the extension and he picked up. Immediately I heard in his voice what Ana had been talking about, a distance, a seriousness.

'Come straight up to my office at the end of the day, Brendan. I'd rather talk to you in person.'

6

Do You Love Me?

WHAT MAKES A good principal? For me, that's an easy question to answer. It's when they're a teacher in their heart. They can be a businessperson and a politician and an economist and a leader, but love of the children must come first. And that was David Carver, tall, easy-smiling, a veteran of The School who had been one of my teachers when I was in Year 7.

That day had passed in a weary miasma of niggling worry. Tessa, I noted, was not in English, though Lonnie had returned. I spent the period focusing on Grace, who still had no aide, though she was getting occasional support from Helen's kind-hearted undergraduates. Three o'clock could not come soon enough, and when it did I went straight to David's office.

He immediately motioned for me to sit. His presence, as always, was disarming. Behind his dark suit and spectacles was still the man whose classes I had adored as a twelve-year-old. The subject had been Egyptian History. I remember David – then Mr Carver – carefully drawing ancient wonders on the board in coloured chalk. To me those simple sketches had seemed magical, the chalk sending tiny spots of dust tumbling down the black of the board like distant

143

meteorites. That blank space at the front of the room was a window, and as Mr Carver spoke in his warm and gentle way it would light up with wonders: dehydrated mummies, cat worshippers, great slabs dragged through the sand by blistering slaves.

'How was your day, Brendan?' His office was adorned with pictures of students alongside several photos of his own children. 'Feel as though you got somewhere? Not too distracted by NAPLAN, I hope?'

'No – well, yes. It was a good day. Tiring, but good.'

'I'm glad. Now, I won't make you sweat this any longer than you need to.' He took a sheet from his desk and handed it to me. 'I want you to have a look at an email that came in this morning about your work with the Year 8s.'

As I scanned the page, he added, 'It's not complimentary.'

The letter – written by Robert, the father of a completely unexpected 8G girl – stunned me like none has since. It began by accusing me of traumatising the class, attributing to me numerous examples from the bullying article Paul had told me to read aloud, as well as a few things I hadn't said at all. It finished by pointing out that this man's daughter had never had any involvement in bullying Tessa whatsoever.

I felt nauseous. David waited, smiling sadly.

'God.' I may actually have held my head in my hands. 'One thing is true – his daughter *hasn't* bullied Tessa. Adriana's a great kid. I feel horrible.'

'Talk me through it.'

I explained that most of what had 'traumatised' the class came from the article Paul had instructed me to read. It was, I conceded, a hard-hitting piece of writing, though I did not feel any of the kids had been particularly affected. I also pointed out the claims that were untrue. Later – much later – it would emerge that Adriana had conflated schoolyard conversations about bullying with our class discussion.

Still smiling, David removed his glasses and took back the email. 'Listen, Brendan. All I'm seeing here is a pastoral care teacher who is working hard to protect one of his students who *is* being bullied. Was the article you read too much? Perhaps, but you were working under the directions of a far more experienced colleague.'

'I just wish . . . I don't know. I wish I could go back and do it differently, but now I'm not even sure what I *should* do.'

'Your problem, Brendan, if any, is that you're too reflective.' He corrected himself. 'You're *very* reflective. The question is, what would you like to do from here?'

I didn't even need to think. 'I'd like the parent to come in for a meeting. So I can talk to him in person. Explain everything.'

David promised that he would give him a call.

There are principals (perhaps few of them, but they exist) who would have asked me to call the parent immediately and apologise, regardless of the veracity of the letter. Such principals adhere to a 'customer is always right' philosophy, choosing the easy option – placation – in the face of parent upset. David was different. In the interest of his staff as well as the parents and their children, he was prepared to do the hard work, to talk, to be honest, to restore all those relationships.

Adriana's father was worried about her, and I knew there was nothing stronger than parental love. Charlie's mother was really not his mother when she did the things she did. And what of Lonnie's? Why wasn't *she* answering calls, writing letters, visiting the school? Perhaps this was her way of protecting her daughter. Perhaps she saw us as the enemy.

I spent several days thinking deeply about these questions. Soon though, a distraction was to enter my classroom – bizarrely, in the shape of a fish.

*

What can disappear?

People. Places. Memories.

'The Beaumont children,' Claire said. In the last few lessons I'd noticed her becoming increasingly quiet, withdrawn. She did not make eye contact as she spoke. 'They disappeared without a trace. I read a book about it. And then years pass, and people forget, and so they kind of disappear all over again.'

Tim was looking out the window. The ocean was not visible but I knew he was seeing it nonetheless, glassy grey pyramids collapsing in veils of white. 'The Great Barrier Reef. It's disappearing.'

The School's heating had failed that day, and I blew into my hands. 'What else?'

'*We* can disappear,' Mya said. 'All or just parts of us.'

The class murmured, nodded in the way they invariably did when Mya spoke.

And she was right, both literally and figuratively. In that sense, we agreed, the entire universe was transient, fleeting. The only certainty was an all-encompassing impermanence.

We were studying the next Peter Carey story on our list, 'Do You Love Me?', about a world where the things that are not valued slowly fade from existence. It climaxes with the protagonist watching his father dissolve in his favourite chair.

'Carey shows us in a nightmarish way that if we don't value

things we can lose them,' I said. 'But what are *our* values? I think that's what he really wants us to consider.'

When I invited the class to share stories about moments when their values had been unexpectedly illuminated, something remarkable happened.

Christopher was my quietest student that year. He kept entirely to himself, both in Literature and in the yard. Despite this almost hermitic withdrawal from his peers, I found him to be polite, kind, not the bitter outsider of adolescent stereotypes. He thanked me at the end of each lesson, and wrote about Carey's stories with insight and sensitivity. When I had telephoned his grandmother recently about an overdue essay, she had admitted he often played video games into the early hours of the morning. She promised to raise this with his psychologist, who some years earlier had diagnosed him with autism spectrum disorder.

Christopher raised a hand as white as porcelain. The class fell silent. Many of them had never before heard him speak.

He formed his words slowly and carefully, discoursing with an almost erudite precision. 'My father took me fishing, some time ago. We went to Seadale Pier.' His face shone in the sickly overcast. Like Tim, he looked out the window as though in search of the sea, but there was only the brick and glass of more classrooms. 'I remember quite clearly that I did not want to go. It was windy and wet. I wanted to be at home. But I was little then. So I went. He gave me one of his waterproof jackets. It was so big on me it hung like a dress.'

(Another ghost drifted into the room then, and this ghost was a vacuum, a blind spot: Christopher's father. I knew his grandmother was raising him but I did not know why. His father could have died, but it seemed more likely that he was simply absent, like so many of my students' fathers. Maybe the challenges of Christopher had proven too much. Maybe Christopher – insightful, perceptive – played video games at night to stave off the silence in which that knowledge whispered.)

'Nothing really happened for a long time,' he said. 'Then my father caught a flathead. I should add that I had never been fishing before. At first I was excited when he hooked the fish. I think I was happy for him. He reeled it in and put it in an esky that was filled with ice.'

There was not a sound in the room. It was not that the class had previously looked at Christopher and been blind to his depths; it was that many of them had not looked at him at all. In Carey's story the vanished do not return, but here the process seemed to be happening in reverse: a boy was fading into being.

'But then I started to feel different.' He made a face then, perhaps of puzzlement, perhaps of pain. 'I looked at that fish, and I felt sorry for it. I could see its little eyes and its little mouth. Flathead have lips, in a way. Like people. They look sad. I thought about it swimming in the ocean, around the pier's pylons, far out to sea. I think I hadn't seen a *real* fish like that before – not up close, at least. Maybe all the fish I had seen were just food. White meat on a plate. I don't know.

'My father must have caught that fish near the end of the trip, because we headed back down the pier towards the car. And I kept seeing that fish's face, and it just overcame me. I –' He chuckled, shaking his head. 'I did something crazy. I ripped the esky open, right out of my father's hands, grabbed the fish and took off running towards the end of the pier. The strangest thing: I was crying.'

We were all there with Christopher on Seadale Pier. We felt the stinging wind and tears, the wet flapping of his over-sized jacket, the fish that hung too cold and too still in his hands.

'What did you do?'

He smiled and raised his eyebrows as though it was the most obvious thing in the world. 'I threw it back into the ocean.'

And so we saw Christopher then, in a way we had not seen him before.

'It's a double session today.' I began passing out lined paper. 'Plenty of time. We're going to be writing about personal experiences. Think of a time when you were forced to consider your values – forced to confront what's important to you. This is about making links between yourselves and this story. Take for example the issues we've raised about the Year 12 Study Centre. We value equality. That's important to us. And the coordinator's got some of the boys to pull their heads in, right?'

The class nodded, shrugged.

'So let's write. Think hard. That's what Carey wants us to do.'

For the next hour I watched as my Year 12s wrote, their pens scratching and tapping as wind cried through the rotting eaves. There were no questions. Christopher had set the tone, and now each of them was venturing back into moments of forgotten meaning, re-examining, reconsidering. They understood that it had not been the fish that Christopher had cared for – not *exactly* – but something else, something larger, something that perhaps even a writer like Peter Carey would find it impossible to define. They knew, too, what had most likely come next for Christopher, the reprimands, the notes in his doctor's file, the adult confusion over something no adult could really comprehend, or at least not in the way Christopher had at that moment: that to throw that fish back into the sea was not bizarre but the opposite, it was the *only* thing to do in the circumstances, and the fact that adults didn't do such things every day meant only that we all grow into heartlessness.

When I went to collect the responses just before the end of the session, one student – Wambui – was still writing. She waved me away, glancing up momentarily from beneath her dark coppery hair. I pointed at the clock and returned to the front of the room.

'Everybody: don't forget that parent–teacher interviews are on tomorrow. I'd like to see your parents, grandparents and guardians there, if possible. And don't leave them to go it alone. You should be there as well.'

When the bell went and the other students had gone, Wambui handed me a stack of pages. They were all completely filled with her swift, looping handwriting.

'Wow. This looks amazing. Quality, I'm sure, but definitely quantity.'

She shrugged. 'I wrote about some things that happened to me in Kenya. That happened to my family.'

'Can't wait to read it.'

I walked out of that room not having the slightest clue what I was holding, or the profound impact it would have on me.

When she was gone I hurried across the schoolyard, checking my watch. NAPLAN had arrived. It was time for the government to play Guess the Jellybeans.

Back then, The School held the tests in our old Assembly Hall, a draughty brick building with small, high windows and a stage at one end. Though we still used the hall itself, an on-site theatre had rendered that stage obsolete years before.

Looking up into its dusty gloom, I occasionally saw flashes of the long-ago performances of my own childhood, 'Lip Sync', *Oklahoma*, *Romeo and Juliet*, all in lurid colour against a backdrop of black. Now, that space was imbued with a sad, heavy silence. When I attended performances in the new theatre I often thought of the hall, dark, empty and echoing with the sounds of the night.

I stood amongst the students congregating for the Year 9 Writing Test. Some looked nervous, some excited, most utterly indifferent.

'Hi, Murray!' I turned. Cynthia – a tough Maltese girl I had taught the previous year – smiled and waved. ''Sup?'

'Not much. Ready for NAPLAN?'

She came over, accompanied by Teagan and Jada. 'I'm not worried. I'm not going to write anything.'

'Why not?'

'Because you don't have to and Mum told me not to.'

The hall doors had opened and David Carver was waiting with a bullhorn. Any moment now he'd start giving directions. 'I reckon it'll be pretty boring sitting there and not writing anything.'

She rolled her eyes. 'I won't be bored. I'll *draw*. Seeya.'

I looked at Teagan and Jada as Cynthia weaved off into the crowd. 'You two better make sure you write something.'

'We will.' Jada was actually trembling. I didn't know if it was the cold or her nerves.

'Don't stress about it,' I said. 'If you bomb out, the only person who will look bad is me.'

'We don't want you to look bad.'

The principal spoke into the bullhorn. His instructions came out garbled, crackly, and were mostly stolen by the wind.

Soon though, he had the students lined up and preparing to enter. I wished them luck.

The corridor that led back towards my office was a dim clutter of impressions: downcast eyes, toppled bins, cling wrap, orange peel, the smell of BO and cheap deodorant, a thousand years of conversation reverberating in a throat of low ceiling and linoleum. I was thinking about Christopher's memory of the fish when Tessa appeared.

It was the first I had seen of her in weeks. As usual she moved awkwardly, barely managing the weight of the books hugged to her chest. Grace trailed behind her.

'Tessa!' Her laptop was about to slip from her grasp, so I took it and passed it to Grace. We stood to the side of the corridor as the adolescent river poured and rushed and bubbled past. 'Great to see you back!'

'Thanks, Mr Murray.'

She sighed the words out, smiling weakly, and I saw then in a flash of insight what had no doubt preceded her attendance: a sleepless night and a tearful morning, pleas, appeals, loving insistence from her parents, first in the kitchen and perhaps later in the carpark. She was at school but it had been a challenge, and that challenge might continue tomorrow, and the day after, and the day after that.

'What do you think, Grace?' I turned to her. 'It's great having Tessa here, isn't it?'

Grace – poor, illiterate, unfunded Grace, Grace who really didn't even *know* Tessa – nodded. 'School is way less boring when Tessa is here. I wish she'd come every day.'

And there it was again: the banality of kindness.

7

Parent–teacher interviews

I READ WAMBUI'S story that night. I still remember the final line all these years later, a simple question put to the universe by a girl struggling for an answer: *Where had the humanity gone?*

I recall that at one point she slightly misused the word 'ambush'. I circled it, wrote a note in the margin, felt utterly absurd. The power of that memory was such that grammatical slip-ups were trivial. I felt like a witness to some miracle turning to the person beside them and remarking that they're not holding the camera correctly. Not that Wambui's experience was a miracle; in many ways it was the opposite. But it transformed her in my eyes, just as Christopher's story had transformed him. There was nothing banal about the compassion Wambui had shown as a twelve-year-old. It marked her as the type of person we all like to think we are, but may not be. Mercifully, few of us ever have to find out.

No classes ran on parent–teacher interview day, and the interviews themselves started in the early afternoon and stretched into the evening. This allowed working parents to attend. Most teachers arrived in the morning anyhow, setting up their classrooms and preparing notes on the key issues to raise for each student.

Just before the interviews started, I dashed across the road to the general store and returned with a greasy brown bag. Ana scowled at it. 'Going for dim sim breath today, Brendan?'

'Yeah. I want to move them through quickly.'

'Want a mint for later?'

'Sure.'

There are several sad realities of government education that teachers rarely talk about openly. One is that the guardians of the most problematic students almost never attend parent–teacher interviews. I knew I would not see Lonnie's mother, or probably Connor's, or any of the other disruptive, disengaged or habitually absent students these pages do not have the space to hold. The odd one will appear, but for the most part such days are spent singing the praises of wonderful children.

Teachers occasionally observe that some of the greatest critics of schools are non-participants in their children's educations. I recall a boy I once taught who was disruptive, sometimes abusive and rarely submitted any work. I must have contacted his parents a dozen times, by every means available, yet they never replied or attended a single parent–teacher interview. The moment that boy received what he saw as an 'unfair detention', however, his mother was at the front office raging for an immediate explanation. Any experienced teacher (and certainly principal) will have dozens of stories like this.

Of course, the satisfying rush of moral superiority that we teachers can feel in these situations is problematic. It's easy to look at these social problems in a reductionist way: 'His parents didn't come to interviews, so they don't care about his education.'

A confession. At the beginning of my career, I would inwardly roll my eyes at children who had no schoolbooks but the latest mobile phones or sneakers. *My* parents had no money, I would think, and Ana's had even less, but they at least had the sense – the selflessness – to prioritise their children's educations. I would sometimes look at a girl's designer hoodie and wonder how her father could afford that but not the textbook. Such thoughts usually came at moments of tiredness (exhaustion even, in my first year of teaching) but I am nonetheless ashamed. I should have known better.

In my naivety and inexperience I had misunderstood many things. The first was that a poor but stable family is very different from a poor and unstable one. Though economically lacking, my parents offered me a home that was wealthy beyond measure in other ways.

I also failed to see that things like mobile phones and hoodies sometimes carry far more meaning than their superficial appearance. It was a more experienced colleague who explained it to me. Parents who have very little can carry enormous burdens of guilt born of love; their hearts ache with the knowledge of the happiness that is missing in a childhood that is, after all, painfully fleeting. Such parents often remember the privations and suffering of their own youth, and don't want that to be repeated.

Still, there are parents who are selfish and disinterested. Sometimes their children are almost uncontrollable as a result, but sometimes they are lovely – damaged, but lovely.

They streamed through, children with their mothers and fathers, uncles and aunties, grandmothers and grandfathers. It was a joy. When Kelvin came in with his mother I could only shake my head.

'This boy is a nightmare,' I said, and they were both laughing, because no teacher had ever said such a thing in all his years of schooling. 'He's a monster. I normally wouldn't say that of one so young, but there just isn't any way around it.'

'Sorry, sir.' He had a basketball with him and kept spinning it in his hands. 'I'll try to improve.'

'How's the team coming along? The . . . ?'

'The Spuds.'

His mother – Sue – rolled her eyes.

'It's coming along nicely, sir.'

I turned to Sue. 'Honestly, if all the students were like Kelvin, this job would be an absolute dream.' I waited. 'All the students *aren't* like Kelvin.'

It was my standard line and always got a laugh. I offered a few tips for reading at home and sent them off for more praise elsewhere.

Not long afterwards Tessa appeared with her family: mother, father and a host of younger siblings, one of them barely a toddler. Tessa seemed cheerful, and had brought back my copy of *Alice's Adventures in Wonderland*.

'What'd you think?' I asked, seeing behind her parents' smiles the worry, the echoes of conversations stretching well into the night over many weeks.

'I *loved* it! It's maybe even my favourite book!'

Her father – a tall, broad man with dark hair swept back from his face – put his arm around her. 'You haven't put it down, have you, Tess? Not just reading, but memorising bits.'

After chatting for a while, Tessa's parents sent her out to the corridor. It was as I'd thought; they were finding it extremely hard getting her to school each morning.

'And thank you for being tough with the class,' Tessa's

mother said. She was much like Tessa, small and soft-spoken and bespectacled. 'I know there was some backlash. But I've spoken with plenty of other mums. A lot of the girls were cheering to themselves when you did that speech. We just need them to get a bit more confident to speak up at school.'

I promised that we'd try. They moved on and more students came, one after the other with barely a minute's respite.

Then Wambui appeared with her mother.

I looked at them and was awed for a moment. Knowing what they had seen, what they had *experienced*, instilled a familiar sense of distance that left me wondering how much of their lives I could ever truly understand. My world of essay structures and grammatical pedantry wilted into insignificance by comparison.

We talked about Wambui's writing and reading, her contributions in class, the progress she was making. It was all positive and her mother smiled, nodded in a way that told me she already knew all the things I was saying. 'She has always wanted to be a lawyer,' she told me. 'Since she was a little girl.'

I wanted to tell them both what was in my heart. I wanted to tell Wambui that I'd never before read anything like what she had written; I wanted to say that I was sorry for what had happened to her and her family; I wanted to say that if I ever had a daughter I hoped she would have Wambui's courage and kindness; I wanted to tell her that she had reminded me what a privilege it was to do this job.

For some reason, I could not. So I smiled, and said, 'If all the students were like Wambui, this job would be an absolute dream.'

8

The night men

WAMBUI AWOKE.

That meant two things: first, that she had actually managed to fall asleep (the night before, in her terror, it had seemed impossible that she would ever be able to close her eyes again); and second, that she had survived. Somehow, this thing had happened to her and she was still alive.

The sunlight through the curtains was weak and cold. Rolling over, she was momentarily confused. Wambui should have been on the top bunk, with her sister below and the maid across the room. Everything had transformed. It was as if she were caught in the mechanism of some three-dimensional puzzle, which had clicked into a new configuration just before she woke.

It came back in fleeting, impressionistic jolts. Shrieks. Chopping pangas. Her mother's pleas. Blood.

Wambui remembered that she was in her grandparents' spare room. After those men left she had been too frightened to return to her own home. The fear came back then in a roaring surge, and it carried her out of bed and to the kitchen, which was full of light and clattering with the everyday sounds of morning.

Her grandmother was there. The old woman turned and embraced her in soap-smells and warmth. Wambui could hear her heart, and that must have meant that she had survived, too.

'*Habari za asubuhi*, my darling.'

It was hard to imagine that the arms in which Wambui nestled were the same ones that had swung with gardening tools only hours earlier. 'Good morning, Cucu.'

When she stepped back, Wambui saw the swollen slit of one black eye hovering above her grandmother's smile. 'Come, darling. Let's get you ready for school.'

Later – much later – what would strike Wambui as one of the most extraordinary things about the whole ordeal was that she had gone to class the very next day.

They had breakfast and then walked across to Wambui's house. The door seemed to loom as they approached it, something so ordinary now infused with an ominousness that might never be dispelled, and might leak like a poison into every aspect of their lives and futures.

Cucu lay a hand on her back. 'Get your things quickly. Straight in and out. You know where your bag is?'

'Yes.'

'Good girl.'

She opened the door. There was blood everywhere. Pools of it congealed on the carpet, while smears held fingerprints on dully glinting doorknobs. It was splashed across the walls. In the gloom some of it was almost black.

Wambui hurried through the silent watchfulness of the house, collected her books, then headed out into the day.

*

In the weeks leading up to the attack Wambui had spent her nights trembling in bed, waiting for the sounds that would inevitably come as midnight reached its zenith and ticked on into early morning. The police had not improved and the people of Kaandiki still had to rely on community solidarity. If it wasn't that piercing scream (part terror and part war cry) it would be the pealing of an electronic house alarm.

For Wambui, the days were an antidote: classrooms bright with welcome, the dusty scent of her grandfather's animals, insistent hammering as her father worked to extend the bungalow. She understood that the people of Kaandiki were good, almost to a soul. They were the same people who, despite the risks, raced into the darkness night after night to protect one another. In the golden glow of morning and early afternoon, there was a sense of what the village truly was, not a collection of individuals but a deeper and more complex network of belonging, responsibility, even love. Far from being deficient, Kaandiki possessed something lacking in some of the most populous cities in the Western world.

Inevitably though, as four o'clock turned into five and on to six, the air would cool and the evening would come. Darkness pressed against the windows. Wambui would lie in bed, knowing that her night-fiends were not imaginary.

That night it was screaming that woke her. This time, though, those shrieks were too loud, too close, too familiar. It was, she knew, her mother.

Wambui leapt from bed and pressed herself behind the bedroom door, waiting.

*

After completing a late shift in the kitchen, Wambui's father Jacob had picked up his sister Zira from a baby shower, and she accepted his offer to spend the night at their place. It was after midnight when they pulled up to the gates of the house.

'Wait here.' He reached beneath the seat and took out a heavy stick with a bolt attached to the end. 'I'll get it.'

The car door opened with the creaking pop of old metal. The night was still, but for the frogs and insects that cried mournfully for one another. Jacob moved into the beams of the headlights and swung back the gate.

Next thing he knew, he was blind.

The torch in his face was so bright it painted his eyes with blue-green spectres that blotted the darkness. An instant beforehand, though, he had seen them: six men in masks and balaclavas armed with pangas.

'Work on the bungalow looks good,' one of them said. 'Maybe you have a bit too much money?'

Then they were attacking him, their blades dropping heavily from the dark. He leapt back, stumbled, swung with his stick and missed. They were around him, and he did not even feel when their steel began opening him up.

The men were still laughing, jeering. One of the pangas made a heavy crack as it hit his skull.

Somehow, Zira got out of the car and made it past them and to the house. Wambui's mother opened the door and, screaming, saw what was happening; Zira continued past her and joined Wambui hiding in the children's bedroom.

Jacob kept fighting as the blades of the pangas shone watery in the moonlight. He was intent on protecting his family. He kicked, punched, swung with his club. The night itself seemed to be babbling with taunts and laughter. He managed to get to his feet but then immediately tripped once more, thudding into the grass. Somehow he needed to turn the fight to his advantage. Across the way was a rectangle of light and he hopped to his feet once more, dodging blows and running towards it. As he drew near, he saw the silhouette of his wife in the doorway.

The men knew as well as everyone that those screams were a call to action, and they raced up to silence her. Jacob staggered and tripped back into the house. One of the men stepped into that box of light, raised his panga and slapped the flat of the blade against Wambui's mother's chest.

'*Shut up, woman!*' He lifted the weapon again and stepped further into the house, forcing her back. His eyes through the balaclava showed no fear. 'Make another sound and I'll kill you all.'

Wambui was reduced to little more than her blazing senses, eyes, ears and pounding heart. She heard her mother's voice: 'Please. What do you want? If you want anything, just take it and get out.'

The rest of the men came into the house now. Another spoke, his voice thick and muffled behind his mask. 'We saw your bungalow extension. Your family is pretending.'

'Yeah. You pretending to be rich and important?'

There were thuds, shrieks, the sounds of tripping and scuffling: six armed attackers against an injured man and his terrified, sleep-addled wife.

Behind the door with her aunt and the maid, Wambui realised that these men had not come to rob. They were there to inflict pain, probably to kill. It was jealousy that motivated them, and something else, something deeper, lying beyond the grasp of her twelve-year-old understanding. She glanced back at the bunk and saw the one mercy of that night: her little sister, barely five years old, was still asleep.

Jacob was on his feet again, standing as a barrier between those men and his family, the blood that poured over him bright and shimmering under the electric lights.

'You're pretenders,' the first man said again, and he lunged and chopped with his panga, but right as he did there was a sound behind them and an old woman came charging in from the darkness, armed with nothing but a pair of small trowels. She was not screaming but bellowing. The man closest tried to leap aside and raised a hand defensively as she blundered into him, swinging her arms with what strength she could muster.

She was alone. Her husband was away at a cultural event. But she fought with a ferociousness that cowed those men.

Wambui no longer felt fear; she *was* fear. It had transcended all aspects of her being and held total dominion over her. For weeks she had listened to the night, imagining it as something existing *out there*, but now its appalling mass had become too much for the walls and doors to resist, and the darkness had come rushing in, mocking, screaming, chopping with pangas that in their upswings painted the ceiling with constellations of her father.

She raced out.

Everybody, somehow, was on their feet, and the men were retreating. As she emerged into the light Wambui saw – impossibly – her father go after them, pick up their doormat and hurl it into the gloom.

'Dad!' She reached to stop him. 'No!' She hesitated, thought. 'You're getting blood everywhere.'

Jacob turned. His eyes were wide and glassy with shock and anger, his chest heaving. Wambui saw that his forearm muscle was split almost in two. The bloody flesh flopped to and fro in a great rubbery flap.

His head, though, was the worst. Gashes yawned on the scalp. Blood welled. His hair was matted and soaked.

While Jacob had been considering pursuit, his wife had retreated for bandages. Now, calm and methodical, she pressed pads against his head and began binding them in place.

'Why are you bandaging my head? It's my arms they got.'

'Shhh. Sit down. I'm taking you to the hospital.' She finished with his head and began working deftly on his arms. 'Cucu, you stay with the girls.'

Wambui's grandmother nodded. 'You take care of my boy. We'll be fine. The village is starting to arrive.'

Wambui looked out the door and saw that she was right. Men were appearing from the dark, men she recognised from the school, from the fields, from the stalls and shops that were filled with smiling faces in the daylight.

Not long after her parents had driven away, the crowd in their yard had grown to about fifty people. There were no police, though the station was barely a hundred metres away. Wambui stayed with her grandmother and little sister, while several villagers looked in the house and around the yard.

'What did they take?'

Zira spoke, her voice still shaking. 'My phone.'

Eventually somebody had the idea to dial her number.

Wambui watched while one of the nearby men took out his own phone. There was a pause as the crowd fell into silence. The dial tone pulsed into the night, audible to everyone. Then someone answered: 'Yeah?'

The man with the phone seemed caught off-guard. 'Who is this? You shouldn't have Zira's phone.'

'We have it. And we raped her.'

'*Uwongo!*' Zira hissed.

'You're a liar.' The man held the phone upright at arm's length before his face. In the glow Wambui could see his features, the brow knitted, the mouth firm but frightened. They were all frightened. That, in part, was what drove them to band together in defence. 'Why don't you give yourself up?'

'We can see all of you,' the voice said through the phone.

Wambui felt a panga cut icily through her entrails. She looked out into the blackness beyond the crowd. There was nothing, just the wire fences and the rooftops and the night stretching on and on.

'No you can't.'

'Yes we can. We can see all of you. We know who you are. We are going to come and get all of you.'

'*Uwongo.* We don't believe you, coward.'

Wambui had heard enough and retreated to her grandmother.

The night, defiant, continued. More villagers came, some consoling Zira, others searching for clues in their attempts to fill the role of the sleeping police officers. Dogs barked, and cows in a nearby paddock shifted restlessly in the dark.

'Grandmother.' Wambui was crying, shaking with fear and the cold. By then it was almost dawn. 'Will Dad be alright?'

'Of course he will. My son is strong and those cuts were bloody but not vital. He will need a lot of stitches.'

'He hates hospitals.'

Cucu smiled and held her and her sister. 'I know. But your mother will make him stay. And he will be back with us and cooking his pastries before you know it.'

After a while it became clear that there was nothing to be

found that could identify Jacob's attackers. Zira's phone had fallen silent, and somebody said the gang was probably in bed, wherever they were. The first of the men went home, then others began to follow, the crowd thinning.

'What if they come back?' Wambui started to cry again, trembling against her grandmother. 'What if they really have been watching this whole time?'

A friend of her father's overheard. 'They're liars, Wambui. They aren't here. But if anything happens all of us will be back very fast.'

She watched as he spoke in hushed tones with some of the other men and then her grandmother. Eventually those last few stragglers left. The night was silent and once more they were alone.

'It's alright, girls. You will sleep at my house tonight.'

Wambui waited while Cucu went into her son's house, turning out the lights and locking the front door. When she came back she had something in her hand: a panga, still wet with blood. In the chaos, one of the attackers had dropped it.

'Come on. You need some sleep.'

In the doorway to her grandmother's house, though, Wambui stopped. It was as if every part of her seized up. She could not take a step beyond the threshold.

'What if they're here?' Her voice whined, and again her grandmother held her, cooing.

'There's nobody here, my darling. Just us.'

And so, holding her hand, Cucu led her from room to room, checking every shadowed corner and cupboard to prove that they were safe, that the men had gone. Eventually Wambui was in bed, the mattress sagging with her grandmother's reassuring weight as she lay with tears drying on her face.

Cucu's voice defeated the fear. She spoke long of many things (stroking Wambui's hair the whole time), and each thing she mentioned was silently awash with daylight in the stillness of that lingering night. She spoke of the farm animals and of her friends in Kaandiki and of the best spices for making *mutura* – ginger, garlic, chillies. But it did not matter what she spoke about, only that she was there. The image of those masked men persisted behind Wambui's closed eyes, but the more Cucu spoke the more they dissolved, faded. Where were her father's attackers now? There was an invisible strand connecting her to them, she could feel it, but with each word from her grandmother those men retreated, and so that strand stretched and thinned. For now they could still spider-scuttle down its length, but soon it would snap.

She slept.

It was several days before her father came home. Countless stitches made railway tracks of his arms and head. Watching him go about his ordinary chores with those injuries, the reality of what had happened dawned on Wambui.

But it was not this story that so powerfully affected me years later when Wambui wrote about it. It was what she did when the village was once more faced with a gang of thieves in the stillness of a Kenyan night.

9

Perspective

AFTER ALMOST TWO weeks, David Carver managed to arrange a time for himself and me to meet with Robert, the parent who was angry with the way I had managed the bullying in 8G.

I woke before my alarm feeling nervous, listless. I had a quick breakfast then walked from my little rented shack to the beach. The sky was an overcast, milky champagne. If the sun ever broke through it was only for a moment, making the dark sea glitter. An irregular wind fussed at my hair.

I tried to use Wambui's story to remind myself that, really, the challenges of my own life – indeed, the challenges of Robert's life – were minor. We were in a safe, privileged country and would return after the meeting to our safe, privileged homes. One day none of this would matter, but Wambui's experiences would always matter, in some way. Neither the passage of time nor perspective would ever render them irrelevant.

As much as anything, I had come to the beach to try not to be angry. In the days leading up to the meeting I had begun feeling some resentment; I kept thinking that the whole thing was wasted time, that my energy would be better spent looking after Tessa than defending myself. But I pushed those feelings away. I was sure that Robert and I were both coming from a place of goodness and would be able to find common ground.

Just before I left I took a final look over the melancholy, autumnal bay. As a boy I had once seen hundreds of dolphins frolicking at the surface, but today there was nothing, just the murk receding to an indistinct horizon.

I turned my back on it and drove to work.

'It'll be fine, Brendan.' Ana, as always, was ready with support. 'Just remember your notes. When he has the full story he'll see things differently.'

Robert was an angular, succinctly spoken man with thinning hair and business attire. He was confident and intimidating. When David introduced us he was polite but almost severe. Right or wrong, I felt that he was thinking something I had heard from parents before: *What would you know? You hardly look like you're out of school yourself.*

'Thanks so much for coming in.' I took out my notes, smiled, did my best to seem appreciative of his time. 'I wanted to start by addressing the article I read to the class.'

I did not want to sound like I was making excuses. Perhaps sensing this, David rescued me.

'It wasn't Brendan's idea to read that article to the class,' he said. 'He was told to do so by a much more experienced colleague.'

Immediately I could see that Robert was taken aback.

'And some of what you wrote in your email didn't happen.'

Robert blinked. 'Oh. Really? My daughter listed a great many things that were discussed . . . Horrible examples of bullying, for instance, that had no bearing on anything I am aware has occurred in 8G.'

'Yeah,' I said. 'But that sort of thing is common schoolyard talk.'

'Our best guess,' David added, 'is that your daughter has heard a whole lot of chatter about bullying that day, come home and unloaded it all on you. Some of it *was* from Brendan's English class and some of it wasn't.'

'Right. I still think it's inappropriate to be using a broad-brush approach to managing bullying and going after the whole class like that.'

'And your daughter hasn't been a bully, in any way, shape or form,' I agreed.

We talked. Robert was, I thought, eminently reasonable. He was a good father who cared – that was the very reason he had come in for the meeting, and the same reason he had written the email in the first place. His only error was in sending it before speaking with me directly, but then I had made errors, too. In some ways, I *had* punished Robert's daughter for something she had not done. And in my inexperience, I had thought that I was required to do everything senior staff members asked me to do, even if that meant reading articles to junior students that contained details too confronting for their age. Today, if I was asked to read that article to a Year 8 class, I would be unlikely to do so. But Paul cannot be criticised for giving me that advice. Bullying is a major concern amongst parents and in the community, and he was working hard to alleviate student mistreatment. These are exceptionally complex and challenging situations that are too often dismissed by non-teachers who simply declare that schools don't do enough to stop bullying.

What I did see, though, was that Robert had little understanding of who Tessa was or what she was experiencing.

Again, this was no fault of his. He did not see her every day as we did.

'Does Tessa come from a troubled family?' he asked at one point.

I did not know what had inspired this question. What conversations, I wondered, or perhaps assumptions, were circling through the school community? I had my first glimpse then of the strange way that these situations can become the conversational chaff of parents who are inadvertently drawn into the playground dramas of their own children.

'She comes from a very supportive family,' David said.

I like to think we ended on good terms. I felt that Robert was managing his daughter's situation as best he could with the limited information he had, and I think Robert saw me as an inexperienced but ultimately caring teacher.

What the meeting didn't achieve was getting The School any closer to solving the problem of Tessa and Lonnie.

10

Sick

PROBABLY THE MAIN reason parents harbour such deep anxieties around bullying is because it lurks in the periphery of an even greater fear: the prevalence of mental health issues in children.

These fears are not unfounded. Comprehensive surveys conducted by Mission Australia in association with the Black Dog Institute found that almost a quarter of young people were experiencing psychological distress in 2018. Of those, thirty-five per cent reported concerns about suicide, and ten per cent felt they had no control over their own lives.

These were things I understood deeply and personally, both as a teacher and from my own childhood.

As Term Two continued, Claire started visiting our office more and more to chat about Peter Carey, share essays and generally pass the time. She would lie on the couch with her arms folded and her feet up, often sporting non-uniform boots with brightly coloured laces. On the one hand I was glad of her company – it meant I could keep an eye on her – but I knew, too, that she was struggling. When things were going well she was out in the schoolyard with her friends, not listening to

Ana and me chatting interminably about the bureaucracy of school. She was there, I knew, because she felt some reassurance in our adult presence.

'I'm actually conditioning myself to have a fear response to coffee,' she said to me one afternoon. It was lunchtime and Ana was on yard duty. A game of soccer was going on in the windy courtyard, and occasionally the ball would strike the office wall with a sound like a dulled cymbal.

'Good one.'

'I'm serious. I've spent so many nights up way after midnight studying, and the only way I can manage it is with coffee. I smelt coffee coming out of the coordinator's office the other day and I swear, Mr Murray, it kind of panicked me. I felt sick.'

I turned from my desk to face her. 'You shouldn't be up all night like that, Claire. It isn't healthy. I'd rather you hand your work in late.'

'*You* maybe. But I have to push myself hard. I don't have a choice.'

'Why?'

She rolled her eyes, groaned. 'I told you. Except for Lit all my subjects scale down.'

'That doesn't mean you should be missing out on sleep. If you get less sleep you won't be able to think straight when you *are* studying.'

She sat in silence for a while as I resumed correcting Year 9 essays. That soccer ball kept pounding against the wall. At one point it bounced onto the tin roof once, twice, then fell back down past the window to a chorus of cheers and applause.

Claire sat up, shuffled in her schoolbag for a moment and cracked open an energy drink. 'Look. I'll admit it. I compare myself to other students. A lot. I can't help it. Like Mya. I'll never be able to write like her.'

'You're every bit the writer she is.'

'No I'm not.'

'Yes you are.'

'Aren't.'

'Are.'

'*Aren't.*'

'*Are.*'

'You'll quit before I do, Murray.'

'Probably.'

Once again I saw how the Year 12 system can contribute directly to students' mental health challenges. Mission Australia's study also found that thirty per cent of students in psychological distress suffered low self-esteem, and more than half identified school and study problems as their biggest concern. Ranking and competitiveness is a part of this. I completely reject the assertion that the system 'is what it is' or 'is the best we've got'. It is a question of priorities.

Currently, at the Year 12 level, schools are prioritising the expediency of tertiary institutions' selection processes over all else. We are completely beholden to them, and are often focusing on that rather than the health, wellbeing and learning of our children. Schools need to have the courage to stand up to universities, to insist that yes, their selection processes are important, but we also have vital work to do. We need to be turning young adults into good people and healthy human beings.

One of the most troubling but illustrative examples of this bureaucratic pathology involved a girl I had taught some years before. I was deeply concerned that Claire could end up having an experience like hers.

Peta was a highly intelligent and well-liked girl who suffered extraordinarily with mental health issues throughout her schooling. Crippling obsessive-compulsive disorder in the junior years drove her to perform rituals designed to stave off an unknown (but certainly horrific) cosmic retribution. In part, this was a consequence of her mother's diagnosis with cancer when Peta was twelve.

'This is actually going to sound ironic,' she told me recently, 'but I used to have ritualistic behaviours – very well hidden, of course – when you were my English teacher way back in Year 8. I used to have to rewrite sentences over and over again until I'd done it a certain number of times. A paragraph that should take two minutes to write would take me over an hour. I felt crazy because I couldn't tell anyone and I had to hide it so well in class.'

Years 8 through to 11 were an extraordinary challenge for Peta, characterised by endless appointments and interventions, including medication. Ultimately, she would miss months of school.

By the time she reached Year 12, however, things had stabilised. Peta had grown into a focused and dedicated young woman working exceptionally hard to achieve her desired ATAR score. Generalised anxiety and panic attacks persisted, but her mother had recovered, the finish line of secondary education was in sight, and her intelligence and work ethic had more than compensated for the learning she had missed.

Then, just days out from the Year 12 English exam, Peta became so ill that she was taken to hospital by ambulance. Her condition – tonsillitis severe enough to compromise her airway – could well have been exacerbated or even caused by the enormous strain of that year and the ones that had preceded it.

Given her focus on academic success, it is perhaps unsurprising that she was set on completing her English exam, come what may. Her first request was that she be allowed to do so in hospital. This was not possible, so the VCAA gave her only two other options: sit the paper at school (with rest breaks provided) along with her classmates, or forfeit the opportunity entirely and be given a 'derived score'. This would be calculated using data from earlier in the year.

Convinced that her hard work would produce a far stronger result than any derived score, Peta discharged herself against medical advice.

Today, she describes the situation with powerful conciseness: 'They made me choose between my health and my future.'

From a medical perspective, she certainly made the wrong choice. But educationally her decision was validated. Peta achieved an excellent exam result she believes was far higher than her derived score would have been. This is an extraordinary credit to Peta's academic ability; while sitting the English exam, she describes herself as feeling 'the worst I have ever been physically in my life . . . I was in a lot of pain even just breathing. I had this medication that was a syrup that I had to put in my mouth and let sit in my throat and then spit it out into a plastic bag. It was to stop my throat from getting inflamed and closing again. I had to do that to breathe normally.'

Putting a child in this position is patently absurd and insensitive beyond words. Procedures should exist to allow such students to sit exams (even alternate exams) at a later date. After nearly a year of study, an extra week or two would not have given her any unfair advantage, especially given that she would have likely spent much of that time recovering in hospital. And if that added period of time places pressure on tertiary institutions awaiting ATAR scores, we need to have the courage to say, 'Peta matters more.'

In short, we must not allow the machinations of bureaucracy to harm students in these Kafkaesque scenarios.

Looking at Claire, I thought that at the very least I could help her avoid running herself into the ground.

'You should do some of your own writing,' I said. 'Nothing to do with school. Nothing you have to submit for assessment. Just for fun.'

'I've still been doing my poetry,' she said. 'The worst part is, though, because I'm comparing myself to everyone all the time, I'm starting to feel like it's shit.'

'Your poetry is *not* shit, Claire.'

She looked out the window with eyes that might well have been painted on. It was clear that she did not believe me.

*

I saw myself in students like Claire and Peta. I saw myself, too, in some of the ghost children beyond my reach, the ones we call 'school refusers'. Both Claire and Peta had worn that label at various times throughout their education. They had returned, but many do not.

Something happened to me when I was nine years old. I do not know what it was. It could have been external, internal or both. What I do know is that in the early weeks of Grade 4 I became so ill that at one point my mother thought I was going to die. Only years later would I realise that my condition was psychological rather than physical, though in the relatively unenlightened 1990s it was never identified as such.

My memories of that time have the distant, flickering quality of silent films. Our grandparents had bought us an above-ground pool, and I remember it heaped with summer storm clouds in the humid stillness of late afternoon. I remember furiously pedalling a tricycle with my little sister on the back. I remember the local milk bar with its sickly odours of sunscreen, meat pies, and blowflies sizzling on the neon ring hanging above the jangling door.

And I remember a feeling that came over me then. I did not have the words to describe it, so I just told my mother, 'I feel sick.'

On my first day of Grade 4 the primary school called her to come and collect me. We drove to the doctor along the coast road in our juddering Datsun, a dented steel bowl cradled in my lap. I did not throw up, and had no way of explaining that the thing that was wrong with me (the thing that suddenly seemed wrong with the entire world) probably wasn't ever going to make me *physically* sick. I did not have the vocabulary to make the adults understand, did not even have the vocabulary to fully understand it myself.

The doctor studied me with kind eyes hovering above his moustache which, to me, wafted about his face like smoke. He was the same doctor who would identify Non-Hodgkin Lymphoma in Kelvin years later. He took my temperature, felt my abdomen, asked what was wrong. I told him: 'I feel sick.'

The following day I could not go to school. That became the following week. My mother's cold hands rested on my forehead, her face pale and worried as I tried to explain: 'I feel sick.' Whatever was wrong with me I felt all the time, in my stomach and in my bones and in my skin, but elsewhere, too: in the pencil-sharpened stink of my schoolbag, in the fatty sizzling of afternoon pans, in my father's newsreel horrors that signified that this day, like the last, was drawing to a close.

I saw a paediatrician who sent me for myriad tests. There was a barium meal, in which I gulped down a great milkshake cup of what I thought was modelling plaster, and later something I took for acid. From there came ultrasounds and eventually a gastroscopy. They found nothing and I could only tell them that I felt sick. I felt this thing could kill me. The thought of being away from my parents became terrifying. On the one or two days my parents managed to get me to school, I carried rolls of Quick-Eze in my pockets, as though crunching them down would stave off this psychic nausea that oppressed me day and night, sloshing at my ankles like an ever-rising black tide. In desperation my mother resorted to alternative medicines; she bought me grey elastic wristbands with plastic buttons inside designed to activate mysterious pressure points.

None of it worked and I stopped going to school entirely. Then I stopped eating.

Even beforehand I was thin. One Saturday morning I woke feeling worse than usual, and by the Monday I had lost two kilograms. My mother could tell by looking at me that I had little more to lose. I remember the paediatrician's baffled eyes moving from me to my paperwork, all of which declared normal, healthy, average.

What saved me from educational purgatory that year was reading. I read compulsively, day after day, short stories and novels and wildlife encyclopaedias. My health stabilised, though I still insisted that I felt sick, and I *did*. What I did not know (but what my mother gradually began to realise) was that my feelings were childhood anxiety and perhaps depression.

After months away from school she did something

courageous. One morning, despite my protests, she loaded me into the Datsun and drove me to school. We sat in the carpark for some time, with me insisting over and over that I could not go in, that I was sick. I do not remember tears but I know I was pleading, and that as I spoke the nausea was surging with a power that seemed capable of annihilating me and everything else with it.

'Just come over with me to the classroom,' she had said. 'Just that far.'

She got me that far and I stopped. I would not go in. I felt *sick*. But in an extraordinary display of courage and love and strength, she stood her ground. I bargained, reasoned, tried desperately to explain, but she was immovable. I cannot thank her enough for it. I have taught many children whose parents did not have the strength, ability or inclination for the stand she took that day. Eventually she won. I went inside, up the corridor and into my classroom.

I took the only seat available, next to a girl named Joanne.

'Are you sick?' she asked.

'Yeah. Did you see me?'

'Yes.'

I remember looking out the window across the grey school-yard to the very spot where my mother and I had been standing. 'Did Miss say anything?'

'She said just to ignore you.'

I was struck by shame so strong it made my face roar with heat.

I returned to school. Like Peta, I would eventually fight off my nausea with obsessive-compulsive rituals that only resolved themselves (almost spontaneously) shortly before I started high school.

It would be years before my sickness came back. When it did, it was a teacher named Liam who rescued me, though he never knew it. One of my great regrets is that I never told him before he died.

But I try to make up for it each day, if I can, by seeing students like Claire for what they are and showing them that there is a way out.

11

The mosaic

TWO LOVE STORIES:

A teacher for whom I have profound respect finished her Year 11 English class at the end of one day. After she had put her things away and cleaned the board, she found a boy still in his seat: Amardad. He was studious, kind, funny in a self-deprecating and awkward way. Today though, he sat with his head down and his arms straight out on the desk, palms upturned as if in anticipation of some offering.

'Amardad – what's wrong?'

He said nothing, just sat in that same strange pose. His teacher thought she heard him sniff.

'C'mon, Amardad. You've stayed back. You must want to talk.'

Still he did not speak, but she knew to wait, as all good teachers do. Some studies have shown that the average time a teacher waits to allow a child to answer a question is less than a second.

'I'm in love,' Amardad said, not raising his head. The declaration was typical of him: honest, direct, old-fashioned.

'That's not a bad thing.'

'Yes it is.' There was anguish in his voice now. 'Because the person I love is never going to love me.'

His teacher thought about this, took a risk. 'Is it a boy, Amardad?'

He looked up slowly, and as he nodded his brown eyes filled and then spilled over with tears.

Another:

Claire was having a bad day – bad even by her standards. She was exhausted and sick and behind with her work. All her subjects scaled down. Ana and I were both out of the office, so when she came to see us she was greeted only by a locked door and gloomy frosted glass.

She found her friend Ivy, put her head against her shoulder and cried.

Late that evening, there was a knock at Claire's door. She opened it and there was Ivy, her beaten-up station wagon with its crooked P-plates idling in the driveway.

'I got you something,' she said. 'Here.'

There were chocolates, but there was a jar, too, filled with small slips of paper, each scratched with handwriting.

Ivy smiled, her face rain-wet in the dirty porch light. 'A hundred things I love about you.'

*

Two horror stories:

On our electronic rolls, some students have coloured icons alongside their names. A red cross identifies a serious medical condition, and a light blue dot represents a student with a diagnosed disability. Dark blue dots alert teachers to special learning plans. An Indigenous flag, perhaps problematically, is used to identify children with that heritage.

Then there are the more worrying examples. The rare aqua dot carries the ominous warning DO NOT PUBLISH IMAGES, hinting at distant threats. When encountered, this dot is almost always coupled with an icon that is as depressing as it is common: the orange R.

I was overworked, tired, stressed, and wanted to show one of my classes a documentary. Unthinking, I connected my laptop to the projector before marking the roll. As I did so, a little girl made a puzzled face and raised her hand.

'Mr Murray – why is there an orange R beside my name?'

I stopped, turned, realised a wall-sized facsimile of my screen dominated the room. The rest of the class looked, too, and more hands came up. There were orange Rs everywhere, up and down the roll, alongside a spattering of the rest: disabilities, illness, disadvantage. Fortunately the icons themselves betrayed nothing.

'I don't know,' I lied, and then, caught off-guard, added pathetically, 'you would need to ask at the front office.'

I suppose none of them ever did, because that was the end of the matter. The orange R indicates parent access restrictions – that a mother or father is forbidden from seeing their child except at certain times, in some instances supervised. It implies, too, a greater fear: that these parents could show up at The School, perhaps at the front office, perhaps directly at the classroom itself. There are stories of such things taking place.

I did not have the courage to explain that the icon was a bureaucratic manifestation of the fault lines running through the children's hearts and lives.

Some of the tiles of The School's mosaic are bright orange Rs.

Let's examine another tile, singular and terrifying, of glittering onyx.

During Year 12, Claire became so unwell one day that she sought out the Wellbeing Team. By chance none of them were in, so, in desperation, she went to another adult.

'I'm not feeling well,' Claire told them. 'I've been thinking things – bad things.'

'What sort of things?'

She swallowed. 'Like . . . I've been thinking about suicide.'

This person – who has not worked at The School in years – sighed. 'Listen. There's nobody in Wellbeing today.'

Claire, teary, stood and waited.

'It's Friday. It's nearly the end of the day. Come back and see them on Monday.'

Claire stayed at Ivy's that night. She says the incident wasn't ever followed up.

*

Two comedies:

Tim had a reputation: he was always hungry and there wasn't a thing he would not consume. When he wasn't studying Literature he was shovelling food into his paradoxically slender frame. Maybe, as his mother said, he was the clichéd 'growing boy'; maybe it was all the surfing.

Mya watched one day, in horrified hysterics, as another boy gave him a meat pie and a carton of milk. At first the purpose of the milk was unclear, but then the boy peeled the top off the pie, produced a jar of molten chilli sauce and poured half of it inside. Tim, blue-eyed and sunburnt despite the cold, grinned as he ate it in a few enormous mouthfuls.

All the Year 12s had an assigned locker. Somehow Tim had two. The second was purely for food storage and was adorned with a high-quality padlock.

One day he interrupted Mya from her study. 'Hey, Mysie.'

She rolled her eyes. 'What is it, Tim?'

'C'mon. Take a break. Just for one minute. I wanna show you something.'

She crossed the Study Centre to his food storage locker. With a look of sly satisfaction, he swung the door open.

Inside was a full antipasto platter of deli meats, fine cheeses, pickled onions, olives and biscuits.

He winked, making a theatrical clicking sound as he did so, and offered her a piece of *Camembert de Normandie*.

This next comedy is one I should not laugh at. A Year 8 boy downloaded an app that allowed him to switch the school projectors on and off remotely. Not long afterwards, this boy – confident, charming in the manner of some elderly men – convinced a young replacement teacher that the projector was clap-activated. He turned it on and off from his pocket while she clapped, maintaining this charade over several lessons. Then, one day, he stopped.

'Maybe you need to stand closer to it,' he suggested as she clapped and clapped and clapped, hands raised above her head. 'It worked last time.'

*

Two stories of hope:

Charlie had endured traumas every bit the equal of those faced by Wambui on the other side of the world. In some ways they were worse: there was his night of the machete, but there was his mother's death, too. He had been with his little brother when they got the news. The words fell on them like blades on anaesthetised flesh. You watch the destruction, not believing it to be your own.

Xavier collapsed, just toppled straight backwards. Charlie stayed on his feet.

He kept his balance for Xavier, for his aunty, for himself. He would not let his disasters crush him. He would take care of his brother and shake hands with his teachers and box at his gym with a crackling energy a lesser person would have expended tearing their world apart. When he learnt that she had suicided he stayed upright still. At school he held open doors, offered words of encouragement, put his arm around his brother in spite of the watchful eye of the teenage patriarchy. When he joked that I needed to hurry up and marry my girlfriend, he was really saying, people matter most.

And maybe that's why I loved Charlie. He stood and faced the world with a raw, aggressive kindness I could never have summoned in his place.

Then there was Grace. Illiterate Grace who did not qualify for an aide, kind-hearted Grace who insisted that her days at The School were just a little greyer and colder when Tessa was not around.

I discovered gradually that though she could not write, Grace could draw like no person her age I had ever seen. Perhaps it was because she had redirected the energies she might otherwise have spent writing; perhaps it does not need to be analysed.

Her favourite subject, I saw, was the griffin. Their great eagle heads peered over the sterile margins of her exercise books, their wings so meticulously detailed with individual feathers that the curling pages were perfumed with biro ink.

The griffins reared on sleek muscular lions' legs, raising talons ready to tear apart the book, the classroom, the entire School perhaps, laying bare the magical world in which Grace lived.

12

Books

DRIVING TO SCHOOL early one morning towards the end of Term Two, my headlights swept over Charlie Blanco as I rounded a bend. He appeared as a momentary phantasm in the ember-glow of falling raindrops: singlet, headphones, trancelike stare into the darkness of a morning that had not yet arrived.

It occurred to me that I hadn't spoken with him in weeks. He was always training. His fixation on that Australian Title was subjugating every other part of his life. I knew he had won several bouts and was still on track to make his goal a reality, but some of his teachers were becoming worried. I promised myself that I would seek him out and see how he was going. Usually it was Charlie who came to me in the office; it might mean something if the roles were reversed.

That morning, teaching Year 12 Literature, my mind returned again and again to Charlie jogging through the rainy gloom. It was that look on his face – not pained, not worried, but not really the Charlie I knew, either. It had a coldness to it, a distance. I wondered what it was like to be the boy who hated violence training single-mindedly for a fight. I had no idea. I needed to find some common ground across which I could approach him.

'Doc?' Tim raised his hand. 'What's the name of the narrator's girlfriend in "Life and Death in the South Side Pavilion"? I've forgotten.'

I squinted, tried to return to the room. 'I'm . . . You'll have to check. I've forgotten.'

A laughing murmur reverberated through the room.

'Well, well.' Mya raised her eyebrows and pointed to the framed portrait on the PA speaker. 'What would Peter Carey say?'

'Please don't tell him. I'd be heartbroken.'

As the class continued, I decided I would ask Charlie about his reading. That had been his obsession when I first taught him. And *that* I could understand. Like Charlie, books had saved me when I was a child, had sandbagged the dark tide of my sickness. I understood only too well their quiet, patient reassurance, their predictability, their power to dissolve the cold realities of the surrounding world.

Looking around the crowded Literature classroom, I thought of just how many children needed books in that way, to a greater or lesser extent.

I reminisce on that year's Literature class with great fondness. Each year since, the enrolments have been shrinking, and this is not something unique to The School. In Australia, Literature as a Year 12 subject – along with reading generally – is dying. Worst of all, this is primarily affecting government schools.

The problem was noted recently in Western Australia, where the English Teachers Association found the number of public schools offering Literature had dropped from seventy-four to thirty-one between 1998 and 2018.

In Victoria, the decline has been both more recent and more rapid.

In the five years from 2014 to 2019, the number of students sitting the Literature exam fell by almost 1700 – thirty per cent. Given that Literature classes average about fifteen students, this decline represents the equivalent of well over a hundred classes. Students are voting with their feet, and telling us unequivocally that this subject is not for them.

For me, it is not hyperbolic to describe this as a tragedy, both culturally and individually for young people. Our next Peter Carey could be lost. There is no denying the transformative and emancipatory power of books, especially for disadvantaged children. And, as Charlie vividly demonstrates, literature has a protective power. I remember a girl I once taught who was a victim of domestic abuse but found great strength in Karen Levine's *Hana's Suitcase*, a tale of a young girl in the Holocaust.

My own father was not highly educated – he had held half a dozen jobs by the time I reached primary school – but he religiously took my siblings and me to the library. I soon discovered that while the carnival offered a seasonal magic, those rooms spilling with books maintained an enchantment all year round.

The library was an old building right on the beach, gloomy with coastal bottlebrush and haunted by librarians who to me seemed impossibly old. I remember only ever being taken there in the evenings, perhaps because that was when my father was available. It was often empty. In the darkness outside, waves roared. The aisles smelt silently of mystery. Most wondrous of all, it was separated into two huge rooms: a children's section and a grown-ups' section. On the walls of the children's section, Sendakian monsters loomed. As a little boy I sat alone amongst the beanbags for what felt like hours, reading of vampires. This was long before they became figures of teen romance. The vampires of my youth stank of the grave, picked at window-lead in icy European nights, had white faces that bloated pink as they gorged themselves on the living. I would wake sweating and exhilarated, wanting to create my own monsters on the page.

When at last my father said I could venture into the grown-ups' section, that was my life decided. In many ways, I would spend every day as a teacher striving to instil that same magic into the young people in my care.

And for me, the protective power of books extended well beyond the crippling anxiety of my primary school years. As a teenager I was terrible at sport and hated its competitiveness: a guaranteed way to exile yourself as a young man in Australia in the 1990s. I was not like the other boys but did not yet have the perspective or confidence to recognise that as a strength. In PE classes, the volleyball would slap stingingly against my skinny arms and go careening off at unpredictable angles, my blunders followed by the unchallenged bellows of other boys. On one occasion in Year 7, while carrying a chair, my sports teacher muttered to me, 'What's the matter, Brendan? Feeling a bit *weak*?'

So I read, getting most of my books from the library and second-hand bookstores because that was all my parents could afford. When I filled a small bookcase, I began stacking the books two deep. And I wasn't the only reader, I soon found. Many students shared my obsession, and found within those bound covers a world entrancing and safe.

Why, then, is Literature dying in public schools?

First is the cultural issue that Australian children are simply reading less. Mobile devices, obviously, are a huge contributor to this problem. In a touchscreen world of bright colours and dopamine-inducing clickbait, young people are losing the applied focus necessary for extended reading, and society will pay a huge price for that.

Then there is the problem of boys. Ninety per cent of my Literature students in the last decade have been female, and I have taught entire classes without a single boy. Despite the progress we have made socially, young men are often pressured to operate within rigid boundaries.

I remember spending weekends writing creative stories as a fifteen-year-old, then being humiliated when an English teacher asked me about it in the presence of my mates.

'I don't do that anymore,' I had insisted with the vague shame of a recovering addict.

In terms of Literature as a Year 12 subject, however, high-level mismanagement and unprofessionalism is exacerbating these pre-existing cultural conditions.

The last time Literature numbers grew in Victoria (in terms of students sitting the exam) was in 2017. That was the first year of the VCAA's new Year 12 course. For many teachers, it was a time of great optimism.

Ever since then, though, Literature numbers have been plummeting statewide by as much as ten per cent annually. So what went wrong? In many ways, what happened in 2017 was an appalling, high-level abuse of student trust.

That year, the new exam task required students to write an essay applying 'one literary perspective' – for instance, a feminist perspective. I taught my students how to do this, and they worked hard in the lead-up to the exam. Many did very well, one even achieving in the top few per cent of the state.

However, some of my students were disappointed with their results, and one complained to me that she had heard rumours online of students who did not use *one* literary perspective, but *several* getting high results. I reassured her that anybody who did not follow the exam instructions would have been penalised, and promised to confirm this with the VCAA and get back to her. I sent them an email.

What happened next stunned me.

In a reply sent on 20 December 2017, a high-level official at the VCAA admitted that a decision was reached that students would be neither penalised nor rewarded for adopting multiple literary perspectives. Their justification was that it was the first year of a new course.

This may seem reasonable, but only if you forget that ATAR scores are a *ranking*. If you don't penalise Student 1 for doing the wrong thing, you are penalising Student 2, because Student 1's movement *up* the rank has the inevitable consequence of moving Student 2 *down* the rank.

In my opinion, there is little doubt that in 2017, Literature students were penalised for following the rules.

A few months later, the VCAA held their annual 'Meet the Assessors' seminar. An auditorium full of Literature teachers was told that essays employing two literary perspectives were not actually employing two literary perspectives; they were employing just one *hyphenated* perspective. I could not resist raising my hand and asking how many hyphens students could use, to much cynical laughter.

The reason I feel that students were so badly let down in 2017 was not so much because of what occurred, but *when* it occurred. If these decisions had been made and publicised at the beginning of the year, students could have prepared for the exam accordingly. VCAA did not even provide samples of Literary Perspectives essays when the new curriculum was introduced, despite requests from numerous schools. This was another missed opportunity to give students – especially struggling students in government schools – a fair shot at getting the best result they could.

Students talk. To one another, to their teachers and online. They have a nose for fairness and choose their subjects accordingly. Incidents like the one outlined above could be contributing to Literature attrition.

Sadly, this incident is not unique. I have already complained that no dictionary is allowed on the Literature examination, a rule that disadvantages our poorest students. Nonetheless, after the 2019 exam, the VCAA wrote in their Examination Report that a common failing was students confusing words such as 'civil', 'civilised' and 'civilisation', something that resulted in lower-quality responses to the essay topic. Of course, a dictionary could have remedied these misunderstandings.

Then there is just the run-of-the-mill, everyday opacity of the curriculum. Also in the Examination Report, the VCAA warned future students not to use 'slang terms such as "toxic masculinity"'. Later in the same report a series of 'high-scoring' essays was provided, one of which contained exactly that term. This type of thing is extremely confusing for students who use Examination Reports as a guide for how to do well.

At the time of writing, Literature is at a critical stage in government schools across the entire country. I call on curriculum authorities to not only make the subject the best it can be, but also the *fairest* it can be, taking into account the disadvantages of some students and the potential that reading has to set them free.

*

I went looking for Charlie during a free period that afternoon. On the way to his classroom I passed 8G on the basketball courts. Kelvin was sitting cross-legged on the sidelines.

'Oi, Kelvin!'

He turned, grinned in a sudden blush of sunlight. The asphalt seemed to sparkle. He motioned me over.

'How are you, sir?'

'I'm okay.' I glanced at 8G on the court. Tessa, I saw, was playing on the same team as Lonnie; as I watched, Lonnie called out her name, passed the ball to her with a wet slap. Maybe, I thought, things were settling down.

'No class to teach this period?'

'Nope. But what about you? Why aren't you playing? Look – Jen's killing it!' Jen, a budding sportswoman, was always the student against whom Kelvin liked to compete.

He winced, straightened out his back. 'Mum had to take me to the physio the other day. He said I've got an inflamed facet joint. It's killing me.'

'What about The Spuds?'

He laughed, shook a finger. 'Don't you worry about The Spuds, sir. First game's coming up and I'll definitely be playing.'

I found Charlie in a portable classroom that had been dumped on the outer margin of The School. Some of the students watched dreamily as a fluorescent groundskeeper drifted to and fro on his ride-on mower, but Charlie had his head down, studious. I took him out to the corridor.

'I drove past you running this morning, mate. That was pretty early.'

He shrugged. 'Should have honked. I was up running before seven.'

'Wow. If you ever see me running at that time of the morning, something's chasing me.'

'Good one, sir.'

'Still got time for reading with all this training? I remember those fantasy novels you used to devour . . .'

'Always the English teacher, right? 'Course I've got time to read. You remember how hard it was to pry books out of my hand?'

'I remember.'

Charlie smiled, watching me with a quizzical look. He knew I had come for something, so I got to the point. 'Look, some teachers are worried you're over-training. That you're pushing yourself too hard.'

'Ah, so *that's* what this is about. Don't worry, sir. Only two more fights, then if I win those I'll have a shot at the Australian Title.'

For Charlie, I feared there would always be more fights, in one form or another.

'And how about your dad? Is he at home?'

'On and off.'

'And you're sure all this training isn't just a way to get out of the house?'

'Maybe. But that title means a lot to me.'

'I know it does. Just look after yourself.'

He patted me on the shoulder with a hand that was calloused across the knuckles. 'Thanks, sir. Don't worry.'

I watched him walk back into class, seeing not the

broad-shouldered athlete he now was, but what he *had* been: a frightened boy hiding beneath a bed as his mother brandished a machete nearby.

I was worried about him. What I didn't know then was that I should have been far more worried about somebody else.

13

The concrete boy

FOR WAMBUI IT came from outside the home, for Charlie from within. For Kelvin, it was his own body that would become the antagonist of his childhood.

With each passing day, autumn was giving way to winter. Rain pounded the iron roofs of The School, so loud that teachers often had to wait for it to ease before they could continue their lessons. Several classrooms had buckets plinking in damp corners, and one had a section of its roof give way entirely, sending a roaring torrent streaming down the bricks and onto the carpet.

Many PE sessions were cancelled (there was only so much space in the stadium to go around), though for the usually athletic Kelvin this made little difference. The inflamed facet joint his physiotherapist had diagnosed was not improving. To make matters worse, The Spuds' first ever basketball game was coming up and it looked like he would miss it.

Heath, nervous, kept asking if he thought he could play.

'Yeah, yeah, I'll be right.' Kelvin would straighten out his back like an old man, twisting himself this way and that and grimacing. 'Wouldn't miss it.'

And he would not, if there was any way he could avoid it. He and Heath had started the team, even designed the uniform, but all his other mates were involved, too; he hated the thought of letting them down. In training they teased him ceaselessly about the socks he liked to wear pulled up to his knees, but they only did that, he knew, because they were his best friends.

'Of course I'll play,' he told them. 'A few days rest and I reckon I'll be right. What hope have you guys got with me on the bench?'

But as that week continued, so did the pain. Sometimes playing sport at recess would help, but as soon as he stopped his whole lower back would stiffen. He could almost see it in his imagination, his muscles and sinews hardening into a grey, coarse concrete that crept up his spine as class ticked by. When the bell went he would groan and reach to swipe it clear, but all he would feel was the smooth hot skin of his back.

Then the concrete spread further. It groaned and cracked around his chest and gripped ever more tightly, and now it began to smother him. Walking from one class to the next he would find his mouth dry and his heart pounding. He hoped nobody would speak to him lest they notice his panting. He put up with this for a week, thinking it would go away, but if anything – like the pain in his back – it worsened. Eventually he told his mother, who phoned the same doctor who had first suspected Non-Hodgkin Lymphoma three years earlier. She made an appointment for the following day after school.

It did not occur to Kelvin that his cancer could have returned. What he did think, however, was that his breathing issues were caused by something more serious than asthma. His experience in primary school had cured him of any youthful naivety. Bodies, he knew, were fallible, unpredictable, prone to breakdown and perhaps total failure. Plus, he excelled in Science just as he did in English and all his other subjects. It was clear that something was happening inside him.

Kelvin and his mother walked together into that same waiting room: the same antiseptic smell, the same frosted glass, perhaps the very same elderly locals with their dripping umbrellas and *National Geographic*s. They sat there thinking of everything and nothing, and then at last the door clicked open and the doctor called his name.

He listened to the symptoms from behind that familiar greying moustache, though today he made none of his usual jokes. His brow was set as he looked from Kelvin to his computer screen and then back to Kelvin.

'Better hop up onto the bed, mate.'

Kelvin lay back, his heart as rhythmic as a basketball. He tried to transport himself to the court, but it was impossible with the cold of the stethoscope on his chest, then the pressing of the doctor's palms up and down his abdomen. The pain in his lower back had quietened a little, but just then granules of concrete ground against one another and he gasped.

'Okay. You can hop down. Put your shirt back on.'

They sat opposite the doctor who looked at Kelvin's mother from over a desk of modelled joints and organs. Plastic; dead.

'I'm going to make some calls.' He clicked his computer mouse, rattled on the keyboard. 'You need to go straight to the hospital. Tonight.'

While many young people grapple with who they are, Kelvin would soon be battling with whether or not he would continue to be.

Term Three:
Winter

1

A story about death

LIAM WAS MURDERED in 2014, about a decade after he had come into my life at precisely the moment I needed him. He was my teacher, but his role transcended that in ways he never knew (though perhaps occasionally suspected).

I regret not telling him on the final day we spoke; I regret not sending him the email I always promised myself I would; I regret not dropping into his office the thousand times I drove past in the ensuing years. If I had, I would have told him he was the type of teacher I wanted to be – *want* to be – and that I still think of him often, sometimes when my day has been hard, sometimes when it has been such a joy that I know I have the best job in the world.

*

My road to Liam's classroom began when I was completing Year 12 at The School. As with so many young people, I had been convinced that this was the most important twelve months of my life, the moment when I would either stoke the fires of a bright future or condemn myself to a lifetime of disappointment. To add to the pressure, my brother had achieved the highest score in The School's history just the year before.

Though the sickness of my primary years was forgotten, I was afflicted with an almost pathological lack of self-esteem. My brother had studied Physics, Specialist Mathematics, Mathematical Methods, while all my subjects scaled down. I wanted to be a writer but felt that to be an impossible dream, so decided to aim for a score that would admit me into a science degree. I became so focused on achieving that score that I could see very little beyond it. It was the year 2000; we watched Cathy Freeman win gold at the Sydney Olympics; there was a sense of the epic and the momentous. When December came around, my results overshot my expectations by such a margin that I spent the week before Christmas convinced there had been an error.

I actually think my eighteen-year-old self believed closing credits would roll when I finished Year 12. They did not. High school was over and I found the real world waiting. I deferred my university course and decided to spend a year writing. Things were fine for a couple of months, then I crashed.

What I did not see then but can recognise now is that the sickness returned. I suddenly felt I had spent the last few years wandering towards a mirage and was now stranded in a water-less desert. I stopped writing. Whenever I sat at the keyboard I was overcome with a nauseous horror, convinced my efforts were futile. The Arts, after all, scaled down. Descriptive writing was a hobby at best. Science, mathematics and engi-neering were the pathways to real accomplishment. Yet when my gap year ended and my science degree arrived, I dropped out in the first week.

Those next twelve months were characterised by an

overwhelming sense that I had been left behind. Many of my friends were into the second years of their degrees, and all I had to show for my disconnection from education were a couple of short story–writing awards. When I spied people from high school on the street I would actively avoid them. I was not then able to see the real source of my existential disorientation: the Year 12 system had encouraged a super-ficial, short-sighted obsession with my final score, while simultaneously convincing me that the Arts were of little value. It was almost inevitable that I would enrol in the wrong course and develop ambivalence towards my real passion.

Almost two years out of formal education (and insistent that I would not spend my life stacking shelves), I enrolled in university once more. When the academic year began, however, I could not face it. I would wake with a feeling of suffocation in the hours before dawn, convinced I was dying. I could barely summon the energy necessary to complete the paperwork for yet another twelve-month deferral.

Years later, I would be stunned when Claire told me of her reluctance to seek help, even when suicidal. I should not have been surprised; I didn't seek that help myself.

The best way I can describe that time is as a kind of torturous mindfulness. When a soul is at peace, life seems to glide by. During those weeks and months, I was dragged through the suffocating grey of each lingering moment. It was pain and exhaustion and an ever-present sense of futility. I couldn't escape those feelings and they seemed to make time stop, so that even menial tasks were experienced in every aching detail: unwrapping the bread, walking across the kitchen, turning on the power point, pushing down the toaster, listening to the buzz of glowing filaments, smelling the burn of old crumbs.

I knew I could not endure this forever and yet I never sought help of any kind.

People ceaselessly analyse why young men fail to reach out. All I can say is that it never even occurred to me. The possibility of help was blotted out by some insidious blind spot that had perhaps metastasised from the condition itself.

I don't profess to have the solutions to these problems. Liam saved me, which was really just luck, a 'protective factor' dealt by fate. What I do know is that the years immediately after high school are an extremely high-risk time for young people, particularly academic young people who have deferred or otherwise disengaged from formal education. And we cannot expect them to ask for help, any more than we would expect a paralysed person to stand and run from an approaching bushfire.

Again, it was my mother who sensed something was wrong. At her insistence I signed up to study Professional and Creative Writing at the local TAFE.

By the time I started the course it was already several weeks underway. My first class – a night subject filled with students ranging in age from eighteen to (it seemed) eighty – was Short Story 1A. When the teacher walked in I had no idea who he was. He was tall and smiling with a checked shirt tucked in at the waist and neat white hair. A girl in the class told me in a whisper that he was Liam Davison, shortlisted countless times for such honours as the Victorian Premier's Literary Award and *The Age* Book of the Year Award. Most impressive of all, he had actually *won* the Banjo Award for Fiction – an accolade he shared with Tim Winton and Peter Carey.

Liam was everything I wanted to be. After class that night I stayed to introduce myself and apologise for my late appearance.

'Nothing to apologise for at all.' His voice had a slight nasally twang, and he spoke through an unwavering smile. 'You're more than welcome, Brendan. I look forward to reading your work.'

I knew somehow that he meant what he said. Driving home, I was already thinking of which of my stories I would show him.

*

I came to spend my weeks anticipating Liam's lessons. The sickness persisted, often waking me with its choking hands in the small hours before dawn, but it was weakening. I read the stories Liam assigned and tried to apply their lessons in my own work. When he recommended Raymond Carver's *Where I'm Calling From* during a conversation one evening after class, I went out the very next day and bought it, reading every story in the collection before the next week arrived.

Liam was kind, patient, humble. Once he read the opening sentence of a story aloud, invited us all to tear it to pieces – to be as brutal as possible – then laughingly admitted it was his own writing.

The moment that really saved me, I think, was when it came time for me to workshop one of my stories. Anyone who has ever studied creative writing will know the anxiety and intimidation of reading your work aloud for criticism. That evening, I sat in the carpark for half an hour before the lesson began, convinced I couldn't do it. I remember trying to persuade myself, even absurdly taking a coin from my wallet and tossing it: heads I go in, tails I drive home. Eventually it was my love of Liam's teaching that got me inside.

I passed out the copies. The story was about sailors in World War II training in mine disposal. I said, 'It's not very deep.' Liam, ever-smiling, gave me a nod of encouragement. I lowered my head and began to read.

When I reached the end, he sat back and looked at me. I still remember his words. 'You call *that* not very deep?'

In that moment I felt my life had become possible. He praised my writing, but he challenged me, too, pointed out ways I could improve, develop. The rest of the class followed his lead.

From then on I wrote ceaselessly. One evening after class I was walking to my car, looking at the underside of a night-lit palm tree, and realised that I was happy. It came as an epiphany after the previous three years. I knew even then that it was Liam with his kindness and patience and honesty who had led me to that point. And I *do* believe he had sensed there was something I needed, something he was in the unique position to offer. He must have reflected on my late entry into the course, the nights in those early weeks when I could not manage that crowded room and had slunk home during the mid-class breaks. I'm sure he recognised the student I was, just as I have recognised such students in my own classes.

I owe Liam Davison more than I can ever repay. Perhaps now, though, I can make a small offering: the story he told me to write that I never did.

*

It was a class focusing on symbolism. That, Liam said, was one way we could all improve our writing, and for us he spoke with great authority. We had seen the symbolic power of his own work, particularly the Banjo Award–winning *Soundings* with its haunting, ethereal landscapes transformed through the aperture of the protagonist's camera.

We were all sitting in a circle. 'A great starting point,' Liam said, 'is to think of the symbols that have resonated with you – either in your own reading or in life.'

We talked of all manner of things, of gifts received and given, of gestures, of the writers that inspired us. Then I remembered something that had happened late the previous year.

'The store I worked at was selling Christmas crackers.' As I spoke, Liam watched me closely, just as he did with all his students. There was never the slightest hint that he was anywhere else. 'You know – the cheap ones. The kind that come with paper hats, cheesy jokes and plastic trinkets.'

'Interesting. And those symbolised something for you?'

'Well, no. But somebody found a symbol inside one, in a way. I was working on Boxing Day and this middle-aged guy came in with a ripped box of crackers demanding an apology and a refund.'

I still remember that man today, stocky and officious with greying temples and spider-veins on a splayed nose. What softened his intimidating demeanour was the quaver in his voice.

'I called my manager,' I said to Liam. 'This man complained that his family had been around the table for Christmas lunch, opening their crackers, and his mother's trinket was a plastic skull. Like a little keyring or something. But the thing is, his mum had terminal cancer. She saw it as a symbol – an omen, maybe. And it had upset her terribly, as well as the rest of the family. It kind of wrecked what was maybe the last Christmas they would be able to spend with her.'

'Wow.' Liam looked around the room. 'What happened?'

'They gave him a refund, and after he left the manager and staff were laughing about it. Saying what a nut he was. But I felt terrible. I almost wanted to go and find him and apologise properly, which I could have done, because people who got refunds had to write down all their details.'

'Did you?'

'No. I think it just would have felt too strange.'

Liam sat forward and spoke with something like urgency in his voice. 'You *have* to write that story, Brendan. Take it further so your protagonist *does* track the man down. See what happens next.'

I shrugged, noncommittal. I was halfway through another story at the time, and had several others planned and waiting.

'I wish I had a story like that to write,' he finished before the conversation moved on.

Not long after that the year ended and I completed the course. By then I had a place studying writing and literature at university. I knew, at last, that I was on the right path. I knew, too, that it was because of Liam, though at the end of that final lesson I did not tell him.

'Invite me to your book launch when it comes around,' he said, shaking my hand. I promised that I would (still not quite believing that such a thing could ever happen), and thanked him for all he had taught us.

I never got the opportunity to stay true to my word. Two years before my first book was published, Liam and his wife Frankie boarded Malaysia Airlines Flight 17 in Amsterdam after a week visiting their children. As their plane passed over the Ukraine, pro-Russian insurgents shot it down with a Buk surface-to-air missile. Two hundred and ninety-eight people were killed.

The School

When I saw Liam's face on the news, I was overcome with rage and despair and regret. I thought of what had been lost, the books unwritten, the lessons untaught. I wondered why I had never told him what he truly did for me, and continues to do, each and every day of my life.

Inevitably, I remembered the conversation Liam and I had shared that day, and the way he had urged me to write the story of that small plastic skull. It was a symbol of compassion, the brevity of life, the sudden unexpectedness with which we can be forced to confront our own mortality. In finally telling the story, I hope I have honoured my old teacher – thanked him, in some small way.

I find it hard to read Liam's books now, though I still do from time to time. I love the sense of place, especially when he writes about the very ocean alongside which I grew up and now teach. One of my favourite stories is 'The Left Man', at the surface a reimagining of William Buckley's colonial exile but really an exploration of history and ephemerality. It ends with a protagonist on a cliff peering across the bay through mounted binoculars, imagining that he can see the past:

Looking from the west, as the coin runs trickling through the slot, you can catch with careful eyes the people moving on the other side. Then the coin runs out. And they are gone.

2

Absences

WHEN I RETURNED to school after the July holidays, I did not initially register Kelvin's absence. There are students missing each day, and it is rare – almost worthy of comment – when every seat in a government classroom is occupied. Besides, there was an additional distraction. Tessa was no longer on the 8G roll.

I looked around the cold grey room, saw that she was missing. 'Anybody know where Tessa is?'

Heath, soaked from a recess on the basketball courts, put up his hand. 'She isn't in this class anymore, sir. I think they put her in 8A.'

'Well, that's the first I'm hearing about it.'

I turned to Lonnie as subtly as I could. She looked neither victorious nor guilty. I couldn't even call her indifferent, for that word implies a reaction that simply was not there. Lonnie just sat with her straight black hair and her battalion of girl-friends, book open, ready for the lesson to begin.

I wondered, not for the first time, if such students' actions are of far less significance to them than they are to the rest of us. Even if I were to someday confront Jude, I thought, he would perhaps squint, scratch his chin and ask: '*Who* are you?' He may even have had a similar reaction the very week after he threw me down those stone steps.

Tessa's relocation, I supposed, had been a decision made by Paul at the end of the previous term, perhaps at the behest of her parents. In some ways it was logical. Even if things had been ostensibly smoothed out, it remained problematic for a girl of that age to spend day after day surrounded by people who had shown her such coldness. An adult would find it challenging. Still, it felt like a partial surrender. Was The School not subjecting Tessa to the very exile Lonnie had desired (either consciously or unconsciously) from the beginning? Plus, there was still the playground to worry about, not to mention the lurid, Goldingesque mindscape of social media.

Once again, I spent the majority of that lesson working with Grace. She still had no aide and it was clear she would never get one. Helen's suggestion was that, next year, she could be put in the same class as a funded student. That way, at least, the aide could be shared.

My anger at this situation had been exacerbated by something I found when I read Grace's midyear report.

'Any griffins for me today?' I asked her.

Flushing slightly, but smiling in a way that showed me she appreciated her talent, Grace reached beneath the table and took out an art portfolio. It was held shut by thread woven around a plastic catch, and she unwound this with practised finesse.

'I done some.' Her words fell as dull and heavy on the table as bricks, but her illustrations were the opposite: light, delicate, precise, griffins now accompanied by goblins, fairies, basilisks staring from the page with the nocturnal pupils of cats.

I had spent the previous few nights reading all of my students' midyear reports. The first thing I had noticed about Grace's was that she was recognised as exceptional – gifted, perhaps – in visual arts. Second was that her abilities were in the junior primary range in all other subjects but one. In that subject, the teacher had put her at the level expected of a child of her age.

Given her literacy challenges, it was immediately clear to me that Grace's result in that subject was completely inaccurate. So what had happened?

I will be blunt: Grace's teacher was not doing his job. Call it laziness, call it incompetence, but this teacher did not know Grace at all, and had simply placed her 'at the expected level'. In all probability, he had put the student at the top of his roll at the expected level, then simply selected the 'fill down' option. Reports done with the literal click of a button.

This frustrated me beyond words. Any slim chance Grace had of getting an aide in the future would be based on a range of data, including reports. One lazy teacher could cause her to miss out.

That morning, I found him in the main staffroom, pontificating on the scourge of NAPLAN. One of my paradoxical observations of the last decade has been that it is the laziest, most disengaged teachers who are often the loudest critics of contemporary education.

The teacher was tall, grey-haired, confident in a blustery way. On more than one occasion I had heard his voice rumbling from behind the principal's closed door, challenging David Carver over some point or other.

I waited until he had wandered over to the water cooler to pull him aside.

'Look, Gary, it's about Grace's report,' I said. 'I'm not sure how this didn't get picked up in proofreading, but you've put her at the expected level.'

He didn't look at me as water from the cooler filled his mug. 'Sure. She doesn't make a sound. Isn't disruptive. Great kid.'

'Well, I've got her for English and she's essentially illiterate.'

'*Illiterate?* Grace?'

'Yeah. I'd be keen to see what she's been doing in your class.'

He stood up straight. 'You're the expert, are you?'

'Look, I'm just saying her data might need to be changed.' I paused, added generously, 'In case there has been a computer error or something.'

Gary looked at me for a moment before shaking his head. 'Listen, mate, I'll have a look back over it when I have a spare minute.'

But I knew what he was thinking. He had been teaching for years, probably since before I was born. In his eyes, I was an upstart.

'Thanks, Gary.'

'Any time. But worry about your own reports first. I'll take care of mine.'

He returned to his seat and resumed lambasting NAPLAN.

I have been critical of standardised testing in these pages, just as many Australian educators have been critical elsewhere. However, if I'm to be fair and honest there is another reality I must address, one we often do not like to acknowledge: that some teachers are opposed to standardised testing because they fear it will bring their incompetence to light.

Like bad police, plumbers, doctors and dentists, there are bad teachers. They're a fractional minority, but they exist in *all* schools, public and private, primary and secondary. It would be all too easy (and self-indulgent) for me to write of teachers as unassailable martyrs. It isn't the reality, and nor am I perfect myself.

Some teachers are bored, some teachers are angry, some teachers are lazy. Some are simply unwell. A few use the classroom as a stage upon which to parade their egos; some dislike children, or only warm to certain *types* of children. And for those of us who *are* teachers, we must be honest and admit that we all fall into these traps occasionally, in one way or another. Usually it doesn't last long. Any teacher who claims to be perfect all of the time is lying to themselves, and unlikely to grow.

Still, every one of us has a story of a truly bad teacher, encountered perhaps as students, perhaps as parents. I will speak plainly: it is extremely difficult to get such teachers out of schools.

On the one hand, administrators work hard to help under-performing teachers develop and improve. This is exactly how it should be. Support must precede harsher measures, provided the teacher's shortcomings are just that – shortcomings. Many a struggling educator has grown into an asset to the profession through suitable mentoring and guidance.

But what about when that fails?

There is a lengthy process administrators must follow. It takes months, sometimes years. Some school leaders choose not to follow this path due to the emotional toll it takes on all involved. I should stress that I am not talking about teachers guilty of egregious failings, who principals always act swiftly to remove. What I am talking about is the ordinary, run-of-the-mill Bad Teacher, the type trudging wearily (and often bitterly) through year after year of tedious mediocrity. In some cases, I think the thing stopping administrators from acting is pity.

But what do we value more? The feelings of such teachers, or the learning, curiosity and passion of their students? In the symbolism of Peter Carey's 'Do You Love Me?', if our hearts go out too much to the teacher then it will be the children who fade from view.

What can teachers do? In short, be better. If they're struggling, they should get help. If they're bored, they should get inspired. If they don't want to be in the classroom, they should make themselves absent.

And administrators need to be courageous. They need to help struggling teachers as much as they can, support them, but be willing to take the next difficult steps if necessary. It's uncomfortable, but avoiding that discomfort simply shifts the burden onto students.

Grace's teacher has been out of the profession for some time now. He never did make the slightest adjustment to her report.

3

Rorschach

THE CHILDREN'S HOSPITAL Cancer Centre was gallantly
striving to present as something it would never quite be:
namely, a playground, a place a young person might actually
want to spend time. Bright colours and cartoonish characters
formed a thin, shifting veil that only partly obscured the more
insistent reality of worry, dread, sometimes despair. Kelvin
walked in feeling small and frightened.

He and his mother checked in at a cool glass counter and
waited. Children passed, some much younger than Kelvin and
insubstantial as wraiths. But for his sore back and breathlessness Kelvin felt perfectly well. He shifted in his seat, feeling his
heart hammering. It had not slowed since they left the doctor's
surgery.

'You alright, Kelvin?' His mother tried not to look at those
sick children, tried not to see in them a forecast of her own
son's future. 'Do you want to stretch your legs?'

'I'm fine, Mum.'

But he was not fine. This was what he had feared since
he was sick the first time, though he had managed to press
down those worries so that they seldom bothered him. A few

years is a long time when you're a little boy, and that golf ball–sized lump seemed to belong to another reality, almost another person.

'You sure? There's a snack machine over there – we could go and get something.'

'I'm okay. Lunch filled me up today.'

He did not want to tell her that his mouth was so dry he probably wouldn't be able to swallow.

They waited. Children made of marble passed in wheelchairs pushed by smiling, chattering parents. Looking around, Kelvin felt suddenly out of place. He was a big kid, muscular for his age and able to run rings around even the senior boys on the basketball court. This was a place for babies. It had the feel of the first-aid room at a Wiggles concert. He felt that at any moment a clown could come cartwheeling by, offering his mother a trick flower that would of course spray water in her face. The clown would wink, chuckle, give him a nickname like 'Muscles'. Kelvin felt utterly separate from it all and was relieved when his name was called.

It all happened in an anxious haze. There was a smiling doctor named Peter whose pinstriped shirt and tie gave him the look of a benevolent Maths teacher; there were corridors and lights and hands as cold as the instruments they clasped. Kelvin was intelligent, something that would be both a boon and a curse in the coming week. He knew there would be tests and one of the first was a PET scan. When he asked, they told him it stood for positron emission tomography.

The radiographer was an older woman with spectacles hanging from her neck on a purple cord.

'Afternoon, sweetie. I'm Karen.' Something in her voice was almost apologetic. 'I'll ask you to pop into the cubicle and strip down to your jocks and socks. There are gowns in there. Take your time and shout out when you're ready.'

Kelvin obeyed. He was cold, the gown scratched his skin, and he fumbled for some minutes trying to get the knot tied at the back.

What came next reminded him that, though he was a person, he was also a *thing*. Karen guided him to a set of scales and wordlessly noted his weight. Next, she had him stand with his back against a wall so she could measure his height, pulling down a tape that she held to the crown of his head.

'What's this for?'

She smelt sweetly of powder. The pencil scratched across her clipboard. 'It's so we know how much of this special mixture you need to drink. It has a tiny amount of radiation in it. A bit like an X-ray. You're not pregnant, are you?'

She went away, and when at last she returned with the concoction, Kelvin studied it dubiously. It was blue-green and looked like it belonged in the fuel tank of a spaceship.

'It's mostly glucose,' Karen reassured him. 'Not much different from the sugar you'd sprinkle on your cereal.'

'What does it do?'

'It helps us see things clearly on the scan.'

His mother, a nurse, knew better: cancer, gluttonous for fuel to sustain its runaway growth, gulps down glucose faster than other tissues in the body. This would combine with the radioactive tracer to paint a picture of what was going on in his body.

Kelvin took the cup and brought it to his lips. It took everything he had not to spit out the first tiny mouthful.

'Wow.' He winced, stuck out his tongue. 'Sugar? Death-liquid, more like.'

Karen smiled sadly. 'Just do your best, hon. Take your time. It isn't a race.'

The taste was so bad that Kelvin was afraid he would throw it up, and that would mean having to start all over again. He went slowly, managing to get down one small cup in about half an hour. He and his mum chatted about school, The Spuds, what time Kelvin's dad would be arriving from work. There were movies playing on a large screen, but Kelvin had little desire to watch them. Other patients came through, some looking sick and others well, some calm and others frightened. Machines whirred and cranked. A draught kept sneaking in the back of his gown. Waiting would be a key feature of the coming months, and at times it was nearly intolerable. If something was happening to you – even something bad – you were at least in the moment, aware of a sense of progress. When you were waiting it was as though the world had stopped, and in that lingering silence, dark possibilities whispered.

Eventually Karen took him through to the room containing the machine itself. It stared back at him with its great manhole of a pupil. The bore was at least fairly shallow.

'Now you lie back and stay as still as you can.' She put a cushion beneath his knees and lowered headphones over his ears. 'Nothing to be afraid of. I'll be just on the other side of the glass, and if you need anything, I'll be able to hear anything you say.'

The bed rolled through that manhole and a red light came on, spreading a grid of lasers that sectioned his abdomen. Kelvin closed his eyes and let the minutes pass as the gurney moved backwards and forwards. The headphones played music he did not recognise, and occasionally cut to traffic reports.

At one point Karen's voice cut in, telling him it wouldn't be much longer.

There was no doubt that he would not be playing in The Spuds' first game. He thought of Heath and the rest of his friends, the uniform they had designed, all the weeks they had spent training and preparing. But he would not let the disappointment or the fear overtake him. He kept his eyes closed and visualised the basketball court with its high ceiling, tiers of spectators and squeaking, gleaming floors. He could almost smell it, sweat and dust and the cold night after the game. Surely, he thought, he would be able to play again soon.

When the scan was over Karen told him the results wouldn't be too long. 'And the tracer will be in your system for a little bit,' she smiled. 'So for the rest of the night stay away from pregnant women and babies.'

'Okay.' He gave a thumbs up. 'Thanks, Karen.'

'Any time, sweetie.'

He hesitated. 'Did you see anything out of the ordinary on your screen?'

Karen's face changed, growing not grave but businesslike, practised. She spat out her response as though she had said it a thousand times, which, Kelvin supposed, she probably had.

'Can't say anything yet. You'll hear from the doctor.'

*

When the scans did come back, Kelvin's mother would not show them to him.

'I don't want you worrying about any of that yet.' She had them in a large envelope that she put on a table across the room. 'Let's wait until we know more. Those pictures just don't really look like anything.'

'If you say so, Mum.'

A few days after the PET scan Kelvin was still in the Children's Cancer Centre. Doctors were monitoring his breathlessness, but he was allowed to wander around, enjoying the outdoor spaces as best he could and watching basketball on his mobile phone. His next ordeal – set for that day – was to have a lymph node removed from his neck for biopsy. The scans alone would not offer a diagnosis.

'Neck dissection.' When he repeated the words to his mother, they had a dark gravity that struck him as almost humorous. 'I'll be asleep, right?'

'Of course you'll be asleep.'

'More cool scars?'

Sue smiled. 'Don't hold your breath. They do it along the folds of the neck so you probably won't even notice it.'

'And I can't have just a quick look at the scans?'

He thought he saw something in her face then, something that was there for the flutter of a moth's wing before she was able to hide it once more. 'There's no point. Let's just wait and talk to the doctor after your biopsy.'

They took him into surgery and he lay chatting with the nurses, anaesthetist, and eventually his own doctor. When you are a child you often forget you are one, but that was exactly what those oncology specialists were looking at, a smiling little boy, mature for his age, who insisted that yes, he was doing quite well, all things considered.

Kelvin felt the oxygen mask cover his face. Somebody pressed the plunger on a syringe and a hot, prickling blush spread up his arm, into his neck and then dwindled away to nothing. He did not even have time to think of basketball before he dropped into the unremembered void of the anaesthetic.

The early years of adolescence are to a large extent a search for self. Children look at the people around them – role models, good and bad – and clutch at fragments of other identities in the formation of their own. Some of those fragments they will discard, others they will keep, fitting them around whatever mysterious potentialities already wait in that ancestral darkness. Gradually, a patchwork begins to form. In that sense, children grow in response to the world *out there*, turning inward from time to time to reflect self-consciously on what they are becoming. Parents and teachers see this same formation and project it into imagined futures, mostly with hope. As Kelvin lay on that bed unconscious, the knife on his neck turned the metaphor concrete: what lay beneath the skin would offer a glimpse of his future, however long or short that may be. And his mother, too, had looked into her son and seen the PET images from which she had protected him, the tumours sucking greedily at the radiated glucose. They seemed to be everywhere, forming a clotted, bulging Rorschach all the way from his throat to his pelvis.

There was more waiting, then at last a diagnosis: T-cell histiocyte-rich large B-cell lymphoma.

It was cancer: stage four.

4

Are you safe?

'HE WAS A lot bigger than me,' Charlie said, palms spread towards our office blow-heater like a storyteller at a campfire. 'And I knew who his dad was. Not a guy to mess around with. But when we squared up I could see he was scared. He wasn't ready.'

Charlie was telling me about his latest fight. This time, it had taken place in the city against the son of a major crime figure, a man I'd seen on the news a few times in the preceding years. The father had decided he wanted his boy to get into kickboxing.

'He was a big dude but he hadn't done the training and didn't have the experience.' From anyone else the words might have been arrogance or bravado, but I could hear the kindness in Charlie's voice – the guilt, almost. 'He was really nervous. He had his dad there and all his dad's mates. I felt for him.'

'What happened?'

'I told him, "Listen, I'm only gonna go as hard as you go. If you just wanna cruise we can cruise."'

'Did he?'

'At first. But then his support crew went mental.'

The men in this boy's corner started bellowing that he should kill him, smash him, knock him out.

'The worst bit was that they were telling him to "do what we talked about".' Charlie looked at me and shook his head. 'I could tell he didn't want to but in the end he did and just started kicking at my bad knee over and over. You could see in his eyes that he didn't want to do it but he kept going, and in the end I had to finish it and wound up knocking him out of the ring.'

Afterwards Charlie collected his trophies, showered, and was headed out with his own team when they ran into the underworld figures in the carpark.

'It was bad, Mr Murray. They were drunk, fed up. There was a scuffle and my mate Tommo ended up getting slashed in the arm with a knife.'

'*What?* Is he –'

'He's fine, he's fine.' Charlie's voice was level, unaffected. 'The police came. And an ambulance. It got sorted. But I feel bad about it. I should have done more – should have defused the situation.'

'Jesus, Charlie.'

'It's all good, sir. Now there's only one more fight and I get a shot at the title. Just have to train hard and win it.'

I was still worried about how hard Charlie was pushing himself, but once again felt so separate from his world that I wondered if it was my place to suggest he slow down. I knew kickboxing was fulfilling a need for him. If the kickboxing stopped, might not that vacuum be occupied by something more destructive? I doubted it, but was sure Charlie would redirect his energies into another obsession nonetheless. His strength in the ring, I had heard, was that he never stopped.

Other fighters would take their time, wear their opponents out, but Charlie went in at a hundred per cent from the moment the bell tolled until the moment the referee held up his arm. He could do it because his training regime was like nobody else's.

As well as the early morning runs, Charlie travelled to his gym in the city four nights a week. When the school bell went he would race home, get changed and then catch a bus. He enjoyed the first ten or so minutes of that trip; forehead rested against the glass, he would look out over the dull steel of the bay where, at that time of year, great clouds amassed and pelagic seabirds dropped like darts into the lace-ruffle of the breakers. Soon, though, he would be on the freeway, and after another thirty minutes he would be sitting on the train. Then, Charlie read. There was no joy to be found beyond that scratched glass, which showed only rusting gantries, graffiti, concrete, weeds nosing up from beneath the crushed stone ballast of the tracks. He retreated into his fantasy novels, perhaps seeing in the characters' journeys struggles analogous to his own.

'*Eragon.*' I nodded to the tome stacked amongst his schoolbooks. The eye of a blue-scaled dragon stared back from its spine. 'Didn't you read that in Year 9?'

'Christopher Paolini.' He took it out and thumped the cover. 'Never get tired of it, sir.'

As we chatted, I sensed that Charlie had more to say. After four years I had developed a sense for when he was holding something back. Normally he was talkative, but today he let the silences linger, staring at that heater and turning his hands this way and that.

I swivelled to face him, took an educated guess. 'Any news on your dad?'

'Funny you ask, sir. He's back.'

'What do you mean?'

'He's moved in with us.' He let out a breath, sat back in the couch. 'Tia couldn't turn her back on him. He's her little brother. She's trying to get him help.'

'So this isn't just on and off? He's moved in?'

'Yep. Full-time.'

There's a question teachers have to ask in these situations, and I asked it: 'Are you safe?'

'Yeah, I'm safe. But I hate being around him.' He made a fist that he moved to thump into his bad knee but stopped himself. 'It's hard to explain. I don't want to be like him. Having him there doesn't help.'

'Look, I haven't met your dad, Charlie. But from what I can tell, you aren't *anything* like the guy.'

His smile was tight-lipped, fleeting. 'Thanks, sir. But the thing is, we don't get along *because* we're alike.'

It struck me as an admission of extraordinary maturity. Charlie hated the traits he saw in his father – violence, destructiveness, selfishness – and had told me numerous times that, while he never blamed his mother for her sickness, his father could not be forgiven so easily. He had clear choices and he had made them. And yet here was Charlie, confessing that when he looked at that man he saw echoes of himself.

'This is why I am this way,' Charlie said, and as he spoke he looked at me in a kind of appeal, though for what I wasn't quite sure. 'Dad never finished anything. Nothing. Not his apprenticeship, not his fight training when he was into it, not anything. So I have to finish *everything*. If I sit back I'll just be *him*.'

The rain started on the tin roof then, a sad sound, like distant applause in some arena that could never be reached.

'There's way more to you than that, Charlie.'

'Maybe, sir.'

I tried to think of what to say. No words seemed right. But then, perhaps there were no words to set Charlie free, only his own outward and inward journeying. I considered *You have huge potential*, but immediately knew it was a trap, felt the weight of every teacher–student conversation pushing my next sentence towards *You can be anything you want to be*. It felt contrived, clichéd, devoid of true meaning. I stopped, weighed up *You should be incredibly proud of what you have achieved so far*, but that was no better. It was as if invisible channels lay before me in the air, and any words I spoke would have no choice but to flow along them.

What I should have said was that all I could see was a young man of whom any parent could be proud.

'Charlie, I think you're being too hard on yourself.'

'Better than too soft.'

We sat there watching the rivulets streaming down the glass, waiting for the weather to clear so Charlie could head to the bus stop. When it didn't ease in time, he folded up the collar of his school jacket and walked out into the rain.

5

The kite

THE RAIN AND the cold continued throughout that week. At lunchtime students crowded the corridors, bunching antlike around the sweet warmth of the heaters. A few of the younger ones braved the weather, pounding through puddles in unlaced shoes and crying with laughter they could scarcely hear over the wind in their ears. It seemed a sin to interrupt the joy of their wild freedom, and they were never going to get any wetter regardless.

When I returned to the office after yard duty, Ana handed me an envelope. It had my name written on the front in thick, sloping texta.

'A little girl came looking for you – a Year 7, I think.' She was gathering her things, laptop and folders and whiteboard markers and a plush die asking *Why, Who, When, Where, How* and *Will?* 'I've forgotten her name.'

I had the afternoon free so sat down and tried to guess the raindrop-blurred handwriting. It looked familiar. Eventually I tore open the envelope and saw a photograph of Tessa grinning from the cover of a handmade card. She held Gonzo the beagle to her cheek, and one lens of her oversized glasses was a blank sheen of reflected light.

Dear Mr Murry, it read. *I wanted to say thanks for making english my favourite subject. You were the nicest teacher and now I have my own alices adventures in wonderland that mum got me. I wont see you around because im going to beachview high now but that dosent have anything to do with you because you were really nice so thanks. I will miss you. From Tessa.*

I stared at the card for several moments then pushed away the stack of correction I had planned for the afternoon. Not bothering with an umbrella, I jogged across the schoolyard to the Year 8 coordinator's office. When I arrived I found Paul squinting at his laptop, the light from its screen making pearls of the water droplets on his face and beard.

'What's the deal with this?' I showed him the card. 'Has Tessa changed schools?'

He nodded, motioning for me to sit. 'Yeah. It all happened pretty quickly. Her parents pulled her out and now she's at Beachview.'

'Why? I thought you'd dealt with the bullying?'

'We had. Apparently Lonnie hasn't caused her any problems in a while. But I suppose the damage was already done.'

'Did you do restorative sessions with the girls?'

'Absolutely.' Paul kept squinting at his screen. I dimly noted that he had not yet turned to face me. 'We got Tessa together with Lonnie, then some of the other girls. Talked about what people had done, why they had done it, how everyone had been affected. It ran like clockwork. But Tessa's parents decided to take her out and that's that.'

I looked at the card again. To me, it was a token of my failure. I felt I had let Tessa down completely.

Then Paul made a sound in his throat, a kind of clucking choke, and when I looked up I realised with a shock that he was on the verge of tears. He had been in the job for decades and carried himself with the confidence of the hulking PE teacher he was. I had never seen a hint of vulnerability in him.

'Shit, Paul, are you okay?'

He took off his glasses and pushed the palms of his hands into his eyes. When he took them away there were no tears, but he cleared his throat thunderously.

'I'm fine, Brendan. Listen, I was drafting an email when you came in. To 8G's teachers. I suppose now is as good a time as any to let you know. Kelvin Lloyd's sick. Very sick.'

'What's wrong with him?'

Paul steadied himself for what seemed a long time. 'He's got stage four cancer, mate.'

Although it would not be the last, that was the first time in my career I had received such terrible news about a child. For a moment I could make no sense of it. The dark, clinical horror of Paul's words seemed completely at odds with the other realities of Kelvin's young life: The Spuds, riding BMX with Heath, helping other students with their work, humorously pronouncing words like 'headache' as *he-darchie* in class. It dropped on me all at once as a kind of cold, despairing exhaustion.

'We're going to tell the kids in small groups,' Paul said. 'The Wellbeing Team are leading the charge. Anyhow, some of the kids are already starting to find out. Not many, but a couple.'

On the wall was a printout of the school's footwear policy. It depicted various types of shoes, some marked with green ticks and others with red crosses. I stared at it hard. 'How? Didn't they get rid of it all when he was in primary school?'

'I'm not sure. Sometimes these things can come back even with good treatment.'

'And what are they doing about it?'

'I suppose they'll start treatment again.'

'And what's the prognosis?'

'I don't know, Brendan. Look, it's been a shit of a day. Why don't you just go home? Take it easy for the afternoon.'

I tucked Tessa's card under my coat, suddenly overcome by a desire to protect it from the weather. As I walked to my car a slack rain was falling through the now windless grey. I thought of the carnival grounds, not as they would be at that moment (skeletal Ferris wheel and knee-high thistles) but as they were in the summer, fibreglass-bright and shadowless in days so long they might have neither beginning nor end.

It occurred to me that Kelvin would not yet be tall enough to be permitted on some of the rides.

*

What is death to most children? Something that happens to old people, perhaps pets that have been in the family as long as they can remember. In that sense it is predictable – frightening but safe, like some terrible rollercoaster they know they are too young to ride.

That was how I saw it as a teenager. I had lost one grandpa years earlier, a man I had scarcely known. To me he was little more than a bright yellow ashtray and the half-remembered scent of tobacco. There was nothing about his sudden absence that challenged my naïve perceptions of the universe. I felt for my father (I still remember him the morning it happened, staring glassily but tearlessly into the brown linoleum of our kitchen floor), but it seemed part of the natural order of things.

My grandpa was old and he had passed away because that was what old people did.

Then, when I was in Year 9 at The School, a senior student died suddenly and tragically.

I didn't know him. We had never spoken. He wasn't friends with my older brother and I could not have related a thing about him, not what football team he followed, what subjects he was good at, who he was dating. I knew him only as a face, and even that face was ill-formed, shifting, something I had to concentrate hard to dredge up. Maybe he hadn't looked like that at all. He was just Some Kid, but, it occurred to me, now he wasn't even *that*. He wasn't an anything, just memories behind the eyes of the people who loved him.

I thought about him day and night. No; I could not think about him because I didn't know who he was. I thought about the concept of him and the towering, unavoidable reality of his cessation. I wanted to feel something other than selfish horror, but the only way I could achieve that was by imagining his parents as my own. *Then* the sadness came. Quickly, though, my mind would return to existential questions that left me feeling nauseous and baffled. Was he really *gone*? Could *all this* – sea and trees and sky and friends and light – just end as pointlessly as a glass bumped from a table? What scared me was that nobody knew, regardless of their claims. Death was beyond the grasp of any adult authority, and if that could not be explained then all the rest of life's explanations were probably just best guesses as well. Question marks bloomed like toadstools over everything. For the first time I felt uncertain, as though every person – my teachers, my parents, scientists, politicians, so-called experts – were really just children themselves, and there were no adults anywhere to provide final solutions to the way things are.

They installed a mural at The School, a large granite block with a plaque on the front. It was unveiled one afternoon while I was waiting for my bus. That day had been cloudless, still, the yard bathed in orange autumnal light. Perhaps twenty or thirty senior students gathered in silence, their shadows seeming somehow more real than the people who cast them. I watched from a distance, feeling once again a sense of incomprehensibility and immensity. It dwarfed me and all I could do was turn away from it.

I forgot, somehow. Teenagers have that capacity. That ghost child (whoever he *really* may have been) lingered for a while and then faded away, receding into the asphalt and brick and litter-strewn gardens. We kicked the footy, played video games and got on with the business of growing up. For a while that boy's memorial carried its awesome magic, but we saw it every recess and lunch and through that repetition it was disenchanted. Somewhere along the way it became just a rock from the local quarry with a rectangle of metal on the front that had some letters on it. We would sit on the benches nearby and chat as we waited for our buses, trying to sneak the names of the girls we liked into the conversation to feel that momentary euphoric rush.

One night that year I stayed over at a friend's place. There was nothing to do in Seadale then, so in the hours after midnight we snuck out and walked the streets. The place was still and dead and silent. We had no destination. After a while we grew bored and decided to head back home via the park.

When we got there we saw something bizarre. It seemed almost staged, though it couldn't possibly have been. A simple diamond-shaped kite – red, yellow, blue and green – had become entangled in the electricity wires, so that it had barely a metre of free movement. It was immediately alongside a streetlight and somehow it was flying. The kite flapped and rippled in the wind, weaving and straining, its colours garish against the blackness beyond. My friend and I watched it for some time, a bright thing shining through the dark mysteries of childhood.

6

The Chance

THE WORLD DID not stop for the news of Kelvin's illness. The next day bells tolled at their designated times and students queued for their classes. The Wellbeing Team would explain everything to 8G in small groups at the end of the final period. I wouldn't see them again until the following morning. By then, at least, they would have had time to process the news and speak with their parents.

Compared with Kelvin and many other students, my problems were trivial. I kept reminding myself of that, and concentrated on delivering the best teaching I could, regardless of how distracted I was by the events of the previous day. In particular, I needed to keep Year 12 Literature at the forefront of my attention. We were already a few weeks into Term Three, and final exams were looming.

That day we'd be studying Peter Carey's 'The Chance'. In the story, a sinister alien species known as the Fastalogians descends to Earth offering an alluring but terrifying technology: a machine that transforms people randomly into new bodies. Widespread social disintegration ensues, at which time a young woman decides to stand up against these extraterrestrial oppressors. Carey's themes of identity, self-image and rebellion always resonate with teenage readers.

Before class I printed and laminated dozens of faces – old and young, male and female, of every conceivable body type and ethnicity – and shuffled them in an old wooden box.

'Let's imagine that you have paid the Fastalogians for a Chance,' I explained, handing out the laminated cards face-down. 'You step into the machine. The aliens turn it on. There are flickering lights and buzzing sounds and maybe a weird sense of distortion. When you step out and look in a mirror you see . . .'

They turned the cards over and instantly the room filled with laughter and chatter.

'Oooh.' Mya grinned. 'I'm a hot guy.'

Somebody corrected her. 'A hot *white* guy.'

Tim held up his picture. It was a woman completely green with ink. Even her eyes had been tattooed. 'What are you doing to me, Doc?' He spun it around and looked more closely. 'I've got horn implants and sharpened teeth. A thousand intergalactic dollars down the drain.'

I let them talk and compare and even trade. They were, I knew, engaging with a key question not only of the story, but of adolescence: Who really *are* we? Who do we *want* to be? And how much control do we have over this? Are manipulative forces shaping us to suit their own agendas?

'In the story the identities are random.' I took a card from the box myself and held it up. It was the green-eyed Afghan girl, Sharbat Gula, immortalised on the June 1985 cover of *National Geographic*. 'But you might like to look at the card you *have* been assigned and wonder: Would my life be better – perhaps *easier* – if I was this person instead?'

'You wouldn't want to change to that girl, Murray.' It was Claire. Whenever she engaged in class I felt a cool breeze of relief. It meant that, for the time being at least, she was feeling alright. 'You've already got the identity that gets the best deal. Middle-aged white guy.'

'I'm deeply offended. How dare you suggest I'm anywhere near middle age?'

Mya screwed up her nose. 'I got a middle-aged white man, but I wouldn't change to this crusty weirdo. He can have his privilege.'

'Actually,' I said, 'that's a photograph of my dad.'

She clapped a hand to her mouth. '*Really?*'

'No.'

'Well, I'd change.' Claire had a woman from a perfume advertisement. 'Don't even need to think about it.'

The class craned their necks to see. 'Would you?' somebody asked.

'One hundred per cent. One hundred and *ten* per cent. Look at her. She's a babe.'

'You're a babe,' Mya said, but Claire just rolled her eyes.

For the first time in a long while I thought of Teagan and the other Year 9 girls with their make-up. I thought, too, of Wambui. Once, she shared her fear that some girls hung out with her only because they wanted a 'sassy black friend'; she admitted to me that she played that role for a time, before realising that she was far more nuanced. Then there was Charlie, fighting his opponents, his past, himself, but – perhaps more than any of these things – the shadow of the father he felt darkening the spaces he had marked for his own independence.

After class Claire hung back. She sat on the edge of a desk, swinging her legs back and forwards as she flicked through 'The Chance', chatting about the characters.

'So,' I said, 'what would you do if those spaceships came down in real life?'

'Bloody Fastalogians. Can't trust 'em. Manipulators.'

'So you wouldn't be saving up for a Chance?'

She straightened and folded her arms. 'Now I never said that, Murray. I wouldn't *save up*. I'd rob a bank to be at the front of the queue.'

I searched her face for humour but found none. 'Why?'

'I'd be happy to be a random other *anyone* at this point.'

I closed my eyes, sat on the table opposite hers. 'Don't say that. Anybody who took a Chance and came out as Claire could count themselves lucky.'

'Thanks. Look, I'm just being melodramatic. It's this year. I want it to be over.'

I saw so much of my younger self in Claire that at times I wanted to tell her but held back. Instead, I strived to give her the advice that might have set me on a better course had I received it at her age. 'Think of Year 12 as being like the Fastalogians.'

She rolled her eyes again, but at least she was smiling. 'How so?'

'Year 12 has tricked everyone into thinking it's something it's not. That if you jump through certain hoops, you'll be the dreamed-of version of yourself at the end. Year 12 will be over before you know it and you'll realise it didn't matter that much.'

'Year 12 is the Fastalogians?'

'Sort of.'

'So I should drop out and rebel? Go to war against the government?'

'That's not what I said.'

'But your metaphor –'

'I have not, in fact, thought this through.'

She laughed then – genuinely, I thought.

'School feels like the whole world when you're in it,' I said. 'Middle-aged or not, it wasn't that long ago I was here. I did Literature right in this room. Sad, right? Never escaped.'

'But you're happy. Everyone can see that.'

'Look. This year will end, the summer will come and you'll be writing poetry on the beach. Or wherever. Like you said to me, you'll be able to forget about all The School's "pathways". Just *be* for a while.'

'Feels a long way off.'

'Maybe, but it isn't.'

*

That afternoon, I had agreed to help supervise a Year 9 group being taken to one of the ocean beaches a few kilometres from Seadale. The weather held – barely – and we packed into a minibus at lunchtime and headed out. Ana was along for the ride. Meg the Geography teacher would do the real work while we made up the staff–student ratio.

When we arrived the wind was roaring. Distant surfers cut incisions through the breakers, moving in and out from gloom to blue-green incandescence. We hurried from the carpark to the protective wall of the sandstone cliffs where the wind fell so silent it was almost eerie. Meg briefed the kids then they all headed off along the cliffs with their notebooks. Ana and I strolled at the rear.

For the most part we talked about Kelvin. There wasn't much to say. It was unfair and horrible and we felt for him and his family. He had a younger brother who Ana thought was in about Grade 4.

'I remember when Aaron was a baby,' she said. 'Not knowing if he was going to die or not. Just waiting. It was awful.'

Ana's little brother, I had always thought, was one of the reasons she was the most empathetic teacher I knew. She had been fifteen when Aaron was born. He had a major heart defect, but it was more than just that; he had been a 'floppy baby', motionlessly tracking the room with his eyes. Doctors quickly detected a major chromosomal abnormality. The day he was born an aunty arrived from Serbia, and Ana sat up with her well into that night, knowing already that something was horribly wrong.

But Aaron survived, and following open-heart surgery at age one he began getting stronger. As he grew, though, the extent of his disability became clear.

When I first met Aaron (then well into his teens) Ana explained that he learnt about one thing every five years or so. He could not speak or understand speech. His most complex social interaction involved dragging people where he wanted them, usually to his television, which played cartoons all day long. He wore a nappy and was prone to fits of screaming and bashing his head against things when he became frustrated. Ana's mother had dedicated herself to caring for him, with support from her two daughters. And they made Aaron's life a joyous one. Ana would take her little brother's hands in hers and kiss them, watching him smile; at such moments he would nuzzle against her, guiding the smooth contours of her chin over his eyelids. And though he could not read – will not ever be able to – the English teacher in Ana used the magic of picture books to enchant her brother. Often he would fall asleep with them clutched to his chest.

'I just keep thinking stupid stuff,' I said to Ana as we stepped over some rock pools and around the bend in a cliff. 'Like, why are there healthy criminals in prison and a kid like Kelvin gets stage four lymphoma?'

'You should sign up for my Philosophy class.'

'Don't you think things like that about Aaron?'

'Of course I do. I think all the time about the things he misses out on. The things other boys his age get to do but he never will. It isn't fair. Life isn't always fair.'

Narrow caves receded into the sandstone cliff beside us, some upward-slanting and glinting with puddles that might have been deposited by the highest of Neolithic tides. Someday, perhaps, the sea would return for them. Two girls peered into one such cave, gingerly using the light from a mobile phone to penetrate the darkness. Neither was Teagan, but both wore as much make-up as her, and more.

'Childhood's so short,' she said, 'yet when you're a kid you just want it to be over.'

Nearby, a group of students was gathered at a rock pool, some standing about, others skylarking. One, I saw, was Connor. His red hair had grown long, almost to his shoulders, and he kept doing handstands while another boy caught his ankles. Ana and I walked over. Despite everything, I was overcome by a momentary peace. The sun had come out and these children were happy. The more studious ones peered into the rock pools, crouching, taking notes. They were silent. The beauty had humbled them. The water in those pools was so clear that to describe it as glass would be inaccurate; it was light. You could not see it, only its effects on other things, its illuminations and distortions.

Driving back on the bus I had an idea. It was not brilliant but it took hold of me. I knew it had come out of my conversation with Ana, as well as teaching 'The Chance'. As soon as we got back to school and the bell went I searched out Teagan.

'I've got a deal for you,' I said to her as she loaded her things into her locker. 'A bribe, actually.'

She had a look of smiling puzzlement. 'Yeah? What, sir?'

'If you and Jada come to school with no make-up – zero – you can have the rest of the week in free periods to watch a movie. You guys won't have to be students. You can just chill out and be kids.'

'I *can't* come to school without make-up, Mr Murray.'

'Yes you can. And anyway, it would be both of you.'

She looked dubious but promised to give it some thought.

7

Cards

8G WALKED INTO the classroom the next morning heavy-lidded, trailing ghosts. Tessa lingered around *Alice's Adventures in Wonderland*, the book's gilded spine visible from the shelf but its pages pressed in darkness. Her absence we could handle; there was some sadness, but we knew she was at Beachview High and would make new friends. The problem was the empty chair beside Heath.

When a traumatic event occurs in a school community, the expert advice dictates that the children need normality. This is certainly true. If boundaries and expectations are removed, it can feel to the students as if that incident – whatever it may be – has jarred their entire world out of kilter. Still, talking is important, and it is disingenuous to carry on as though nothing has happened.

That morning, I felt a strange, unique kind of pain as I skipped Kelvin's name on the roll. When I had finished I stayed quiet and waited.

Even a well-behaved class is never silent. There are rustlings, shufflings, drum-beating fingers. That morning there wasn't a sound.

'Alright, 8G.' I sat on the edge of my desk, hoping that most of the class had spoken with their parents the night before. 'We all know Kelvin's pretty sick and is in the hospital at the moment. Some of you are really close with him – Heath, Jimmy – but others might just know Kelvin from class. Either way, we can all agree he's one of the nicest kids you'll meet.'

There were earnest nods all around the room.

'The obvious thing,' I said, 'would be to make him a card. We could all write messages wishing him a speedy recovery.'

A sense of dishonesty struck me then, of cowardice. It reminded me of the time I had refused to explain the orange R to a class. Were there speedy recoveries from stage four cancer? Were there *any* recoveries?

'We could *each* make him a card,' Heath suggested.

'Sure. There's plenty of materials in the cupboard.'

The students set to work, not a soul complaining. Kelvin's closest friends gave out advice on what they should include – namely, anything to do with basketball. I still remember one girl whose card was almost entirely dominated by a hilarious sketch of a basketballer with an exaggerated monobrow. The caricature's uniform was emblazoned with a number five – Kelvin's number.

At one point a boy called me over. It was Jimmy, one of Kelvin's Spuds teammates. 'I reckon you should send the cards one at a time,' he said. 'So he can open, like, one a day. That'll brighten up his month.'

'I think that's an awesome idea, mate.'

In the end the kids spent several periods on their cards, designing, colouring, ruling faint pencil lines that could be erased after serving as tightropes for their messages of hope.

I bought the envelopes and stamps then stacked all the

cards on my kitchen bench. It was a rare moment when I was thankful for the overcrowded nature of government class-rooms. Recognising the need to care for myself as well as my students, I took to getting up half an hour early each morning and walking along the beach. It helped. Anybody who lives near the coast knows how beautiful it can be in winter, how much is missed by those who visit only in the hotter months. Often the mornings were bright and windy, olive waves spilling with light as they fell, scattering shells, and then smoothing my footprints in retreat. Another wave, two, and there would be no trace that I had passed that way at all. The beach would retain no memory of my presence and there was a calming humility in the knowledge.

When I drew level with a toilet block I would head inland, cross a road and slot that day's card into the lonely postbox.

*

So far, Teagan and Jada had not accepted my anti-make-up bribe. I raised it with them every lesson and could see that they were tempted. A few free periods of watching a film is a serious motivator for most Year 9 students.

'How good will it be?' I would ask, affecting my best sales-person voice. 'Think of it: You get to sleep in. Skip that whole part of your morning routine. *Then* you get to chill out in English and watch whatever you want. What movie would you pick?'

'Hmmm.' Teagan scratched at the foundation on her neck. 'Not sure. Jada and I would have to agree.'

'Fair enough. And who knows – maybe you'll decide that the sleep-in was so great that you don't care about the make-up at all anymore.'

'But people might be mean to us.'

'Good. Then you'll find out who your real friends are.'

I don't know if my approach was the right one. What I do know is that neither Teagan nor Jada *wanted* to wear that make-up – they had told me so – and I certainly wasn't going to send them to the coordinator to have it scrubbed off their faces.

The next task for that class was a standard one in Year 9 English: a persuasive oral presentation on an issue of the student's choice. Often, the toughest part is helping them decide on a topic. Every teacher knows that the question of 'What are you interested in?' is all too often followed by: 'Nothing.'

We watched YouTube clips and looked at newspapers and soon there was everything from abortion laws to whether or not the AFL grand final should be held at night. One student who did not yet have an idea was Connor.

He had changed since the beginning of Year 9. He was still the joker who sometimes overstepped the mark, but the childishness of February was fading. His face had narrowed and he slouched with a long-legged nonchalance. Where previously his red hair was almost clownish, now it hung limp.

'No ideas yet?'

He stretched himself out, yawned. 'Not yet, sir.'

'What are you interested in?'

'Not really much.'

'Wow. Didn't think you were so boring.'

He wasn't too cool to grin. 'Come on, sir. You're hurting my feelings.'

'You're hurting *my* feelings.' I snapped his laptop shut and dropped a stack of newspapers in front of him. 'Have a think. Be interesting.'

I circled the room for a while, keeping everybody on track. When Kelvin, Tessa, Charlie or any of the others drifted into my consciousness I pushed them away, trying my best to be in the present for the students in the room. After the bell went I returned to Connor and saw that he'd written half a page of notes.

'This is what I like to see. What's your topic?'

He shut his book, flicking the cover as he stood to leave. 'Why we should stop boat people from coming to Australia.'

One of my weaknesses as an educator is allowing my own political views to infiltrate my teaching. I almost slumped, almost told Connor that I had thought he was kinder than that, more empathetic. I managed to keep quiet and reminded myself that I was there to facilitate, not indoctrinate.

'Fine. Go away, do some research and try to convince me.'

As I watched him leave I wished that he could meet somebody like Wambui.

8

Mercy

WAMBUI WATCHED AS her father's wounds healed. He came home with a skullcap of bandages, but these were soon peeled away to reveal a shaved scalp and the black barbs of stitches. Before long they too had vanished. Eventually even the hair grew back, rising like wilderness obscuring the remnants of some forgotten battle.

But Wambui would not forget. She felt it even in the smiling bustle of Kaandiki. Watching a man pass in the afternoon heat, she couldn't help but study the swing of his arms, the slouch of his shoulders, and wonder if he was one of them. She would imagine him masked, try to catch a hint of his voice, replay the taunts she had heard that night: *You're pretenders*. At such moments there was no fear, only a dull anger that would colour the rest of her day. Her father was no pretender. He worked hard, as hard as anybody in the village, and she knew his attackers were motivated by jealousy rather than robbery. What were they doing while he spent hours cooking pastries in hot kitchens to provide for his family? Drinking, probably. Drinking and being layabouts.

The anger would darken further when she thought of

her grandmother. Cucu had been hurt that night as badly as anybody, not by the black eye but by seeing what had happened to her son. Wambui knew that mothers felt pain like nobody else.

Ironically, it was a second break-in a few months later that helped her release some of these troubling new feelings. That morning when Wambui's mother rose early to make tea, she discovered the gas cylinder missing. Moving into the lounge room she saw that the television was also gone, along with their DVD player and a radio. While the family slept, some-body had cut the bars off a window then unlocked the front door for their accomplices. The slaughtering of chickens over-night in a nearby shed had helped conceal the noise.

Wambui stood with her mother in the lounge, both with their arms folded. These were not the same men as last time, she realised. They did not want to hurt anyone and were moti-vated only by desperation.

'Look, Mum. They even took our cushions.'

There was silence for a moment, then Wambui started to giggle. Her mother joined her, and soon they were laughing openly as they sat on their cushionless chairs.

Jacob listened but did not smile, looking first at the bare spots in the lounge room and then at the sawed bars of the rear window. He studied it all with cold, hard eyes and in his stare there was an element of patience.

*

With the break-ins increasing, the men of Kaandiki ramped up their community response. Despite the trauma of his own attack (or perhaps because of it), Jacob was happy to help. He knew that the police could not be relied upon and were often drunk when you telephoned them. Plus, he was deeply worried about his own family, particularly his daughters. Eventually it was decided that waiting for screams or house alarms was not good enough. Volunteers would patrol Kaandiki every night between midnight and two. Mobile phone numbers were shared and locals knew not to bother with the police.

Wambui watched this unfold with nervous interest. Most members of the night patrol were middle-aged family men like Jacob, but a few were boys in their early twenties who she knew from the local area. They were farmers and mechanics and students, good-hearted and willing, but naïve. They were not like the men who broke into homes in the night with pangas.

'Hey, Ashura!' Wambui might call to one of them as he passed by the house. 'You going out with Dad tonight?'

'Yeah. Tell him to bring some pastries.'

'Look after him for me!'

'I think he'll be looking after me.'

The best nights were when her father wasn't on patrol. Then sleep came easy, for she knew not only that he was safe but that *somebody* was awake and watchful. It was a cosy feeling. One phone call and men would come, soon to be followed by half the village. They were organised and they were ready. What Wambui had not considered was what would happen when they eventually caught somebody. It did not take long for her to find out.

*

Jacob's alarm sounded a little before midnight. Not wanting to disturb the girls, he turned it off quickly, tripping in the darkness as he put on his trousers, shirt and a heavy jacket. His attempts at silence were no use. His wife sat up in the dark.

'Jacob, get back into bed.'

'I can't.'

'You *can*. I don't want you out there.'

'What about the others? They need me. And what if everyone stayed home?'

'I need you here with me and the girls.'

'I'm sorry. You know I love you. But I have no choice.'

Before leaving he collected his torch and a club.

Outside it was utterly silent. He walked the short distance to the meeting place where already a half-dozen others were milling about. Soon they had broken into groups and spread across the village. Their strategy was simple but effective: they stuck to the shadows, speaking only in whispers and listening for the barking of dogs. Each had a mobile phone that other villagers could use to call for help.

The whole time Jacob thought of his family, and particularly his daughters. The scars on his arms and head did not frighten him, but acted as reminders that he must protect the people he most cared about.

'Hey, Jacob!' It was one of the younger men. For them, the night patrols had a sense of adventure and excitement. Few had the nagging worry of a wife or children at home.

'Keep your voice down. What is it?'

'Over there, by those trees – did you hear something?'

And they would go, and investigate, but so far there had been nothing.

That night there was nobody about and nor was there a breath of wind. As they crisscrossed the village they found dirt still hanging in the air that their own shoes had kicked up half an hour earlier. There wasn't a light on anywhere and cows slept on their feet by the roadside. Eventually they leaned against a barbed-wire fence for a break, watching the constellations pivot across the sky.

Then a vibration came from within Jacob's jacket.

He took out the phone and peered at the dull green glow. The text message was from Ndwiga, a local boy much younger than Wambui but with a reputation for precocious intelligence:

Someone breaking into our house im hiding quick need hlp

The events of the following minute were a chaotic shadow play few could piece together afterwards. Jacob and his partner were only around the corner, and as they ran they phoned other members of the night patrol. Torches hacked at the darkness. As Jacob sprinted he saw more men in his periphery.

'Be careful,' he panted to the others now alongside him. 'Don't run straight into a panga.'

There was shouting, running, gesticulating. For a moment it was unclear who was who but then a lean figure streaked through the darkness trying to escape. Ndwiga came out pointing. Dogs started to bark. Porch lights flicked on. Kaandiki was suddenly as awake as if it were the middle of the afternoon.

The night patrol gave chase. The thief was fast but one of the younger villagers had the sprint of an athlete. Those two men – pursuer and pursued – raced through the night. The thief kept looking over his shoulder and when he realised he was not going to win this race he dashed down the narrow gap between a house and a fence and disappeared into a backyard.

The rest of the night patrol caught up. They moved into that darkness with torches held aloft. There was silence. At the back of the yard were tightly packed banana trees, and as the torch beams slid over them they cast shadows like elongated bones. He was somewhere close by but they all knew he could produce a panga or knife. At any moment he could decide that his only chance of escape was a violent offensive.

'If you're in there, you better come out! Don't make us come in for you!'

More men squeezed down that narrow gap into the backyard. The owners of the home turned on the rear light to help with the search. Then somebody saw him amongst those trees, crouching and cowering and totally unarmed. Three of the men dragged him out and frogmarched him to the crowd on the street.

Jacob, breathless, studied the man now pinned by torchlight. He was in his twenties, sweat-streaked and panting, his bare feet cracked and caked in dust. One of the local men approached him.

'Where's the rest of your gang? Why are you alone?'

In his terror the young thief spoke quickly, honestly. 'We were going to go together but they were too tired.' His eyes were enormous, the whites laced with veins. 'So I came by myself.'

'Why would you do this to us? You've made it so we're too scared to sleep!'

'I was only doing it for my children. I've never hurt anyone.'

The mob circled him. Text messages were still going out and the people of Kaandiki were rising from their beds. There was no thought of calling the police.

'Let's take him to the centre,' somebody said. The place he meant was almost directly outside Wambui's gate.

So they took him.

*

When Wambui woke there was light coming from beneath her door and noise on the street. If there had been music it would have sounded like a festival. She could hear talking, shouting, even laughing. It was nowhere near dawn and when she rolled over the maid's bed was empty, the covers thrown back. Wambui passed through the empty lounge room and into the front yard, joining her mother, who stood looking out into the night.

'Mum, what's happening?'

Then she saw them. There were dozens and dozens of people just outside their gate – as many as seventy, she thought. Her father was there, and a number of other men from the village who she recognised. Most were on their phones, sending texts, making calls, waking anybody in danger of missing whatever spectacle was to follow.

'They've caught one of the bad men,' her mother said. 'The night patrol. Ndwiga was hiding in his house and they rescued him.'

Wambui walked to the gate, peering between the shoulders of the men now leaning on it. The crowd, she saw, had left a few metres of space around a man they had completely encircled. He wore a T-shirt and slacks and already his nose was bloodied. She thought immediately that this was not one of the men who had attacked her father. *This* man – slim and young with fine features and rounded shoulders – seemed more like somebody who would creep into a house silently, if he could. He looked like somebody who would steal cushions.

When her mother joined her, Wambui asked what they were going to do to the man.

'I don't know,' she said.

Just then one of the younger members of the night patrol emerged from the crowd and walked towards the thief. In his hand was something Wambui couldn't quite see – a cord or a whip or a rod. He looked reluctant, but when older voices from the crowd began encouraging him he took another step forward, raised his weapon and brought it down with a sharp crack across the bare skin of the thief's arm.

'Who's in your gang?' The villager raised the weapon again, seemingly as a threat at first but then bringing it down two or three times anyway. 'The ones who break into our homes. Give us all their names.'

Wambui watched, transfixed, as the man listed names one after the other. Somebody produced a pen and pad and wrote them down. When he had finished they started whipping him again, over and over, first on his hands, raised in defence, then across his back as he balled himself up in the dirt.

'Why are they still hitting him?' Wambui turned to her mother. Behind her she could hear that sound, relentless: that rod or cord or whip would cut through the air, a strange sharp zipping sound, then immediately afterwards came the stinging *whap* she almost felt. 'He gave up the names.'

When she turned back to the crowd the man was still on the ground, shirt bloodied, fingers laced over the back of his head. There was a momentary lull, then somebody shouted some-thing from the crowd and one of the boys stepped forward and launched a thudding kick into the thief's exposed back. The sound was far louder than Wambui had expected and it had a hollow echo to it. The crowd cheered. She turned away and heard that thud again and then again and then again.

'The crowd's egging them on!' She went to her mother and took her by the hand, knowing that neither of them could do a thing about what was happening. The sound changed then to a kind of cracking slap that proved to be boots going into his face.

The thief was now moaning, now crying. He spluttered blood and rolled onto his side, raising his hands in surrender.

'Get up and walk! You can walk! So get up!'

Wambui was watching again and it was like a horror film from which she could not turn away. The man made no attempt to move so they began bellowing at him.

'*Get up! Get up on your feet!*' They wrenched him up by his torn shirt but he just splayed panting back to the ground. The boys went on bellowing for him to rise, kicking at his face, back, stomach, anywhere exposed from behind the pale flapping palms.

Eventually the thief tried. Face clenched, he rolled to his knees and began to rise. His head hung forward, chin to chest like a lead weight. All his muscles were in a spasming tremble. He was crying and before he had got even halfway one of the men reached down and began punching him until he slumped down into the dust once more.

The crowd cheered and they resumed the attack. Others joined in. There was stomping, scratching, even open-handed slaps to his blood-streaked scalp.

'Why are they doing this to him?' Wambui looked from one adult face to another. Some glanced at her briefly but most just watched as the beating continued. 'He doesn't *deserve* this!'

It continued. A small number of the most violent young men led the charge. They slapped away the thief's raised hands so they could pummel him, stood back to catch their breath, then resumed once more. One started stomping him, knees knifing almost to his chest.

'*Please! I have children!*'

When Wambui heard that voice floating through the din she thought it was the most horrible thing she had heard in her life.

'Get up! We know you can walk!'

'*I can't get up.*' His words were blood-wet and strained and distorted. '*Please. I have children.*'

At last Wambui raised her voice. 'He's talking about his *family*!' When still nobody paid any attention to her she shouted: 'He's got *kids*! What about *them*?'

In a kind of panic she moved along the fenceline, looking for the faces of adults she knew, who knew *her*. There were plenty, and she could not understand their cruelty, could not reconcile it with the kindness they had shown her as far back as her memory would stretch. They were ordinary people. They weren't murderers or even vengeful. And yet now they would not listen to her. She understood dimly that this man was no longer a man to them but something else, a symbol, the embodiment of their collective months of fear and trauma.

'*Stop!*' Even as she pleaded they kept beating the thief. He was covered in blood and almost unrecognisable now but, worst of all, still pleading and striving vainly to defend himself. '*He doesn't deserve this!*'

Nobody would listen to her, and amongst the adults there wasn't a single dissenting voice.

'We need a tyre,' somebody in the crowd said, breathless.

'We have an old tyre in our yard. What do you want to do?'

'Put it over his head so he can't move his arms and we'll burn him.'

'*I have children.*'

Wambui searched for her mother in the darkness but could not find her. She could have been with her younger sister, she supposed, taking her inside perhaps. Wambui pleaded with anyone who she even vaguely recognised, insisting that they had done enough, that this man deserved mercy, that he was a human being with children and that if they killed him then in some ways they were killing his children, too.

The kicking and slapping and whipping continued. She thought almost every bone in his body must be broken by then. How long ago had she been awoken by this festival? It was a long time, she knew. More than an hour. And they had probably started the moment he was captured.

For the next ten minutes Wambui pleaded for that man's life. Nobody listened to her. Then one of the young men emerged from the darkness rolling an old tyre. It made a hollow rubbery echo as it bounced on the hard earth and it kept wobbling out of control as he approached.

She tried again and again. 'Please!' Nobody listened. 'Let him live.'

Then Wambui's mother embraced her from behind and steered her back towards the house.

'No more. You must go to bed.'

And she did, hands pressed to her ears, waiting for the smell of that burning man to invite itself into her bedroom.

*

They did not burn him but they did kill him. By the morning he had been beaten to death and the only evidence left was trampled soil and pools of blood outside the gate.

The people of Kaandiki had been frightened and exhausted. They had seen their friends beaten, robbed and even killed.

They did not have a police force to rely on and in the righteous frenzy of that night they had acted. Only Wambui – a girl with more reason to feel vengeful than most of that crowd – argued for compassion. When I read her essay about values (ending with that simple question, *Where had the humanity gone?*), I wondered who *I* might have been in that crowd. We all want to believe that we would be Wambui, but know in the deepest recesses of our selves that most of us would be silent at best, holding the whip at worst. Wambui had not only empathy but the courage to speak it, even if her child's voice was ignored, just as the voices of children are so often ignored in our own culture.

Wambui carried that man with her. She carried him when she walked to the market stalls through the red dust, when she sat attentively in her classes, when she went with her grand-father to check on the calves; she carried him sometimes at night when she could not sleep, and sometimes when she could and met him again in dreams; she carried him onto a plane that flew her to a strange new country where girls, perhaps well-meaning, formed rings around her and asked that she say things in her native language. She carries him still, nearing the end of a law degree and giving up hours of her time as a volunteer. She carries him as she continues to live as the type of person most of us want to be but never will.

9

Rule breakers

'WHAT YOU'RE SAYING makes no sense,' Claire said, sitting with her feet up on the couch as she studied the results of her most recent essay. 'You're contradicting yourself.'

Her anger was a relief. I had expected despondency. 'Yes and no.'

'Exactly. Is it yes or is it no?'

'It's no – I'm *not* contradicting myself. But yes, I can see why you'd be confused by what I'm saying.'

'God, Murray. You're driving me nuts.'

'Sorry.'

One of the great challenges of teaching is giving feedback to students – particularly vulnerable students – without discouraging or even crushing them. It's a delicate balance between honesty and sensitivity.

'But I thought you *liked* my essay.'

'I loved it.' It was the truth. 'You were fluent, engaging, thought-provoking. You made me think about Carey's writing in ways I haven't before. You showed a knowledge of the text that was amazing and picked up details I've overlooked, and I've read these stories a thousand times.'

'But then why did I get a *low*?'

It was the first such result Claire had received that year, perhaps ever, and it seemed to have shaken what she saw as the very foundations of her identity. 'Because you weren't fulfilling the requirements of the task. This was supposed to be *passage analysis*. You wrote amazing stuff, but you hardly used the designated passages at all. You just went your own way.'

She fell back into the couch, exasperated. 'So it's possible to write beautifully and get a dud result?'

'Yeah. You need to fit into their boxes. If you produce something like this on the exam – no matter how wonderful it is – they'll give you a low.'

She unzipped her schoolbag and jammed her essay into it, scrunching the paper as she did so. 'See, this is what I don't understand. We study writers like Peter Carey and Virginia Woolf and get told how amazing they are because they broke from what had come before. Modernist. Postmodernism. Whatever. Then *we* get told,' her voice took on a witch-like condescending lilt, 'No, you can't do it like that, you need to follow *our* rules and do everything this way and that way or we'll give you a big cross and you won't get the ATAR you need to go to university.' She paused, thought. 'You won't be able to follow your chosen *pathway*.'

I opened my desk drawer and took out a poem she had given me weeks earlier. It was about a bone-white city emerging from some glittering ocean. 'You're a free thinker, Claire. I see it in everything you write. It will be a real strength in the future.'

'But not on the exam?'

I sighed. 'You need original ideas but you still need to do what they want you to do. There's got to be boundaries on formal assessment, otherwise everyone could just read Carey's stories, stroll into the exam and write whatever they pleased.'

'Would that be a bad thing?'

'For you – for *us* – no. But for the examiners and the system, yes.'

'Right.' The bell went and she stood. 'So we're all just prisoners of The Company. Or actually of *ourselves*, because The Company is keeping us in a pavilion and pavilions don't have walls.'

'Claire –'

'You know the worst bit? So much of what I write I hate. Then I finally feel good about something and it doesn't cut it because I haven't done what the government wants.'

Walking to my Year 9 class I knew that she was right in all the ways that mattered. Her creativity was arcing like electricity from downed wires, and all my advice to her was about getting it insulated, channelled and controlled. And in many ways it was for my own good. Of course I wanted her to succeed (in accordance with bureaucratic metrics), but I knew that *I* was being measured by the system just as much as she was. The moment the final Literature results came in, my pigeonhole would be stuffed with data: graphs comparing my students with the rest of the state; graphs comparing my students' results with their *predicted* results derived from barely relevant 'general achievement tests'; charts telling me if I had marked my students too kindly or too harshly; charts assessing the accuracy of my 'indicative grades' (scores teachers provide shortly before final exams); summaries of whether or not I had got the students' ranking right. At such moments I couldn't help but wonder how many Virginia Woolfs and Peter Careys had been steered from creative freedom onto more conventional tracks by teachers like me cowed by the awesome power of educational bureaucracies.

And then, as is so often the case in teaching, I had to wrench my attention from one plane to another.

'Okay guys, persuasive presentation research.' The Year 9s' laptops swung open, a barrage of surf stickers and taped-on timetables. 'Remember the CRAAP test – currency, relevance, authority, accuracy and purpose. Don't be one of these bone-heads who believe the first thing they read.'

Computers can be a pacifier, and the class fell into a keyboard-clattering hush. Besides, it was getting on towards Term Four and the Year 9s were turning into Year 10s. They were becoming less silly, more focused, the disengaged students transitioning from clownish to apathetic. Connor sat in a corner on the room's only desktop computer (his laptop had broken months earlier), studying pictures of boats crowded with asylum seekers.

I walked over. Nearby hung a poster declaring ONLY BABIES SCRIBBLE ON WALLS; somebody had drawn an enormous penis on it. When I tore the poster down Connor turned.

'Oh. Hey, sir.'

'How's your research going, Connor?'

He angled his book towards me. It did seem to be filled with notes. 'Smashing it. Focusing on the crime angle at the moment.'

'What do you mean?'

'You know. Boat people coming to this country and committing crimes.'

'Boat people? What are we talking about here? Illegal immigrants?'

'Yeah.'

'Pretty sure most illegal immigrants in Australia come by plane. They're usually backpackers on holidays who've over-stayed their visas.'

He bent over his book, wrote something down. 'Thanks, sir. I'll google it.'

I looked around the room, from Teagan with her stencilled brows to the rest of my Year 9 class. This group, I knew, was the centre of Connor's narrow world. There wasn't a non-white face amongst them. 'Thorough research, mate. Remember, it's your job to persuade me.'

'Don't you worry, sir.' He gave me a thumbs up and then tapped his notes. 'I will.'

He did not. However, what he did do was even more extraordinary.

10

Glimpses of sky

THE VIEW FROM Kelvin's window offered little – no trees, no ocean, no passing people (though he could sometimes hear them in the courtyard below). There were a few geometric slices of sky, but at this time of year they were as grey as the hospital itself. Opposite he could see the concrete and brick facade of another wing, its rows of small dark windows perhaps hiding children like him in various states of treatment, recovery and decline. For Kelvin that process was yet to begin and he sat on the bed fully clothed, waiting to discover what it would be like.

'I know it's not much to look at.' Jane was one of the social workers. She was young with wide-spaced eyes that squinted almost to closing when she smiled, as now. 'But there's always the telly.'

It was a small room with a narrow bed in the centre. On one side there was space for the doctors and nurses and on the other a hard couch that looked as though it had been carried up from the foyer. An adjoining bathroom with an outward-opening door contained a sink and shower. He supposed the door opened that way so they would be able to get to him if he collapsed inside.

'It's fine, Jane. Not too bad at all. Thanks.'

'Well, you are polite.' She came around the bed and opened the curtains a little wider. 'But it's no good you lying in here all day. Up you hop. Let's go meet Steve.'

Ever since those first terrible minutes in the waiting room, Kelvin had been unable to shake a feeling of disconnection from the other patients in the ward. To him, they all seemed like little kids. Most looked to be primary aged and some were far younger. This combined with the decorations in the corridors to create a strange, sickly sweet atmosphere of juvenility from which he felt totally separate. Recognising this, Jane had decided to introduce him to one of the oldest patients.

She led Kelvin down the corridor and into a lift. As they went, they passed children in wheelchairs and gowns and some striding fully clothed with the wind at their backs. Some smiled, browless and lashless, from beneath signed beanies.

'Steve is the veteran of the ward,' Jane said as the lift chimed and let them out. 'He's just lovely. I think you two will really get along.'

Kelvin's stomach cramped slightly as they came to the room, but the moment they entered his nerves vanished.

'Hey, Kelvin.' Steve stood from his bed and extended a hand. He was tall, broad-shouldered and fit-looking with a shaved head. Kelvin thought he was probably around eighteen. 'Welcome to the ward.'

Jane played chaperone until it was clear the boys were getting on fine without her.

'Are you into cricket?' Steve asked, gesticulating with his thumb at the stacks of cricketing magazines beside his bed. 'I'm a bit of a tragic.'

'Yeah, cricket's cool. But basketball is really my thing.'

'Sweet. I don't mind a bit of basketball myself.'

It occurred to Kelvin as they chatted that, to Steve, he must have appeared like the little kids from whom Kelvin felt so removed. The realisation came with a rush of gratitude.

'My treatment has been going on for years.' Steve moved from the bed to the couch and motioned for Kelvin to sit. Out the window, he noticed, was a bleak vista almost identical to his own. 'But I'm doing okay at the moment, so I can get out and have a hit of cricket every now and again. Get down to the nets with Dad.'

'That's awesome. I've only just arrived, so I guess I haven't . . .' Kelvin struggled for the word. '*Acclimatised* yet.'

Steve smiled. 'Jane said you were pretty bright. I'm actually hoping to go to university when I eventually get out of here.'

They talked some more. Eventually Steve asked him if he had started treatment yet.

'No. I think it will be soon though. What will it be like?'

'It's going to suck a bit,' Steve said. 'You having chemo?'

'Yeah.'

'The first round is usually the strongest. But it's over before you know it. The nurses are cool. And everyone around here knows what you're going through.'

In the coming days it became clear that Steve – calm, soft-spoken – was not talking with Kelvin purely out of a sense of obligation to Jane. For hours at a time he would come to Kelvin's room or Kelvin would go to his, and they mostly talked about sport. It was an escape. The more they reminisced and debated and discussed, the more those brick and concrete facades dissolved, giving way to roaring green fields and tiered stadiums.

'When Donald Bradman was a kid, he used to practise with a stump and a golf ball,' Steve said. 'He'd hit it back and forwards against a corrugated iron water tank. *That's* the way to learn. Then later on they give you a big flat bat and a ball the size of an apple and you can't fail.'

The comfort Steve offered extended beyond Kelvin himself. Soon, the boys' parents had met, and their mothers began sharing their pain and their hope. When they weren't doing that, they would simply sit on the ward, looking out at all that concrete and brick and wondering if their children would ever escape it.

*

Kelvin's first round of chemotherapy was more frightening than he had anticipated.

He slept fitfully the night before, waking early and watching television for a while but then staring out through the steely overcast to the ward opposite. A dove moved about on one of the sills, occasionally sweeping down and out of his view. The hospital awoke: heels on tiles, chatting nurses, traffic on the street below as people navigated the everyday world from which Kelvin had been so unceremoniously exiled.

Sue sat on the couch, patting his hand. 'I'm just glad it's starting,' she said. 'The sooner the better, I reckon.'

'Yeah.' Kelvin watched that dove. Its head bobbed and its tiny black eyes seemed sightless. 'That's what I reckon.'

Then the nurse arrived. At first he thought she was in a hazmat suit. She had full surgical scrubs, including gloves pulled up over the sleeves, as well as a plastic face shield. Behind it her features were obscured by glare, and when she spoke her voice was muffled.

'Sorry, Kelvin. We need to wear all this when we're handling the chemicals. It's called OH and S – occupational health and safety.' She moved around the bed and to the window. 'Nothing to worry about. We just want to make sure the medicine only goes where it's supposed to.'

'That's cool.'

It wasn't entirely cool, though; he knew that meant that the chemicals must be dangerous, and there was something confronting about the outfit itself. It was like a costume almost, something from a science-fiction film.

The nurse laid a rubber hand on Sue's shoulder. 'Mum, you'll have to step out for the time being, too. Sorry. OH and S.'

Sue stood and bent over Kelvin, kissing his forehead and wishing him luck. 'I'll be right outside.'

'Don't worry. I'll be fine.'

The nurse nodded, welder-like. 'That he will.'

Once his mother had gone the nurse closed the curtains. The room was surprisingly dark, and for the first time Kelvin wished he could look at that concrete building.

'The chemicals are sensitive,' she said. 'Doxorubicin and methotrexate. We need to keep the light off them as much as we can.'

She left him and the room was silent. Steve would be on one of the floors below, Kelvin knew; Steve, who had probably sat in darkness just like this and come out the other side. What had he said? That chemo wasn't really so bad? The nurse wasn't poisoning him, despite the hazmat suit and all the OH and S. She was helping him.

'Alright, Kelvin.' Now she held two packages that he knew would contain the chemicals. Each was wrapped in black garbage bags. If they were trying to make the process seem sinister, they were succeeding. 'This one's the doxorubicin.'

She tore away the plastic and in the light from the corridor Kelvin saw what was going into his body. The bag was clear and filled with a bright red liquid, almost the colour of the mercury thermometers he had used in science. A blue sticker proclaimed CHEMOTHERAPY: DISPOSE OF PROPERLY.

'Now all you need to do,' the nurse said, jabbing the IV into his arm, 'is sit and relax.'

So he did. They put the television on but there was something stifling about the breakfast news presenters laughing out into that darkened room. Instead, he found himself watching the dripping IV. That fluid made him uneasy. It was like nothing he had really seen before. It *looked* toxic. He imagined it mixing with his blood, being gulped into the ventricles of his heart then pumped everywhere else, lungs and liver and kidney and brain. The nurse couldn't touch it without a space-suit, yet here he was, lying in the dark with it invading every part of his being. When it was time for the methotrexate he found it just as bad – acid yellow, spider venom yellow, wolf piss yellow.

She's not poisoning me, he thought again. I might hate this but the cancer will hate it more. And Steve has done it.

Finally it was over. The nurse took everything away and his mother was allowed back into the room. She opened the curtains, and once again Kelvin was given his narrow slice of sky.

11

His father's voice

CHARLIE'S FATHER FILLED the house.

There was no escaping him; even with the door shut Charlie heard the old man's voice through the wall, or the heels of his bare feet thudding as he made his way across Tia's kitchen, rattling cups on their hooks. Concentrating on his school-work, Charlie would turn up the volume on his earphones so loud it hurt. It didn't work. His father's presence remained, pressing outwards so that it seemed to leach into the carpet, the curtains, the now-claustrophobic plaster. It wasn't a smell or anything that could be named, just an essence to which Charlie felt himself painfully attuned. There was only one solution and that was to get out and train.

He ran through the grey morning light before school, wrapped once more in garbage bags to draw out the fluids. He passed shuttered holiday houses, a milk bar with a decaying striped awning, the bus stop where boys had bullied him long ago. Nobody would dare now. Charlie had turned eighteen and there wasn't a single person at his gym who could beat him. His next bout was in the city and he was determined to win that, too. After that, he would have a shot at the Australian Title.

He sensed his father at his back and ran faster. Even Charlie knew he was pushing himself harder than he should, close to limits he had never tested before and beyond which lay significant dangers.

The ocean came into view, a great plain of misted slate. Charlie went still faster towards it, aware of a light rain falling now, then paralleled the hissing waterline as he reached the foreshore. He dodged in and out between tilting moonah trees whose sinuous trunks were like the windblown shrouds of wraiths. He overtook one jogger after another and ended up running far longer than he had planned.

Back at home he had a quick breakfast and shower and let his eyes slide over his father. Tia saw him to the door.

'You be good, Charlie.' She kissed him, looking in the direction of the bus stop as though dangers still lurked there. 'And have a big lunch. That was no breakfast for a growing boy.'

'Thanks, Tia. Love you.'

He spent the whole bus ride thinking about Tia and his father. How could a brother and sister grow to be so different? They were like branches from a shared trunk, each having speared so far in opposing directions that they now bore completely different fruit. It was both frightening and reassuring: frightening because Charlie knew that he, too, grew from the same soil as his father, reassuring because it meant people had choices. If they were smart and good and above all hardworking, they could take control of their destinies.

As he walked to class Charlie saw a teacher waving to him.

'Earphones out, Charlie. Put them away.'

'Sorry, sir.'

'If I see them again you'll lose them.'

The bell went and he sat down to study electrical diagrams.

The rest of the students in his class were also part of the trade stream, preparing to be plumbers and mechanics and builders.

While he tried to work the other kids talked and joked. He wanted to put his earphones back in but remembered the warning he had received that morning. His father would have mouthed off at the teacher, argued back, but Charlie would not. He focused.

Resistor. Potentiometer. Vacuum tube cathode. Fixed capacitor. He followed the map of lines, connections and breaks, highlighter in hand. Then it all became entangled and he felt sick. His ears started to ring.

'Miss Khatri – may I please go to the bathroom?'

'Quickly, Charlie.'

He floated across the schoolyard to the boys' toilet. It was damp and cold and smelt of piss and urinal cakes. Far away he could hear a game of soccer being played. He closed his eyes, head buzzing. When he opened them he was flat on his stomach, one cheek pressed into the concrete. He didn't know how long he had been out but he was aching. He rose slowly, was seized in a monstrous bear hug of nausea and vomited into the steel sink.

Gripping onto what he could, he made his way back towards class through a schoolyard that was blanched of colour and trembling in and out of being. It was like a dream. He thought of his upcoming bout, his father, the fluids he had been cutting, Tia, the fifteen-year-old Eragon finding a dragon egg while hunting in the Spine Mountains. Then there was someone with him – Miss Khatri – and he was sitting somewhere, on a bench, he thought, and by the time his head cleared the ambulance had arrived and he was on his way to Seadale Hospital.

'Your teacher said you're in training?' The paramedic was a pretty girl in overalls with a pencil behind her ear. 'You're a kickboxer?'

'Yeah.' He shook his head, feeling utterly humiliated. At least it didn't happen in the classroom, he thought.

'You are severely dehydrated.' The hospital was just up the road from The School and they were already parking. 'They'll be giving you lots of fluids.'

'But I need to keep my weight *down*. I have an important fight in a couple of days.'

'You won't be doing much of anything in a couple of days if your kidneys pack it in. Think they'll let you take a dialysis machine into the ring?'

Charlie was polite to the nurses and did as he was told. He lay back on a bed in the emergency department while they put him on a saline drip and got him something to eat and drink. He was not a swearer – Tia had raised him not to be – but he just kept thinking, over and over: *Fuck*.

'Will I be able to go back to school today?'

'Definitely not.' The nurse was busy, moving back and forwards between him and other patients. 'You're going to be on that drip for some time. Then you're going home to rest.'

He lay back, glaring at the bag bulging with fluids by his side. It looked like a jellyfish with a single stinging tentacle pressing his arm. *Fuck*. His fight was coming up and there wasn't a chance he was going to withdraw from it or change his training regime. He was not going to quit.

Then he heard his father's voice from somewhere beyond the curtain.

It was deep, gravel-spitting, nothing like Tia's. It hurt Charlie in some literal sense that he would have struggled to articulate. He hated it. In one motion Charlie stood from the bed and pulled the IV out of his arm. The nurses saw him and rushed over, crowding him, trying to get him to lie back down.

'I'm fine.' He slunk around them. 'I was just dehydrated from training too hard. I know what I did wrong and won't make that mistake again. Thanks for looking after me.'

His father was there but Charlie would not look at him. He was just a dark form in the periphery of his vision. Charlie walked around him wordlessly and back out into the grey morning, thinking once again of his fight.

12

The hero's journey

TOWARDS THE END of Grade 4, after I had temporarily overcome the sickness that had kept me at home for almost six
months, my friends and I found an arrow engraved into a
wooden bench in a corner of our primary school.

Hardly anybody ever went to that spot. It was called the
'Quiet Area', and for that reason repelled most of us who
preferred to run, shout, play bat tennis with handmade wooden
paddles on the asphalt courts. But one day we went in there
and found it.

The bench was shaded by trees and partly obscured by
a huge caged water meter. We could see that the arrow had
been there for a long time, probably longer than we had been
alive. It was the same colour as the bench with its dark wood
and rusted bolts. Its surface had been smoothed by years of
use, arrow included. And it was no small arrow; the thing was
nearly as long as our young hands and had been gouged deep
into the timber, so deep that on wet days it filled with rain-
water on which crimson bottlebrush filaments floated.

We became obsessed with it. If there was an arrow then it
had to be pointing to something. What that something was

enchanted us. We talked of it ceaselessly. In class I found my mind drifting. I looked out the wall-sized grid of windows at the trees, whose leaves seemed to form arrows in the quiet sunshine. I imagined the engraver. To me she was always an older girl or woman, sitting alone on that bench with her head down and some sharp object in her hand, gouging and scratching and picking. I could never see her face; it was concealed by long straight hair. Love was her inspiration, I thought.

At recess and lunch we would take turns placing our heads on the bench to follow the direction of its flight. The arrow pointed straight out of the Quiet Area, over a basketball court, past a sundial (bizarrely situated to be in the perpetual shade of gum and pine trees) and to the wall of a portable classroom.

We walked, following the line as straight as we could. Sometimes one of us would stay at the bench, standing tall on that arrow with arms pointed out straight, palms pressed together in horizontal prayer. When the rest of us reached the wall at just the right spot, our guide would hop off the bench and run to join us. Together, we three or four boys would crawl on our hands and knees in the dirt and peer between a narrow gap in the planks.

Underneath it was dark. Cool dust breathed into our eyes, making it hard to see. Shapes were indistinct, shifting. There might have been a tennis ball or the white bone of an exposed pipe, but there seemed to be other things, too, things we could not identify but which each of our imaginations lifted into the light and examined. The arrow was urging us on but those boards seemed inevitable and impassable.

It was a tingling mystery but it was a game, too. Our search extended. Maybe, somebody thought, the arrow did not terminate at that classroom wall. Maybe the forgotten engraver wanted us to bounce from surface to surface. To a nine-year-old it made perfect sense. We followed it once more to the classroom wall then ricocheted to another, then another, bouncing like pinballs from red brick to glass to steep dirt embankments. We covered half the school before turning to one another in awed wonder when we ran directly into a hundred-year-old pine tree in the school's centre. If you climbed to the first branching of huge limbs you found yourself on a platform like a floor. Beneath it, we thought, something must be hidden. We imagined gold, descending stairways, portals into other dimensions, the curled skeletons of lost loves. That platform was thick and hard but seemed hollow.

We began making maps on scraps of paper. Our parents would burn the edges then let us store them, carefully folded, in empty matchboxes. We coloured them with thick gold texta so that our hands smelt of paint and sulphur. And those maps (on which the arrow always dominated) did not plot the school but other places, some commingling of our inner and outer landscapes as we searched and wondered.

At some point we agreed that the rebound theory of the arrow was wrong. Surely, we thought, it was intended to be straight. That portable classroom looked far newer than the arrow so we decided we needed to continue beyond it. We rounded the building (shouting at one another through those planks to ensure the line stayed true) then went on. We crossed a playground, gardens, passed through more buildings, then inevitably reached the perimeter fence.

There was something out there, we were all sure. Something to which the arrow was guiding us.

What lay beyond that low wire fence? Back then there

wasn't much on that street, which terminated in a cul-de-sac where the land sloped steeply upwards to the freeway. Opposite, there were a few empty lots and sad-looking fibro houses. One bore the triangular yellow 'Safety House' logo, though a graffiti artist had inked legs protruding from its grinning mouth.

What intrigued us particularly was a narrow strip of overgrown land that ran parallel with the freeway and receded into an immeasurable distance. It began at the end of the cul-de-sac with a broken-down fence that was almost entirely covered in grass. One lunchtime a friend (infinitely more courageous than I) leapt the school fence, sprinted across the cul-de-sac to that rustling wall of grass. It seemed a barrier into another world, flimsy and close but somehow utterly impassable. He returned to us and we helped him over the fence and back into the real world, awed that he had followed that arrow further than any of the rest of us had yet dared.

Even when we grew too old for such games we thought of that arrow sometimes, sitting there in the peaceful shade as the tea-trees whispered and the water meter ticked away the months and then the years. We did not know that there was not a single arrow, but one for each of us; that it did not matter where it pointed, only that it did.

*

So much student learning lies somewhere beyond the documented curriculum, floating outside and around it, often uncontained by the walls of the classroom. At university they explained this to us as the 'hidden curriculum'. It's true that I remember almost nothing of what I was taught in Grade 4, but can see that arrow with perfect clarity, from its crude fletching right down to an infuriating kink in the shaft that made it difficult to follow. Despite this, I spent my undergraduate years convinced that all my most important teacher–student interactions would occur over a desk, or as I stood pontificating at a whiteboard.

When a student visited the office to see me it was usually Claire or Charlie. It surprised me one afternoon that term when Mya appeared.

As usual, I had essays spread across my desk in a foaming tide. With just her head tilted through the door she looked at the mess and offered to come back tomorrow.

'No, no.' I had a headache and hours of work ahead of me. 'Any opportunity to procrastinate. I need a break.'

She sat on the couch, placing her books neatly on the cushion beside her and brushing droplets of rain from her blazer. Hardly anybody at The School wore blazers, only senior students with leadership positions. Mya's rattled with badges. I had little doubt she would be my top Literature performer and probably one of the most academically successful students at The School.

'Thanks, Mr Murray. I actually wanted to get your opinion on my pathway.'

'Archaeology? I'm not an expert at all. You're better off asking the Careers Team.'

'It's more of a general question.'

'Oh. Sure.'

She took a breath. 'All through school I've been adamant that I wanted to study history, but especially archaeology.'

It was true. Mya was one of those students who teachers discussed often and with pride. She devoured history books, visited museums, corrected her teachers, exceeded tenfold the requirements of any assignment related to the past. Years later, after I published a book about the taipan, she would send me a photograph of a carved stone snake, explaining that serpents were a protective symbol for ancient Egyptians.

'*Archaeologist.*' I tried to conjure in my tone vast bright landscapes of excavations and wonder. 'I think it would be a dream job, Mya. You'd be amazing at it.'

'I vividly remember Mr Di Stasio teaching us about Ancient Egypt in Year 7,' she said. 'I became super obsessed with it. I made an Egyptian fashion magazine and a gold clay hiero-glyph tablet with my name on it for a project.'

'Why do you love it, do you think?'

'I guess I've always been interested in knowing where humans came from and what makes us human . . . And in Philosophy we're doing Plato, Socrates and Aristotle . . . Like, examining the way those ancient people tried to conceptualise the world . . . And *mythology.* I *love* mythology.'

'I'm only hearing positives.'

She cracked. For a brief, fleeting moment – less than the time it took her to reach up and sweep a stray hair from her eyes – the muscles in her face contracted and she was crying. No tears came and before I knew it she was once more the Mya she presented to the world, blazer and braids and immaculate books and not a single piece of homework unfinished in six years of secondary education.

'It's my dad.' She steadied herself for a moment and then went on. 'He's not a big fan of it.'

'Why not?'

'He says that it's really hard to get jobs in archaeology. Employment isn't guaranteed. He wants me to find something more stable.'

I had not met Mya's father in person but had spoken with

him on the phone. He was a gruff, no-nonsense fisherman working the waters alongside the small Queensland town in which he had been born. I was sure he had known hardship and wanted only security for his daughter. However, I knew too that his world was a small one. When his daughter spoke on the telephone of lost tombs and scarab-etched papyrus, I imagined these things would seem as tangible to him as fairy-tale characters or the landscapes of other planets. His was a world of fishing permits, gross catches, the fear of hard seasons that might result in mortgages going unpaid.

'It was fine when I was younger.' She maintained her composure as she spoke, but all the while her eyes glistened under the fluorescent tubes. 'But I think now that I'm eighteen and I'll be going to university next year he's kind of like, "Why haven't you grown out of that yet?" Do you know what he wants me to do?'

I shook my head.

'He thinks I should become a cook. There's nothing wrong with that but when have I *ever* given him the impression I'd want to do that for a job?'

'I think he's scared for you,' I said. 'He's putting his anxieties onto you. Adults do that to kids a lot.'

'But what should I do? He's my *dad*. And what if he's right?'

I knew I was on dangerous ground. It was the type of conversation that could easily result in an angry voicemail waiting first thing the next morning, or maybe another invitation to David Carver's office. Still, I didn't hesitate. I knew exactly how she felt because I had been in a similar position in Year 12 (though the pressure on me had not come from a parent). At eighteen I had chosen the wrong path for the wrong reasons, and it had almost cost me dearly.

'Let me put it this way. You love mythology, right?'

Mya nodded. I could see she was at a point where if she tried to speak she would cry.

'Ever heard of Joseph Campbell?'

She shook her head.

'So Campbell was a professor of Literature who did a lot of work on mythology. His most famous book is called *The Hero with a Thousand Faces*. Basically, he thought that almost all myths retell variations of the same story, and that we can learn really important lessons from this. It sounds cheesy, but he believed that each of us is on our own heroic journey. Campbell has a quote that I really love: *If the path before you is clear, you're probably on someone else's.*'

Still Mya didn't speak. I felt – hoped – that she had come to me for advice because she knew I would disagree with her father and just needed to hear an adult validate her dream.

'Maybe the path to archaeology isn't so clear. Who knows? Maybe there are dangers. And I'm sure the path to being a chef will be clear and smooth and a guaranteed job 'til retirement. But that is somebody else's path. Then there's the whole threshold guardian idea.'

'What's a threshold guardian?'

'Campbell says that every hero will reach certain thresholds they need to cross – like borders or doorways leading from one place to another. Like just before you start your archaeology degree.' I deliberately phrased it as a certainty. 'And at those moments, threshold guardians always appear to bar the way. They can be critics, parents, even ourselves. But it's the hero's job to overcome these guardians so she can continue on her journey.'

'That makes so much sense.'

'Joseph Campbell's the smart one, not me.'

'Well – thanks to Joseph, then.'

Wanting to finish with something concrete, I took a final risk. 'If you were to become a chef I can pretty much guarantee what would happen. You'd get a stable job. You'd earn money. You'd be safe. Then one day, maybe when you were thirty or forty, you would wake up and think, *I wonder what would have happened if I'd studied archaeology?* And the moment that happens, you'll start to resent your dad.'

Watching her leave, I realised with a lurch of sadness where I had first learnt of Joseph Campbell. I hadn't been much older than Mya. Liam Davison had taught me.

13

Side effects

AFTER A FEW weeks, Kelvin Lloyd's days fell into a pattern.

At nine o'clock the oncologist would come, bracelets jangling as she felt his neck, armpits, stomach and groin, tracing a landscape of subterranean mysteries. The tumours could be shrinking, growing or staying as they were. Kelvin had no way of knowing. The oncologist was kind and warm but she was also efficient, completing her duties in only minutes before moving on to other children. She would check his drip and surgery sites while asking how he'd slept and if Sue was visiting that day.

'Yeah, Mum'll be in just before lunch.' He was sick now, exhausted and nauseous with scalding ulcers beginning to burrow from his gums. 'She has to take my little brother Marcus to school then drive up from Seadale.'

Once the oncologist had gone he would try to eat breakfast. It was nearly impossible. Those chemicals had stripped and rearranged his senses. The hospital food tasted of steel filings. He knew he needed energy so sometimes managed to force down a biscuit or perhaps a small carton of milk. Afterwards he would go down and chat with Steve until his mother arrived.

Though he saw himself as being on the verge of adulthood, there was no denying the immense reassurance that came from his mother's presence. There was little they could do; occasionally they would go for a walk around the ward, or head down to the larger treatment room and read magazines together. Mostly they stayed in Kelvin's room and talked. They had always been close, but in those lingering afternoons the two discovered new avenues of connection perhaps closed to all but mothers and their dying children. She had quit her job and if it wasn't for her nine-year-old would have spent every minute with Kelvin.

'How's Marcus?' Kelvin would ask, trying his best to hide the discomfort that came from speaking. So far, the mouth ulcers were the worst side effect of the chemotherapy.

'He's been better. He's lost a lot of weight. But he's coping.'

'I can't imagine Dad would be especially comforting.'

Kelvin soon saw that the cliché of cancer bringing families together was just that – a cliché. For the Lloyds it was a solvent, melting whatever adhesive held them to one another. Kelvin's father worked ceaselessly, perhaps because he had to and perhaps as a means of coping. As he grew increasingly distant Kelvin sometimes sensed that the man wanted to visit more but felt helpless, perhaps afraid. Kelvin did not have the strength to process these complexities, observing them with the same passivity viewers bring to overplayed footage of historical disasters.

When his mother left he turned to the nurses for company. They were mostly young, in their late twenties, and one – Bridgette – competed in athletics like him. He came to anticipate her shifts, enjoying the glimpses of reality she offered as she spoke of heptathlons and relays. Inevitably though, she would leave and he would be alone once more. At night the pain of the mouth ulcers leaked dully into his dreams. Sometimes his sleep would be deep and serene, dreamless, and then he would be woken by a nurse tugging at his cords or checking his drip. Sometimes it would be Bridgette and sometimes it would be little more than a formless shadow that hovered then moved away. Often he would not sleep again, and before long the oncologist would come on her rounds.

Then the letters started arriving.

One by one they came, fragments of a world to which he had once belonged and might belong again. They were meant to be heartfelt and they were, but more often than not he laughed at their contents: cartoon figures with bulging eyes; five-pointed stars; basketballs of orange texta, the pinpricks at their centres betraying the compass used to craft them; stickers; sketches of teachers intended to be offensive; stamps; well-wishes in block letters that grew small and cramped at the nearing of the page's edge; smudges; spelling errors; a basketballer with an absurd monobrow; and an illustration of The Spuds' uniform, complete with red trim and flaming potato.

For the first time he wondered if any of his friends would visit him in the hospital. It became something he would wonder again and again in the coming weeks. For the time being, he had to rely only on the inhabitants of his strange, closed world.

One day he found a girl he thought he knew sitting in the treatment room. Pale eyes and a straight, thoughtful mouth smiled at him from below hair cut short in anticipation of baldness. The recognition was mutual and simultaneous, and they quickly realised they were both from Seadale.

'I go to the Catholic school.' Her voice was so loud Kelvin was sure the nurses would hear it up the corridor. 'We have some of the same friends.'

'I thought so! Wow. Not much fun in here, right?'

Margaret had Hodgkin Lymphoma and had been in the hospital a month longer than Kelvin. She had an open confidence he came to envy. She maintained it even as she grew sicker, steroid treatments leading to water retention that gave her a bloated, almost grandmotherly look.

Despite the efforts of the staff to engineer friendships amongst all the children in the Cancer Centre, Margaret and Steve soon emerged as the only other patients to whom Kelvin felt he could relate.

Soon afterwards, Steve found Kelvin in the ward and led him back towards his room.

'You're going to love this, mate.' He was taking huge strides. 'I asked Jane for it – for you and me.'

Waiting at the foot of his bed, defying the bleak concrete wall outside, was an Xbox.

'And I've got a game,' Steve said, his quiet voice making him almost Margaret's opposite. '*FIFA*. You keen?'

When Kelvin grinned he didn't even feel the mouth ulcers.

14

Making sense

I DID NOT hear of Charlie's collapse through the school grapevine but directly from Charlie himself. He came by the office just before the end of one recess, quizzing me about my marital status as though nothing out of the ordinary had occurred.

'When I propose to Greta,' I assured him, 'you will be the first to know.'

'I'll hold you to that, sir.'

I gathered my Literature essays and books and glanced at the clock. 'We might have to walk and talk. What's new in your world?'

He avoided eye contact. 'Ah. Well. About that. I kinda . . . Passed out in the toilets the other day and ended up in an ambulance.'

I dumped my things on the desk and sat down once more. '*What?*'

'Sir, it wasn't as bad as it sounds, I swear. I got up on my own and Miss Khatri found me on my way back to class. It was just a bit of dehydration and over-training.'

'*Just?* What did the doctor say?'

He laughed in the manner of one who has just executed a cunning but innocuous prank. 'Well, I kinda discharged myself.'

The bell tolled. I stood, a kind of Pavlovian response, then immediately sat again. 'Why?'

'Dad showed up. I guess The School called and he answered instead of Tia. I didn't want his judgement.'

'And what did *Tia* say about you bailing out of the hospital?'

'She wasn't too impressed.'

'Neither am I, Charlie. It doesn't make sense. You're training so hard you're going to make yourself sick – what good would that do?'

He said nothing. I could see he was conflicted, caught between feelings of guilt at the stress he had caused Tia and his single-minded drive to live life on his own terms.

'You've got to take it easier.' I realised I did not want to sound angry – *wasn't* angry – and smoothed my voice. 'I'm no kickboxing expert but surely you know this.'

'Yeah.' Streams of students were passing the window. We both knew the conversation had to end, and with the Literature room on the other side of The School I was already late. 'But I had that fight anyway – just a few days out of hospital. And I won it, sir. So now I get a shot at the title – a shot at the *belt*. I get to fly interstate and everything. My first five-round bout.'

Everything that could be done for Charlie, I knew, was being done. Calling an ambulance for a student was as serious as it got; all the key staff would have known it happened, from the principal to the Wellbeing Team. Charlie would now be swatting away more adult support than he wanted. I reminded myself that he was visiting the office by choice, and that I did not want to push him away.

'That's awesome, mate. I'm happy for you. Really. But just please be careful.'

'I will, sir. I promise.'

We parted ways somewhere amongst the crowds of pale-faced, wintery-eyed children. He wasn't the only one pushing himself too hard, I knew, though for others it was less a matter of choice. Wambui had two part-time jobs, one in a restaurant and one in a newsagent; her parents were also working long hours, and this often left Wambui to cook dinners and care for her little sister. The pressure on many of my students was immense, and I was distracted by the thought as I came to the Literature room to find Tim waiting outside.

'Hey, Doc. We were starting to think you weren't coming.'

It was odd for him to be waiting like that but I didn't register it at the time. 'Sorry. Just sorting a few things out.'

Then I walked inside and knew something was up.

The first thing I noticed was that the room was packed. All the seats were full and there were students sitting on the floor and in the aisles between tables. Half of The School's English teachers were in the room, too: Ana, filming me with her mobile phone; white-haired Richard who we all wanted as our grandfather; Jason the graduate, tattooed from neck to wrists to ankles; Sebastian with his cockatoo laugh; Tina the Head of Department, who cared for all of us like we were her own children.

'Right. What's going on?'

Laughter. '*Nothing*, Mr Murray.'

'It doesn't *look* like nothing.'

I came to the desk and saw that Ana was not the only one filming. All around the room students' faces were lit by their phone screens as they angled the devices towards me. Mya approached holding a large blue card.

'Thanks, Mya.' It had been a long time since I had felt self-conscious or unsure of myself at the front of a classroom. 'Usually classes give cards after the exams, but I appreciate it.'

'Just open it.'

I did. It was filled with student signatures, as well as a strange paper flap below a handwritten message.

'Read it out loud,' Mya said, returning to her seat and getting out her own phone.

I looked across the room at all the smiling faces and recording phones and began to read.

'To Mr Murray. As a class we wanted to say thank you for being our Literature teacher these past two years so we wanted to set up a surprise for you. We got in touch with someone special to set up something for the end of the year. However they got back to us sooner than expected and would love to have a chat with you. So you will be getting a phone call from none other than . . .'

I had to lift the paper flap to read the name below.

'*Peter Carey!*'

There was riotous laughter and applause. When it subsided I was able to read the final line.

'We all appreciate everything you do for us Mr Murray and we all love coming to Literature classes as you make them so much fun.'

There's nothing I can write that will capture what that moment meant to me. I knew right then that it would always tower above not only all my memories of teaching, but my memories of life. As my last grains of sand skitter through that narrow glass neck to join the silent heap below, I will remember that luminous gesture of kindness.

Teachers play with time. We reach into the past and drag it into the present, from the cool limestone vaults of the pyramids to the almost unimaginable prehistory four billion years ago, when the Earth was a nameless molten ball snarling with fire. We want our students not only to see and understand these things but to be moved by them, as Mya was once during Mr Di Stasio's History lessons at The School. But it isn't only about the past. We journey into the future, too, inviting children to speculate less on the species' unfolding narrative as on their own; cooking dinner for her brother in a small rented flat, we want a little girl to see not herself reflected in the dark window, but an archaeologist twenty years from now, dusting sand from the bones of a past as vital and powerful as her own. We want her to see that possible future and aim for it as surely as an archer peering down the shaft of an arrow.

Writers play with time, too. I have gathered these students together from my own past, selecting them for the power of the lessons they have taught me. I have changed names and distorted details to protect them. Now, though, I want to use real names, for though I never thanked Liam Davison properly for his kindness, that is not a mistake I will make again.

The two students who decided to contact Peter Carey were Emily Opie and Shae Evans. After giving me the card, Shae showed me the email they had sent. I reproduce it here verbatim not to boast about their compliments (the students were far kinder than they should have been) but to highlight their kindness:

Dear Mr Carey,

Our names are Shae and Emily and we are currently studying Year 12 Literature at our secondary collage. We have studied your book 'Collected Stories' and focused on American Dreams, Do You Love Me?, Peeling, Shadow Industry, Conversations with Unicorns and Life and Death in the South Side Pavilion. We had a great time reading them and loved your writing.

Our teacher Mr Murray absolutely loves your writing and looks up to you as an author himself. We even got him to admit his favourite author and you were on top. Mr Murray is everyone's favourite teacher and makes studying Literature really interesting and entertaining. We love coming to class and exploring the complexities of texts. Mr Murray puts his heart and soul into teaching us and we really want to give back to him when we graduate this year.

So we as a class are enquiring if it's possible to please organise a signed book by Peter Carey or a phone call. We are really open to all ideas and options on how we can make this dream a reality. We are willing to pay as we all believe our teacher deserves this experience as he has truly made Year 12 incredible.

Thank you so much,
Shae and Emily.

I noted that they had misspelt the word 'college' as 'collage', something I found endearing and heartwarming, even in a subject where bureaucrats forbid dictionaries in the exam.

Today Emily is nearing the end of her paramedic qualifications. By the time this goes to print she will likely be on the road in an ambulance. There is no person in this world I would rather have turn up to help in a crisis. Her extraordinary kindness will buoy countless patients and their families through difficult moments.

Shae was completing a hairdressing apprenticeship but was let go as a result of the coronavirus pandemic. While she waits for Victoria to open back up, she is working as a streamer on Twitch, getting paid to play video games while chatting with online viewers.

Interviewing her for this book, I asked her what her biggest passion is these days.

'My biggest passion is finding happiness and giving people happiness in return,' she replied. 'As cheesy as it is, my biggest passion is making those around me smile, comfortable and content. Same as myself – searching for happiness.

'I hope that makes sense.'

15

Night-time at the
Children's Hospital

THE WORST PART of Kelvin's day was when his mother left. He knew she had to look after Marcus, so he never broke down or pleaded with her to stay. Still, watching her go left him with an empty feeling that was deeper than simple loneliness. It was as though she carried something with her when she arrived each morning that she had no power to leave behind. With her departure the hospital seemed to take on a menacing quality, from the steel rails encircling the bed to his outward-opening bathroom door.

If he was well enough he would go down and play *FIFA* with Steve or chat with Margaret, but for the most part he just sat in his room. Then the evening would come.

On the wall was an electric clock similar to the ones in his classrooms at The School. A red second hand seemed to drift through a viscous fluid. He watched it. Played with his phone. Watched it some more. Turned on the television. Clicked it off and then looked at the clock again. There was nothing to do but wait for bedtime.

The ward was always busy during the day, with visitors, patients and staff moving about. Once the lights dimmed, that changed. A new silence descended on the Children's Hospital. Soon all Kelvin could hear was the beeping of the IV pump. When the bag ran empty that beep would become rapid and panicked, and a nurse would need to see to it.

Sleep had become even more difficult in recent weeks. Following another surgery, he could only lie comfortably on his back or left side. Worst of all, though, were his stores of unspent energy. Not long ago he had been playing basketball every day, doing athletics, riding BMX with Heath. Now he was spending his days in bed, and by midnight he was often so acutely awake that the tiniest details of the room were brought into sharp focus. The ceiling with its speckled panels glared down at him like a negative of space, a million dead black stars in an infinity of Dulux white.

During those long nights everything turned strange, alien. It was a sickly, haunted landscape.

Through gaps in the curtains he could see squares of light: windows in the wing opposite. They hovered in the darkness like lanterns that slowly burnt out. Sometimes one might light up again in the deepest night, when it was too dark for Kelvin even to see the clock; at such moments he would wonder about the child there, and about the children in those unlit windows who might be staring out into the night, just as he was.

Then he would think.

Lately he had started feeling a strange bitterness. It was not a trait he liked in himself but there was no denying it. Why, he wondered, hadn't his friends visited him? Why weren't they calling more? The cards meant a lot, but they weren't the same as speaking to real human beings. Lying in that darkness he had a strong sense of being left behind. He felt himself to be a fading memory that no longer mattered.

'In two days I'll get to see Marcus,' he would say to the room, trying to be optimistic. 'In a few months I'll be done with this forever.'

But even if he did survive, what would his life be like? Kelvin did not know if he would ever be fit and healthy again. At that young age he already defined himself to a large degree by his athleticism. He kept thinking of The Spuds, but didn't know if he'd have the strength to throw a basketball, let alone play an entire game.

Then other thoughts would come. He would think of a fight with his brother and wonder why he did what he did, said what he said. Guilt and regret clenched at him. Interactions with classmates resurfaced, some years old, and he would wish that he had behaved differently. Was he ever cruel? No. Not Kelvin. But he felt he could have been kinder. He thought of his friends, for instance, and that made him think of the people he *didn't* talk to, not because he disliked them but simply because he had little in common with them. He felt that he could have been friends with far more people. There are countless ways in which a person can be better, can strive for happiness and give others happiness in return.

Kelvin would roll over, wires tugging at him as the IV beeped and his mouth ulcers throbbed. Sleep would not come, but nonetheless he felt weak. Often he was hungry, but the feeling was combined with an oily nausea he knew would prevent him from eating anything. On the wall, that red second hand kept gliding through the viscous night.

There were others sicker than him in the hospital, he knew. Many were younger. When things had been offered to him by the staff – opportunities, gifts – he always said no, give it to somebody who is sicker. He hoped that they would get well. He thought, too, of the kids who did not have the benefits he enjoyed in life, the kids who struggled with their school-work or came in uniform on free-dress days because they had nothing else to wear.

Lying there, the remembered faces of students from The School drifted in and out of the silence. Often, they were nameless. He wished he had reached out more, and promised that if he survived he would live a better life. He understood too young that nobody had much time.

The nights were long but had nothing on those great gulfs of time he knew preceded his birth and would follow his death. Those voids of nothingness. He understood that each person was a bushwalker passing momentarily into a stripe of sunlight. Enjoying the warmth for an instant. Disappearing once more into shadow.

Term Four:
Spring

1

Being kids

I HAD POSTED the last of Kelvin's cards long ago. Nonetheless, as a kind of ritual, I began each day walking along the beach as far as the postbox before turning back. No word had come to The School about how he was going and I found myself thinking of him often. To clear my head before a day of teaching I focused on the ocean.

Some mornings the waves were sharp, hissing with foam, while other times they had a silent, hulking glassiness. Looking beyond them, the sea was often a patchwork of shadows interspersed with awesome fields of light. Kelvin would leap into my thoughts, or Charlie, or Tessa at her new school, but I pushed them away. I wanted to care, but knew my future in the profession could be truncated if I didn't find ways of silencing these phantoms.

Gradually the weather changed. Pigface blossomed in the dunes and the smell of hay blew from the pastures inland. There were mornings when the bay stretched away with the smoothness of a melted mirror. On such days the oyster farm was cut a vivid black out of the silver and I would remember my grandfather pointing it out to me when I was Kelvin's age.

Like the Ferris wheel, the anchored boat looked to be the same one I had watched decades earlier. There was a sense of entanglement with the past and I sometimes wondered if I should be teaching at the same school where I had grown up.

'You've had the holidays to research your oral presentations,' I told my Year 9s early that term. 'You should be experts by now on your chosen topic. *Now* you're allowed to have opinions.'

It was the beginning of the lesson and I saw that there were two new students in the class. They would be well behind everybody else.

'The big question, though, is this: *how* are you going to convince the audience that your opinion is the correct one?'

I looked at those two new students again, blinked, and saw all at once that they were not new students at all. It was Teagan and Jada. Both had come to school without their make-up.

Though it may seem like exaggeration, there truly was a moment of non-recognition. Both girls wore as much make-up as anyone can feasibly apply, and I had only ever seen them that way. I remember Teagan in particular. The tough, streetwise car-wreck survivor was gone, replaced by a grinning kid with a faint blush of freckles.

'Bet you thought we'd never do it.'

'No. You got me there. To be honest I'd forgotten all about our deal.'

'Now we get to watch a movie though, right?'

I reached across and closed her laptop. 'Totally. What do you want to watch?'

She and Jada looked at one another and nodded. 'Do you have *Shrek*?'

I did, and the girls spent the next few lessons watching a film we usually reserve for Year 7s. It didn't bother me in the least that they were off-task for a while, even falling behind. I knew they would catch up, and, more importantly, I remembered what Ana had said. Childhood is fleeting and as the seasons marched on and the end of the year loomed, I found it moving to see them just being kids for a little while.

*

That term, I saw Lonnie's mother for the first and only time.

Late one afternoon, I was crossing the schoolyard towards the carpark when I spotted Lonnie far ahead with her back to me. With her was a woman, tall, straight-backed and with the same black hair as her daughter. She wore a shawl and pointed tan boots. Both walked with a strange, jerking briskness, though I did not have a sense that they were arguing. It just looked as if they were in retreat, eager to get out of The School and as far away as possible.

When I reached my own car I saw Paul coming out of the front office and waited for him. He was smiling and shaking his head.

'You'll love this, Brendan. More issues with Lonnie over the holidays.'

I slumped, thinking it had to involve Tessa. He seemed to read my thoughts.

'Don't worry. Nothing to do with 8G. I won't go into details but let's just say another girl is claiming Lonnie is giving her a hard time.'

'And what does Lonnie say?'

'All just a big misunderstanding.' Paul opened his boot and

heaved in an armload of folders. 'And her mum's supporting her.'

'Do you need me to do anything?'

'No, no. This one's nearly out of *my* pay grade. Just keep a sharp eye out and let me know if there are any issues in class.'

There were no more issues with Lonnie that year in my class. With Tessa gone she seemed to recede into the background, still surrounded by her group of friends but being neither disruptive nor cruel in English. She was punctual, completed her work, on rare occasions even raised her hand and contributed to discussions. But there still hovered around her a sense of a world I did not – perhaps *could* not – ever understand.

And that was Lonnie for the next few years. I never taught her again, though I heard of the challenges she both posed and faced. Always she had difficulties with other girls, usually because they felt she was bullying them, occasionally because she felt they were bullying her. Sometimes there might be a month or even a term when things would settle, but then it would happen: a telephone call from a parent, or a student (sometimes Lonnie herself) blustering into a coordinator's office with tears streaming down their face.

She likes the drama, some of the older teachers would say, though I never believed it.

Years later, when her cohort graduated, she was not among them. I supposed she had secured full-time work, or was completing an apprenticeship. She would be on one pathway or another, and I hoped it would lead her smoothly to a good life.

Watching those former twelve-year-olds – now young adults – walk out of The School for the last time, I thought of the story about kindness that Lonnie had written all those years ago. That's what I tried to remember: Lonnie on the shoulders of her grandfather, high above a roaring crowd at a football match, knowing that there was somebody who would never drop her, somebody to whom she really mattered.

2

Peter Carey

IN THE EVENINGS, I liked to correct essays under a green-shaded desk lamp my mother had given me as a gift. That lamp, I thought, added a little culture to my otherwise humble beach shack with its wooden floorboards, leaky spouting and top-loader washing machine. I was working under that lamp late one evening when my phone rang. Glancing at the screen, I saw a string of unfamiliar numbers with two words beneath: *New York*.

Peter Carey's call came a day earlier than I was expecting, which worked perfectly. I think my nerves might have got the better of me otherwise.

After unveiling their surprise, the girls had asked for my number and passed it on to Carey's manager. From there, they had gone through a back-and-forth process of scheduling (New York is fifteen hours behind Melbourne) before arriving at a time. With the piles of correction I was wading through and my preoccupation with Kelvin, Charlie and all the rest, it is almost certain that I was the one who got confused about the date. In the lead-up, Ana had teased me incessantly, asking day after day when 'my friend Peter' would be calling. When he did, it was far more than just an opportunity to chat with one of my idols: I was to learn something significant that I passed on to my own students, and have done every year since.

'Hi.' It was the same voice I had heard in countless interviews, and echoing from the pages of *Wrong About Japan*, which I had just finished reading. 'This is Peter Carey.'

I thanked him for his call, of course, and in particular for his willingness to respond to my students amid all the correspondence I was sure he received. We talked about the kindness of young people, and the way their generation is so often misrepresented and misunderstood. 'I've spent some time teaching creative writing at New York University,' he told me. 'Sometimes the students do nice things for me at the end of the year. They might give me a bottle of wine or a card. But nothing like your kids!'

I wanted to ask questions with answers I could bring back to the students, but allowed myself a moment of indulgence. I told Carey how much his stories had meant to me, what they meant to my students, and asked if he planned on writing in that form again. He said that he preferred novels for the time being; that they were like adventures for him, journeys.

'But back then I just couldn't stop writing short stories.' I imagined Carey as I had seen him in pictures from the seventies and eighties, slim with wild hair and thick-framed glasses. I was overcome with a sense of surreality. It seemed impossible that the talkative, friendly man at the other end of the phone had written the stories my students and I obsessed over in class each day. 'I'm self-conscious of them now, though. I read them and think, here's a guy who knows about five words, and keeps using them over and over.'

313

I thought he was being humble but did not say so. I promised not to let myself slip into sycophancy.

'Maybe it's an obvious question,' I said, 'but I wonder what advice you would give to young people trying to improve their writing?'

'Keep doing it. Read a lot and write a lot. Just keep going.' He paused before adding in an almost embarrassed tone, 'But you know all that. You don't need me telling you.'

We chatted for some time. Carey was open, warm, and never for a moment gave the impression that the call was an inconvenience. He answered questions about his books and reiterated how moved he was by the kindness of my students. Somehow, we reached the topic that would become an invaluable teaching tool: confidence.

'I constantly feel self-doubt,' he admitted. The moment he said it I thought of Claire. 'A little while ago I threw a novel in the bin that I'd been working on for a year. I've started a new one now but already I'm doubting myself.'

Though I again kept silent, I was stunned that an author who had won the Booker Prize twice could question his abilities in this way. To me, Carey didn't need to strive for good writing; he defined it.

'That will be good for some of my students to hear,' I told him. 'Sometimes I feel like Literature attracts the students who lack confidence.'

'Oh, I don't believe any of my good reviews. But I believe every bad one.'

Before that call, I had a story that I would always tell my Literature and senior English students who were lacking confidence. Before he had published a single novel, Stephen King was living with his wife in a caravan while he worked on a manuscript with the working title of *Carrie*, about a teenage girl with telekinetic powers. King eventually became so disgusted with his own writing that he tossed the entire typewritten thing in a wastepaper basket. His wife rescued it, read over the incomplete manuscript and encouraged him to continue. A few months later, he would sell *Carrie* to Doubleday for a colossal sum and begin his career as one of the most popular writers of the twentieth century. 'If *Stephen King* can be a bad judge of his own work,' I would tell my students, 'you need to be open to the possibility that your writing is nowhere near as bad as you might think.'

Now, I was armed with an even better story, one about a multi Booker Prize–winning Australian who completed his secondary education not too far up the road from The School itself.

Before long I thanked Carey once again for calling. I knew he had done it for me, but he had done it for my students, too. I like to think they may have made him reminisce about his own schooling at Bacchus Marsh, and perhaps some of the teachers he had there.

'I appreciate it, Peter,' I said. 'This has been . . . a really nice thing.'

'It's been a really nice thing for me, too. Keep up all the wonderful work you're doing. And thanks for teaching my stories.'

After hanging up, I sat in silence for some time in the light of that green-shaded desk lamp. As usual, I had hours of work ahead of me before I could turn in, from Literature essays to progress checks on my Year 9s' draft oral presentations. In that moment, though, none of it bothered me in the slightest.

I knew then, as I still know now, that teaching is the greatest job in the world.

3

The visit

KELVIN WOKE TO find his pillow covered in hair.

Propped on one elbow, he half-turned and swept it up with his fingertips, tossing the golden bundle into the bin. He was not yet bald but knew he soon would be. Walking into the little bathroom and flicking on the light, he ran his fingers across his head, sifting what little hair remained to trace the ancient contours of the skull itself.

The hair loss did not bother him. He had always kept it short anyhow. The problem lay in those reflected glimpses (in mirrors, chrome hospital fittings, darkened windows at night) when he would be suddenly reminded that he was sick – *very* sick, so sick that the word itself, short and simple and somehow childish, could not capture the gravity of his condition. That's *me*, he would think when he saw that strange face peering back at him. Since his admission he had drawn a line between himself and the sickest children. They frightened him somehow, with their angular shoulders and translucent, doorknob skulls. Now he was becoming one of them.

Sitting in Steve's room, thumbs clicking at the Xbox controllers, the older boy asked him how he was going.

'I'm alright.' He was, he supposed – by the standards of the Children's Hospital Cancer Centre, at least. 'Gonna be bald like you soon.'

'Who needs hair anyway, right?'

They went on playing for several more minutes before Steve asked a question out of the silence: 'You ever go down to the counselling sessions?'

About once a month, the psychologists and social workers held a meet-up for the kids on the ward. Kelvin had not attended any of them yet; he found it too confronting and kept insisting to himself that *they* needed it because *they* were sicker than him. It was a conviction growing weaker by the day.

'Nah. I'm happy just hanging with you and Margaret.'

'Fair enough.'

That was one of the things that Kelvin loved about Steve: he never pushed, not like the adults. The staff were never callous and Kelvin knew they only wanted what was best for him, but he always sensed an invisible chasm between the children and the grown-ups. He supposed that was true everywhere, from cancer wards to classrooms. Children would always inhabit a world that adults had forgotten, or reconstructed in their own minds to such a degree that only hints of its true essence remained.

Their game ended and Kelvin set down his controller. 'I have my big chemo coming up, though.'

'Yeah?'

'Yeah. Mother-of-all chemo. They're going to take out some of my stem cells first then put them back in afterwards. I guess they're worried they'll get fried or something.'

'It'll help with your recovery.'

Kelvin shrugged.

'How long does it last for?'

317

'Just two days. So it will be over pretty quick.'

Steve turned off the TV and lay back on his bed. He was unwell today, tired and wan, but he never complained or asked his young friend to leave. 'You'll be right, mate. Hundred per cent. How's Margaret?'

'She's good.' Kelvin grinned. 'You know. A motor-mouth. We'll worry about her when she's quiet.'

Kelvin left Steve to rest. His mother soon arrived, bringing food that the nurses let her store in the staff refrigerator. The band of flavours he could stomach was growing narrower by the day. More significant, though, was the news she would bring with her that morning.

Steve and Margaret had gradually transformed the ward into a place Kelvin felt safe. No child could ever be happy under such circumstances – there would be no nostalgia for any of them if they survived – but there could be comfort, and a feeling of kinship. Still, for Kelvin there was an aching absence: his friends from The School, from the real world. For weeks now he had felt forgotten, even if he exchanged text messages with the boys almost every day. Thinking about it would make him feel bitter, then guilty for his bitterness, then bitter all over again.

After he had finished eating his breakfast that morning (one slow, tiny mouthful at a time), his mother pulled her chair to the side of the bed.

'I have some exciting news. Heath and Jimmy are going to be paying you a visit on Saturday.'

In those few fleeting moments while he processed the news, Kelvin didn't have cancer anymore. He forgot the hair loss, the nausea, the dull brick facade pressing ever closer to his own window.

'Really? What, they're coming *here*?'

'For the whole day.'

'Yes!' He pumped his fist, tugging slightly at his IV so its wheels rattled.

'Just make sure you don't tire yourself out.'

'Oh, I won't.' He turned to his bedside table. 'I'm going to text them.'

Years later, Kelvin's mother would still remember Heath's parents in particular for their kindness at that time. Seadale was a long way from the Children's Hospital, but it was never too far and nothing was ever too hard.

The last time Kelvin and Heath had been in the same hospital together was immediately after they were born. Now, both on the cusp of adulthood, one would be supporting the other through what could prove to be the final months of his life.

*

So much of life at Seadale was about leaving, either out of desire or necessity. When teachers quizzed Year 12s about their plans, the answer – more often than not – was a derisive, 'Move away from *here*.' The young people up the road at Beachview were the same. Where tourists saw foaming tide lines, the local children saw shackles and impassable boundaries. They dreamt of the city (visible over the water on clear days), and of the cities beyond.

Heath's parents woke him early that Saturday, though he did not complain. He knew the drive to the Children's Hospital was a long one and every minute he slept was a minute he would not spend with his friend. They picked up Jimmy on the way and drove out of Seadale as dawn was rising. The sky turned pale and after a while they were passing beneath steel gantries and through choked city traffic.

'Be patient with him, boys.' Heath's mother wore sunglasses that now reflected a glary spring morning. 'He could be feeling pretty sick but might not want to admit it to you. Don't let him tire himself out.'

They reached the hospital and the two boys passed through large glass doors from their world into Kelvin's. There was a brief chat at reception (like Kelvin, Heath was unsettled slightly by the waiting room with its strange carnival atmosphere), then they were in a lift going up to the ward.

Heath and Kelvin had been friends for so long that Heath had no first memory of their meeting. Kelvin was just always there, as permanent a fixture in his life as his parents. Heath had grown up without brothers or sisters, and had spent his primary years loving school for the time it gave him with his friends. In his mind, childhood and Kelvin Lloyd were synonymous, indistinguishable. Heath remembered them together as little boys (backpacks on hooks, the smell of clag, the miniscule scraps of paper they were ordered to pick up from the carpet) and then later when they saw high school on the horizon. During those years Heath had known that his friend was sick for a while, but he never fully grasped the seriousness of the situation and it seemed to be over before it had really begun.

'It'll be good to see him,' Jimmy said suddenly, and the nervousness in his voice had the paradoxical effect of calming Heath a little. 'It's been ages.'

'Yeah. Let's hope he's feeling alright.'

The lift rose. They had been texting their friend for weeks but did not know what they would find when they finally got to the ward.

Heath had been there that day in Grade 4 when a boy named Pete Salinger was being bullied. He remembered it vividly. For some reason that he never quite understood, the boys did not want Pete to play football with them. He at first asked, then pleaded, then eventually just watched them glumly as they raced across the oval with the ball. Had Heath felt guilty? He could not remember. Those memories were just like old photographs, devoid of sound and sensation and feeling: the ball, the grass, a little smear in the distance that was Pete. But Kelvin had got them together and said, Pete should play, there's no reason to leave him out. And so they had let him. One day not long after, though, one of the boys tackled Pete so hard that his trousers split, revealing the bright red, appalling humiliation of his undies. The rest of the boys had been in hysterics, pointing, almost wailing. It went on and on, and that day Heath knew it had gone too far. Again, Kelvin was the voice of empathy.

When Heath and Kelvin did start Year 7, they discovered they were the only two from their primary school in the same class. Though they made new friends quickly, it solidified their own friendship further. Time passed; they learnt, changed; formed The Spuds; wondered about girls; and now there was this, unexpected and terrifying, barrelling both boys into adulthood years before their time.

Heath remembered the moment he had learnt Kelvin was sick again. His mother had sat him down after getting the news and repeated Sue Lloyd's words: 'It looks like the real deal this time.'

He had known exactly what that meant.

The trip up in the lift seemed an eternity but then it was over. They walked to Kelvin's room and there he was.

'Hey, Kelvin!' They shook hands, retreating to the safety of adult rituals.

'Hey, Heath! Hey, Jimmy! Thanks for coming.'

Heath gave two thumbs up. 'We've been looking forward to it all week.'

For an instant he looked like the old Kelvin. He was out of bed, grinning in shorts and a Golden State Warriors T-shirt. He even had his characteristic pulled-up socks. Then, though, the other details fell into place. His hair was thinning and his face seemed somehow bloated. This, combined with an almost complete absence of eyebrows and eyelashes, gave his eyes a narrow, slotted look. A cord extended from one arm to a drip mounted on a steel trolley.

The last time Heath had seen his friend was at the height of their basketball playing, with Kelvin streaking back and forth the full length of the court and barely breaking a sweat. Now he was utterly transformed. He looked poisoned, almost.

Neither Heath nor Jimmy's unease lasted. Kelvin bombarded them with questions about footy, basketball, school. They sat on the little couch and made an AFL SuperCoach team. Sue left them alone and before long they were joking and sharing stories just as they always had.

'There's an outdoor section with a basketball ring.' When Kelvin said it he was half-smiling. 'You guys wanna do some training?'

'Sure.' Jimmy was on his feet. 'Didn't expect basketball in here.'

Kelvin led the way through the ward, rattling his drip alongside him. They passed through a door and entered a patio busy with pot plants and garden chairs. A steel fence at the opposite end was decorated with stars, and a yellow scooter leaned discarded against it.

'What do you think?' Now Kelvin was laughing. 'Ready for some training?'

The basketball ring was plastic and barely as high as their chests.

'For sure. Let's do it.'

There was an undersized basketball, and they took turns sitting in one of the chairs while trying to bounce it through the ring. After a while Sue joined them, using her phone to film them play. If she appreciated those boys and their families before, that sense of gratitude now came into an even sharper focus. Her son was happy. He may not have been the day before and he may not be the day after, but right then, in that simple moment with the sound of traffic grumbling from the street below, he was able to be a child.

That night after Heath and Jimmy had gone, Kelvin looked at his clean white pillow knowing it would be a mess of hairs again in the morning. He knew that, soon, the doctors would suck stem cells from his body and then pump him with new and vicious chemicals. In some ways he felt it was a test of endurance between himself and the cancer: who could withstand the poison the longest. Who would buckle first.

'Hi, Kelvin.'

He turned and Steve was leaning against the doorframe, a smile on his colourless lips.

'Oh – hey.'

'How did your visit go today?'

Kelvin looked back down at that pillow. Whatever was going to happen, he knew he could handle it. In the morning he would just sweep those loose hairs away as flippantly as crumbs from his lap.

'Awesome.'

Steve nodded and backed into the corridor, swaying slightly but then regaining himself. 'Cool. *FIFA* tomorrow?'

'You know it.'

Perhaps because he was tired, perhaps because he was at ease, Kelvin slept that night like he hadn't in a long time. After the boys' visit he never felt any bitterness again. He knew he had not been forgotten.

4

Impossible things

CLAIRE WAS FIRST through the door. She stopped, raised an eyebrow, looked at me. 'Um, what is *this*?'

'What does it look like?'

'A test.'

'You got it.'

The rest of the Year 12s followed, most groaning or rolling their eyes. The easiest way to send a class into a panic is to separate the tables, stack them with lined paper and put the chairs end-to-end.

'The exam countdown isn't months anymore, it's weeks.' I tapped the board, where I had written a series of lines that would only increase their anxiety further:

10 mins: Planning
5 mins: Introduction
12ish mins: Body paragraph one
12ish mins: Body paragraph two
12ish mins: Body paragraph three
5 mins: Conclusion
Leftover: Proofreading

'You'll have two hours to write two essays on the exam,' I reminded them. 'It doesn't matter how well you know the texts or how well you can write. If you can't do it under time pressure – if you can't finish the responses – you aren't going to get a good result.'

Claire put up her hand. 'If your friend Peter Carey were to come in, do you think he could write an essay in one hour – twelve minutes per body paragraph?'

'I'm not sure. Maybe he couldn't.'

'So you're saying that *Peter Carey himself* might not do well on an exam about his own book, just because he can't conform to these arbitrary timeframes? I mean, why two essays in two hours? Why not one in an hour and a half? Why not three in two hours and forty minutes?'

'The people upstairs give us the hoops,' I said. 'We jump through them.'

I started the timer and they got to writing. A few minutes in, Tim raised his hand. I swatted it back down.

'Nope. You won't be able to ask me questions on the exam. As much as I'd like to, I'm not allowed to come in and help.'

'Just *one* question, Doc.'

'Not today. You're flying solo.'

He moaned and cradled his head in his hands, a few grains of sand trickling from his wild hair onto the blank page. After a moment, he picked up the pen.

I wandered the room, looking over shoulders and raising my eyebrows at anyone who stared for just a little too long out the windows. They hated timed writing, but I had no choice other than to put them through this kind of training. If I didn't, they would not perform on their exams.

'Right!' I clapped. 'If you haven't finished your introduction, you need to get there urgently. You're falling behind.'

All across the room the kids shared glances, mouths open, panicked. Somebody moaned, 'This is *impossible*.'

'No it isn't. A few practices and you'll be able to do it easy.'

At some point it became clear that Claire had stopped. Her pen was flat on the desk and she had nestled her head into the crook of her elbow. The stripe of purple hair I had noticed long ago had faded now to a bluish-grey.

I gave her a few minutes, but when her position hadn't changed I knelt beside her.

'Psst. Do you want to take a break?'

She raised her head just enough that I could see her eyes. 'I *am* taking a break.'

'I meant outside. Did you want some fresh air?'

Those eyes – a moment ago heavy with sarcasm and irritation – softened. 'I'm fine, Murray. I'm just not feeling it today.'

'Okay, Claire. Just do the best you can.'

When the session ended she swept up her things and was out the door before I could stop her. On her page was a single sentence: *In his often disturbing collection of short stories, Peter Carey levels a scathing critique on the cruelty and selfishness of the modern world.* That was it. Though she was far more competent than most of the class, she was the only student that day who wouldn't score a single mark.

Collecting up her paper, I thought back to that day in Year 10 when she had presented me with her bloodied forearms mid-lesson. The memory was so vivid I could almost see it again, the pale skin, the rivulets she must have allowed to trickle for some time under the table before rising and revealing them to the world.

I went straight to the office and telephoned both her mother and the Wellbeing Team to let them know I thought she was struggling.

It was a few days (including one missed Literature session) before I saw Claire again. I found her in a corner of the Year 12 Study Centre. It seemed a lifetime ago that I had gone to the coordinator with complaints about misogynistic boys; today there was no evidence of that, just a scattering of students quietly eating noodle cups as they squinted over notes and laptops.

'Hi, Claire.' A Biology textbook was open on her desk. 'Am I interrupting?'

'Nah.' She pushed a chair out with her foot. 'I owe you an apology.'

'No you don't. If anything I owe you an apology for springing that timed task on you. I could have given you the heads-up.'

'We have to do it. I get that. But I'm sorry I ran out and skipped Lit yesterday.'

Claire was so pale as to be almost grey. Beside her textbook were some sandwich crusts in a ziplock bag; much of the sandwich remained attached. 'Timed writing gets easier. Do it a few times and you'll find you can write just as well as when you're *not* under pressure.'

'I suck at Biol,' she said, nodding at a winding double-helix in her textbook. 'But you know what? I don't care. Because I don't *like* Biol. I suck at Literature and that's awful because I love it.'

'You do *not* suck at Lit, Claire. You feel like you suck and that's holding you back. You wrote one brilliant sentence the other day. A lot of other people wrote a hundred average sentences. You just need to keep going.'

'But every idea I think of seems crap.'

It was my first opportunity to share what Peter Carey had told me, and I did. Claire listened, at first indifferent but then surprised and even, I thought, a little relieved.

'If we fished Carey's discarded manuscript out of the bin,' I asked, 'do you think it would be trash?'

She smiled on one side of her mouth and slotted her eyes. 'I would have taken it. He could have let me put my name on the cover and submit it to an Aussie publisher. Then *I* could have a bestseller. Get myself some coin.'

'Totally. Now *you* have to remember that when you think your writing sucks. Trust me: it doesn't. I'm the one with the degree around here so I'll be the judge.'

After that conversation I phoned Claire's mother again. We had spoken many times before, including two years earlier when her daughter had been even less well. Everything was being done – family support, friends, counselling sessions, even medication.

'We're close,' her mother said. 'It's just a matter of getting her through the exams.'

The next time we attempted a practice exam I reminded Claire of Peter Carey, and it seemed to work. She completed two full pages of writing. Mya and Tim did equally well.

'See, nothing to it.' The three of us were in the Literature room, the rest of the students having headed home after the final bell. Year 7s shouted and jostled in the corridor. 'The only difference between today and the exam is that you'll be sitting in a bigger room.'

'And guess what, Mr Murray?' Mya flipped open a folder and spun it around to reveal her university preferences. 'My first preference is Melbourne University. I want to do a double major in History and Ancient World Studies.'

'Brilliant.'

'Assuming I get the score I need.'

'You're doing all the right things.'

'Maybe. But I still wonder about the system.' Her braids swung like pendula as she leaned conspiratorially across the desk. 'I heard a rumour that some students in elite schools actually write the name of their school on their exam papers, because they know they'll get special treatment from the assessors.'

I just laughed. 'No way. That's an urban legend for sure.'

Tim said, 'Private schools aren't that great anyway, Mya. Remember Fletcher went to Pinewood Grammar in Year 9? He said the only difference there is that every teacher is like a solid seven out of ten. But there aren't any ten out of ten teachers like we have here at The School. Not like Doc and Ms Nikolic.'

'You're too kind.'

'Plus,' Tim finished, standing to leave and looking out the window, his eyes perhaps studying the wind for its impact on the surf. 'We just need to beat the kids up the road at Beachview High.'

The rivalry between Seadale and Beachview high schools was as absurd as it was well known. Students, parents and staff squabbled about which school was better, while teachers who had worked at both (a significant number) insisted again and again that they were identical: same kids, same strengths, same weaknesses. When the rivalry was at its worst, both schools poured huge amounts of time and money into marketing themselves; time and money that could and should have been spent on our students. It became more about adult egos than the needs of the children. It was shamefully wasteful on both sides, and illuminated the absurdity of government school enrolments being based on anything besides postcodes.

'We don't have to beat the kids at Beachview,' I said. 'You guys just need to focus on doing the very best that you can. Now go home and annoy your parents so I can read these essays.'

They left, and I sat at my desk correcting until my eyes grew tired. The afternoon stretched on and the sky turned orange. What looked to be hundreds of cockatoos gathered in a huge elm tree on the other side of the asphalt. That elm tree was far older than The School itself, its first sprouts probably peeking up from the sandy soil at the beginning of the last century.

I packed my things and walked out into the long shadows of afternoon. Then I saw it: a small, lonely figure at one of the lockers in the Year 8 area.

At first I didn't recognise her. By the uniform I could see the student was one of our supposed rivals from Beachview. I detoured the short distance across the asphalt to the lockers. She turned on my approach, and then I saw the short hair, the big glasses, and realised that it was Tessa. It was the first time I had seen her in months.

'Mr Murray!' She let loose a wild, flailing wave. 'How are you?'

Seeing her so happy overcame me with a heavy, relieved sadness. 'I'm good, Tessa – how are you?'

'I'm good. Just clearing out the last things from my locker. They've been in here for ages.'

I wondered if it had taken her this long to build up the courage. Perhaps that was also the reason she had come in the late afternoon. Lonnie, perhaps, remained the Jude of her childhood, a figure to be avoided wherever possible. 'Did your mum drive you down?'

'Nah, I walked. Just live around the block.'

I passed her the last of her books. The locker yawned its steel emptiness as those cockatoos continued to scream. 'Thanks for your card. I'm sorry I missed you on your last day.'

'That's alright. Check this out.'

She took out her mobile phone and began swiping at the screen. After a moment she showed me a photograph of several girls sitting on a sunlit lawn with a beagle sniffing at their shoes. 'These are all the friends I've made at Beachview.'

'Looks like Gonzo has given them his approval.'

As we walked together to the front gate, she told me about her continuing love of Lewis Carroll. 'I have a book now called *The Wonderland Collection*,' she said. 'It has *Alice's Adventures in Wonderland*, *A Tangled Tale* and *Through the Looking-Glass*. There's a rabbit on the spine.'

'Memorised any more?'

She thought a moment. '*Why, sometimes I've believed as many as six impossible things before breakfast*. That quote is on the back cover.'

'Nice. I like it.'

We had reached the school gate. Without warning she wrapped her arms around me and said, 'A hug for my favourite teacher.'

I watched her walk out the gates and up the footpath, soon disappearing into the suburban maze beyond. I have not seen her since, but I wish her all the best this world has to offer.

5

Home

KELVIN HAD BEEN having chemotherapy for months, but in the lead-up to his 'mother-of-all' treatment they gave him a two-week break. He knew that he needed to be as strong as possible to stand a chance.

During that fortnight he started to remember what it was like to be well. His sense of taste remained distorted, but after a few days he could stomach a little more food and found his energy levels increasing. He was able to play *FIFA* with Steve or chat with Margaret without needing to shuffle exhausted to his room after half an hour. Those two remained the only friends he needed, he felt, aside from Heath and the kids from The School, who he still texted daily.

'Thank God for phones.' Margaret sat cross-legged on Kelvin's bed while he lay back on the couch. Like him, she was bald and pale. 'Imagine fifty years ago. You would have needed to write letters. Snail mail.'

'Yeah. Not to mention all the treatments they didn't have back in the day.'

She leaned forward, cupping her chin in her hands. Her eyes were bright and she spoke with the same speed and energy she always had. 'We're lucky, I guess. You ready for the big one?'

'Yeah.' He rubbed his smooth head, winced. 'Well, I guess. They're moving me to the bigger Children's Hospital for a month or so. They're going to harvest my stem cells.'

'Sounds kinda disturbing.'

'What isn't kinda disturbing around here?'

'Good point.'

Kelvin looked over the windowsill and through the dusty glass to the world below. 'I just want to get it over with.'

Each day that passed without chemotherapy was another when Kelvin felt himself growing stronger. Then, like a miracle, the doctors allowed him a sojourn home.

In some ways that time was like a dream. He worried he could suddenly awaken to cords tugging at his arms and the hospital ceiling looming over him. But the dream persisted. He played basketball with his little brother in the driveway, at last able to throw a full-sized ball the height of a full-sized ring; he and Marcus trash-talked one another, playing on as the backboard rattled and the afternoons gave way to hushed spring evenings. Kelvin's mother told him to be careful, and he was, taking breaks and lying down even when he did not yet feel tired, but now there was a sense of hope. The real world had returned. He was able to eat at the table, tag along to the shops and spin a basketball on his fingertip until it was numb.

When they arrived at the larger Children's Hospital, the first thing that struck them was the room.

Sue whistled. 'Check this out! Luxury!'

It was bright, spacious and twice the size of his room at the previous hospital. The window overlooked a sweeping park where joggers moved in and out of view amongst golden wattle and blackwood.

'It's nice.' Kelvin watched those joggers, feeling for the first time in months as though he could almost join them. 'There's a lot of light.'

After several days of injections to coax stem cells from his bone marrow to his blood, a sharp-faced young nurse wheeled an unfamiliar machine into the room. Medical devices were becoming such a feature of Kelvin's life that he barely paid them attention by then. They were all a little alike, with their clean white plastic, dials and indecipherable screens.

'We're going to pass all the blood in your body through this – it's called an anaphoresis machine.' She barely looked at Kelvin as she spoke, moving her hands swiftly over the panels and dials. 'It will separate out the plasma, then we can get at the stem cells.'

He watched his blood dart through a tube and to the machine. There, the tube knotted amongst others in a kind of cereal-box maze. Soon half of that maze was red and the other half bright yellow. He closed his eyes.

'Your next lot of chemotherapy is going to be very strong.' She sounded far away. He missed Bridgette and the other familiar nurses from the old ward. 'It's called conditioning therapy. It'll attack the cancer and make a bit of room in your bone marrow for these stem cells to grow when we put them back in. You had no donor matches in your family?'

'No.' Kelvin did not open his eyes. 'My grandparents and mum and dad all had blood tests and didn't match. And my little brother. He nearly passed out from the needle. They had to put blankets on him and everything.'

'That can happen.'

He waited for her to say more, but she did not. The machine whirred. In the park below, he imagined joggers moving through the shade of leaves and wattle. He imagined overtaking them, one after the other, his legs strong and the wind cold on his face.

*

Kelvin discovered that he had not previously known what being sick meant.

At first it seemed just like before. The chemicals dripped innocuously, running down their plastic tubes while he read magazines or watched basketball on his phone. Occasionally a message would come through from Heath or Jimmy and he would grin, thumbs tapping at the screen. Then it hit him, and he understood why the doctors had needed him to be as strong as possible before commencing the treatment.

The nausea was worse than anything he had experienced in his life. Soon he was vomiting almost uncontrollably, Sue at his back in the little bathroom as tears streamed down his burning face. When the spasms receded he would collapse into bed, the room swirling with the mad endlessness of the basketballs he had so recently balanced on his fingers.

'Try to get some sleep, sweetheart.' His mother's hand on his forehead was soft but damp. 'I'm here.'

Sometimes, though, he drifted so far from that room that he was only dimly aware of her presence. He thought he sensed her pressing the buzzer beside the bed, asking the nurses to give him something. A little while later there might be a shuffling of feet, a dim pulsing of lights, a burning sensation in one arm or a bitter taste in his mouth. He couldn't move; there wasn't a chance of him getting out of bed.

A strange, acrid pain filled every part of him, arms, legs, eyes, teeth and toenails. It seemed to reach into his past and future, so that if he tried to cheer himself up by thinking of driveway basketball with Marcus the pain was even *there*, in the hard steel of the ring and the slapping bounce of ball on concrete. All this contributed to a fatigue so strong that it transcended the mere physical: it was a mental, even a psychic exhaustion. Those chemicals seemed to be unlatching the very bonds that held his cells together, so that before long he could come apart entirely, dissolving into an aching mist that would drift out over the night-time park, past the lights of the city and back towards the distant dark spot across the bay that was Seadale.

When at last it could not be avoided and he had to shower, a nurse would help him. The trip from the bed to the bathroom was agony. He would hold on to whatever arm was there, feeling as if the entire building was trying to buck him from his feet. Even the water drumming on his scalp hurt.

During those weeks he considered seriously for the first time that he could be dying, that there might be no 'other side' of his cancer. His pain was such that the thought was not frightening, though a crushing sadness overcame him when he imagined Marcus and his parents after he had gone. He would be reduced to a signpost in all their lives, a before and after. Someday their pain might lessen, but always that marker would be there, so that in fifty years one of them might begin a reminiscence with, 'Before Kelvin died,' situating the memory within that long-lost, sunlit moment.

Then he would think of Steve. Steve was eighteen, tall and strong. He had been sick for far longer than Kelvin. If Steve could make it, then so could he.

The treatment continued. When the nurses weren't around Sue would help her son go to the toilet and brush his teeth. Even the energy needed to lift a toothbrush was difficult to summon. He had become a baby again, utterly vulnerable and utterly dependent.

Often, she would simply sit by the bed and watch him sleep. More than anything, she wanted to take him home.

6

Projects

CONNOR HAD SPENT the last few lessons in exile on the desktop computer in the corner of the room. As I addressed the class a few days before their persuasive oral presentations, I saw him listening with an unusual attentiveness.

'Remember, this is a *major assessment item*,' I said. 'In other words, it's going to make a big contribution to what goes on your report. You're showing me you can research, write, persuade, present. This is serious.' For the first time I saw a glimmer of something behind Connor's usual cocky nonchalance: worry. 'When your name is pulled out of the hat you need to be ready. If you're not, you'll be up the creek, *sans* paddle.'

'What's a sands paddle?' he asked. He was not joking and nobody laughed.

'*Sans*. S-A-N-S. It means you won't have a paddle.'

Most of the students were ready and only needed time to rehearse. The sun was shining so I sent them out to quiet corners of the schoolyard to practise with their friends. Soon only a handful of students remained. One of them was Connor, elbows on the desk, head in his hands as he stared into the screen.

'How are you going, mate?' I looked at the pages of notes spread across his desk, complete with scribbling, highlighting and sketches of waves crashing in the margins. 'Surely you of all people aren't nervous about speaking in front of the class?'

'No, sir. It isn't that.'

'Well, what's up?'

He turned to me and spoke with a seriousness I had never seen in him before. 'It's the topic. The refugees.'

'What about it?'

'It's hard to argue that these people don't deserve a second chance.'

There are moments from my career so far that I know I will not forget, some as major as the telephone call from Peter Carey, some as minor as a brief conversation with a roguish but kind Year 9 boy. This was one of those moments. Connor, I felt, had gone through an epiphany of sorts, had unearthed a previously hidden vein of empathy in the landscape of his self. I had not led him to it. He had been his own guide as he sat, lesson after lesson at that computer with its keyboard of rearranged letters, reading about people he did not know searching for a new life.

'Do you need to change your speech?'

'Is there time?'

'There's always time. It's better than standing up there and trying to convince me of something you don't believe.'

That lesson and the next, I saw Connor work harder than ever before – perhaps harder than any student I had ever seen before. Perhaps it was his newfound realisation; perhaps it was simply his fear of being unprepared for the major assessment item. Whatever the case, he said not one word to any of his classmates from that moment on. Instead, he researched, taking notes while he circled, crossed out and amended the work he had already done, even bundling up whole pages of notes at one point and dumping them in the bin.

I thought of him months earlier, mouthing off, disrupting the class, using every opportunity he could find to derail my lessons in the name of an easy laugh. It would have been easy to write him off – take the punitive approach – and I was glad I had not.

*

The cockatoos I had seen the day Tessa visited lingered around The School. Usually they would be in that elm, or pecking about on the oval, waddling off when the Year 11s' footy game strayed too close. Sometimes they wheeled screaming into the sky, their white feathers and yellow crests bright against the deepening blue of a spring afternoon.

Watching them on yard duty, I suddenly noticed Wambui hurrying towards the Study Centre, several folders clutched to her chest. Once again I was awed by the image of her in the darkness of Kaandiki, arguing for the life of a man she had never met. Though I did not know it at the time, things were becoming increasingly difficult at home. Like many teenagers, she was clashing with her parents; their domestic expectations, she felt, were getting in the way of her learning. She wanted to be more like her friends, some of whom did not need to work and were allowed the freedom to study for hours each night. Only later would she come to appreciate her parents' predicament, that they were under enormous strain themselves in their efforts to start again in a new country.

When Charlie wandered across the asphalt towards me, I cut him off before he even opened his mouth.

'No, I have not yet proposed to Greta. How's life?'

He raised his eyebrows and cocked his head to one side as though considering the question. 'Not bad, sir. Better if you'd get yourself sorted out. I'm sure Greta will make an honest man of you someday.'

'God, Charlie.' Sometimes it was like speaking to an old man trapped in a teenager's body – or liberated into one. 'How's your prep for the title going?'

'It's okay. But I actually wanted to ask you a bit of a favour. It's to do with my studies.'

I should have noticed how quickly he changed the topic. Ordinarily, Charlie would happily talk about kickboxing for as long as I offered a willing ear. What I did not know that day – and what I would not know until years later – was that he was fighting a separate battle as the title drew near. He was beginning to wonder if he was fighting for the wrong reasons. All he wanted to do was fight, night and day, and he found himself ceaselessly challenging the other members of the gym though he had beaten them all and knew he would beat them again. Once, a long time ago, he had taken up kickboxing because he was tired of being bullied, and because he wanted a way to feel less angry. Charlie achieved both of those things. He found an outlet. Now, though, he was using the anger as fuel. It would begin long before he entered the ring, a kind of hot sickness that welled and throbbed somewhere deep inside. With a little focus he would press it down, but was always careful not to extinguish it entirely. He needed the pressure to grow, like the bubbling, steaming darkness in the belly of a kettle. Then, when the time was right, he would unleash, driving that rage into his opponents with thunderous punches and snapping kicks. And it was satisfying. It felt good doing that to another human being.

Charlie felt that in this he was becoming more like his father. But his father was a quitter, too, so there was no way he could back down from a shot at the title. More importantly, he didn't want to.

'I need a project to build my electrical knowledge.' His white school shirt was perfectly ironed and buttoned to the neck. 'Something I can completely take apart and put back together again. I wondered if you had anything lying around you don't want? Something I can tinker with?'

I thought. 'Well, I have an old telly in the shed. Like, really old. Probably from the sixties. You can have it if you like, but it's massive.'

'Perfect. Thanks, sir.'

We agreed that I would drop it at Tia's place the following day after school.

Next morning there was no stroll on the beach, just a wrestle with that ancient television. I walked it on its wooden legs and heaved it into the boot, seeing my own face reflected in its long-dead, green-grey screen. For a lot of that day I wondered if I would meet Charlie's father when I delivered the television. I wondered if I *wanted* to meet him. I had never seen him before and to me he wasn't even a voice on the telephone. Over the years it had been Tia at every parent–teacher interview and at the other end of every telephone call. In the end I asked Ana to tag along.

We drove out to Tia's house after the staff meeting. It was modest but immaculate, the garden a neat strip of roses fronting a manicured lawn. There was a birdbath, a hose on a reel, gnomes peering from the bushes. Charlie was already waiting out the front.

'So this is the beast?' he asked, helping Ana and me untie

343

the straps keeping the boot down. 'It's old alright. You weren't kidding.'

'I think it was my grandpa's,' I said. 'I reckon that screen has shown everything from the West Gate Bridge collapse to –'

'The West Gate Bridge collapsed?'

'Yeah. Way before even I was born.'

Ana and I were struggling to get the television out of the boot so Charlie lifted it on his own, manoeuvring it onto the porch. Right as he did so, Tia came out.

'Hello, Mr Murray – and thanks. This will keep him very busy.'

I was struck, not for the first time, by how old she was. Tia was small and stooped with slender hands bulging with veins. A strip of silver ran down the centre of her head where her dyed hair was growing out. She had sacrificed so much to raise Charlie and Xavier, and now to look after her own little brother as he battled his demons.

While Tia, Ana and I chatted, Charlie opened the garage and took the television inside. Once – for just a fleeting moment – I thought I saw movement behind a curtain, a stirring of shadows, but then it was gone. I thought of Lonnie's mother, and of all the other parents of the students I taught, sometimes closely involved in their children's lives, sometimes so distant they existed in my mind only as spectres, their impacts seen but their true presence never felt.

As I was getting into the car Charlie shook my hand.

'Well, sir, you won't see me again until after the title fight.'

I smiled, glanced briefly back at the house and wished him luck.

7

Change

TEACHERS LIE TO their students. Usually, it's for the right reasons.

I lied to my entire Year 9 class that year when I told them the oral presentation order would be random. For me, this is a common deceit. If a child is almost sick with anxiety, I will often 'draw their name out of the hat' first to spare them lesson after lesson of agony. On occasion I will choose the strongest, most passionate student to go first, knowing their talent will set a high standard that the rest will strive to follow. Often, if somebody isn't quite ready but has worked hard, I will push them to the end of the queue to give them every chance to succeed.

I chose the latter option for Connor that year, deciding not to call him up until near the end. His last-minute change of opinion was something I wanted to reward and celebrate – how many of our politicians (indeed, how many of *us*) have the strength of character to say, *No, I was wrong, I have rethought my position and changed my mind*? I had listened to persuasive speeches about refugees before and have since, but Connor is the only student to ever change positions due to empathy.

So, one by one, I drew other names from the hat.

There were students so nervous their voices warbled like theremins, and students with the confidence of seasoned thespians. Some were desperately cutting their cue cards as they walked into the classroom; others needed no cue cards at all. A few talked so long the class began to drift, and a few puttered to a halt after thirty seconds, red-faced, guiltily turning to me and confessing, 'That's it, sir.'

Then, at last, it was Connor's turn.

He did not strut or swagger to the front of the room but moved slowly, ignoring his mates and studying a neatly stacked deck of cue cards in the palm of one hand.

'Okay, Connor.' I took out a blank criteria sheet, pen poised. 'What's your topic?'

'Refugees.' He tugged at his shirt, looked at his cue cards again. 'Refugees coming to Australia illegally and how we should respond.'

'Sounds good. As soon as you start speaking, I'll start the timer.'

He seemed to hesitate for a long time. It was the most serious I had ever seen him, though his red hair was wild and long and I should have been challenging him for the sneakers he was wearing and the stud glinting in his nose.

'Imagine you're a mother,' he said.

I waited for the laughter. There was none. He took a breath and continued.

'Imagine you're a mother with a small child. Small enough that you can pick them up but, like, big enough to understand what's going on around them and that.'

I was sitting off to one side, and he had his head almost at right angles to face me as he spoke. I subtly pointed to the rest of the class and he turned to his peers.

346

'Now imagine they don't scream for you at night because they think there's a monster under the bed. Imagine they scream at night because on the way home from school yesterday they saw this.'

He pressed a button on the computer and the projector screen lit up, opening a window to a universe utterly divorced from most students of The School. The black hulk of a burning car sat on the side of a street covered in debris: broken brick and steel, clothing, a few bright red mounds that Connor had hidden behind pixelation but we all knew were corpses.

'So you go to everyone you know and beg for money. Everyone. Your whole family and all your neighbours. Nobody has much but they all scrape and search and give you what they can. Then you pick up your kid and run as hard as you can and the next thing you know you're on a boat trying to escape.'

He had the entire class, every last student. They listened like they had never listened to me. As he continued his confidence grew; he spread his hands, cue cards forgotten. This boy who was only vaguely reminiscent of the boy we had once known took us across the sea. We felt the slippery, salt-smelling deck beneath our bare feet, the weight of that faceless child in our arms. We saw bloated storms over the Indian Ocean intent on nothing but our destruction, and we retreated into stinking holds so jammed full of people we couldn't even sit down.

'Then you get here.' His slide changed and now we saw one of Seadale's surf beaches. 'The best country in the world. And you know what happens? You've done all that, come all this way, and a bunch of men in suits are waiting for you. And you know what they say?'

There was a lull. Connor looked at me then back to the class. 'They tell you to *fuck off*.'

Every face in the room – aside from Connor's – turned to me. I didn't say a word. Again I thought there would be laughter, or perhaps applause, but instead there was silence. They saw in Connor's hard white lips and flat eyes that his declaration came from somewhere else entirely, some place Connor himself had perhaps only recently discovered.

'I reckon that's wrong. I reckon everyone deserves a second chance.'

I want to tell you a *Dead Poets Society* story. I want to tell you that Connor's speech was perfect, that it reduced the class to awed silence; I want to tell you that first one student began to clap, then another, and soon all of them were drumming their palms against the tables as they cheered.

Of course, that wouldn't be quite true.

The speech was good, but he had been forced to throw it together over just a few days. Occasionally during the presentation he became muddled and needed to search through his cue cards. He mispronounced the names of countries. A few times he apologised and said he needed to go back to a point that he had missed. When it was over I led the applause, and the class followed with a brief smattering of their own. We went on to the next presentation and the moment passed. Students resumed glancing at the clock, the cockatoos outside, the graffiti carved into the table by long-forgotten children now approaching middle age.

When the bell went I stopped Connor on his way out the door. He had another class to get to; there wasn't much time.

'Oh yeah,' he said before I had a chance to speak. 'Sorry about the profanity.'

'That's okay, mate. Audience and purpose. Sometimes you need stuff like that to break through the wall with these guys.'

'Reckon I did okay? All things considered?'

'Absolutely. I loved it. It had a lot of heart.'

He seemed surprised. 'Awesome! Thanks, sir.'

'Pleasure.'

The rest of the students had disappeared into the jabbering roar of the corridor. Connor moved to follow them but then stopped. 'I meant what I said, too. About that mum and all that.'

I nodded. 'I know you did.'

*

In the lead-up to the exams, Year 12 classes stopped running. The idea was to allow the students time to prepare in ways that best suited them. By that stage I had got my class to the point where most of them were able to consistently complete the required tasks under time pressure. They were as ready as they were ever likely to get.

A few days out from the exam itself, I held an optional revision session after school. It was really more of a morale booster for the kids. I brought along cake and soft drinks and most of them attended. One notable absence was Claire.

'Quick question.' I looked around the room before we made a start. 'Has anyone spoken with Claire lately? I haven't seen her around.'

Nobody had. It did not augur well but there was little more I could do. I had spoken with her, her mother and the Wellbeing Staff. Now it was just a matter of waiting for the big day.

The revision session proved to be a light-hearted affair.

We talked about Peter Carey's stories, but more in the manner of fans than students about to undertake a formal examination. I reminded the class that we were all there for a reason: because we loved books, and writing. That, I hoped, was why they had all signed up for the course. I told them to remember that and to try to enjoy the process as much as was possible. 'You've all got something to say,' I told them, 'and there's an examiner out there ready to listen. Take your passion for the stories and put it on the page.'

It was after five by the time we finished. Mya stayed to help clean up, carrying plates and mugs from the classroom to the staff kitchen and loading them into a dishwasher. When we were done she folded her arms and looked at me squarely.

'Mr Murray – I just have to ask. I'm ranked at the top of the class, right?'

I let out a long breath and smiled. 'What difference does it make? You're still going to walk into the exam and do your best. Your ranking shouldn't change anything.'

'I know that.' She closed her eyes. 'Look, this isn't an arrogance thing. I don't need to know that I've done better than anyone else. I just need –'

'Yes,' I said. 'Fine. You're ranked number one.'

'That's what I thought. And I'm scared. Because if I have a bad day on the exam, everyone else's results will get pushed down.'

'You're not going to have a bad day on the exam.'

'But what if I do?'

We walked to the carpark, talking the whole way. All I could do was remind Mya that she was ranked number one for a reason: because she worked hard, and had performed exceptionally on every task I had assigned, including those completed under time pressure. There was no reason to think the day of the examination would be any different.

'I just hope you're right, Mr Murray.' She climbed into her car and wound the window down. 'It's one thing to screw my own marks up. I don't want to affect anyone else's.'

'I promise that you'll be fine. Maybe take a day off studying. Go to the beach tomorrow or something.'

And I knew that she would be fine, that she was experiencing little more than last-minute jitters. I was less sure about Claire.

8

Running

FINALLY THE TREATMENT was finished. Kelvin had been walked to the precipice of his physical and mental endurance but had not fallen over the edge. Still, he felt that the boy he had once been was gone, replaced by an insubstantial ghost at risk of fading in even the weakest of sunlight.

'Good morning, Kelvin.' The nurses at the bigger hospital were brisk, direct. 'How are you feeling today?'

'Sick.' He would swallow, throat clicking dryly, eyes half-closed. 'But maybe a tiny bit better.'

'That's because the chemo part is done with.'

Soon they had thawed and then reinfused his healthy stem cells, which saturated his bone marrow and began producing new, clean blood. The improvement was far from miraculous but after a few days he was sitting up and getting himself to and from the toilet unaided. Next came three weeks of rehabilitation.

Sick as he was, Kelvin had spent months dreaming of returning to school. He knew that any possibility of regular attendance was a significant distance away, but thought he might be allowed in for a day, or even just half a day. It was about feeling normal as much as anything else. That brief period of respite at home had made him realise that, though his cure existed in the complexities of paediatric oncology, it existed *out there*, too; in conversations with his friends, in schoolwork, in parties, in rooms that didn't beep and in bathroom doors that opened inwards. He needed to escape.

Thinking in this way, Kelvin brought an athlete's mindset to his rehabilitation. The medical staff were coaches and he did everything they asked. He ate in spite of the nausea, strained, sweated and pushed himself, but rested when he needed to, understanding that the only thing worse than laziness was over-exertion. Lying in the dark with his eyes closed, he would feel that new blood thudding through him and *will* his body to heal, re-stitching its atrophied muscles and flushing clean the poisoned bone. There was an imaginary scoreboard somewhere and he sensed for the first time that the cancer could be losing. He imagined the tumours shrivelling like dead things left too long on the sun-hot boards of Seadale Pier.

At the end of the rehabilitation he was allowed to go home to continue his recovery. Part of that recovery, he decided, would be a day of attending classes at The School. Sue agreed.

'Only when you're ready, though.' She looked at Kelvin not only as a mother but as a nurse. 'It's no good getting ahead of yourself and winding up back in hospital.'

'For sure. But when you think about it, I wouldn't be doing much more than I do at home. I'd spend most of the day just sitting around.'

They talked about it, and after some more time recovering eventually agreed that he was ready. Sue informed The School and arrangements were put in place.

I remember when I first saw Kelvin again. I had just pulled

into the carpark and spotted him walking below the limp flags at The School's entrance. He was barely recognisable as the boy I had once taught. A purple, bloated face peered from beneath a beanie that seemed too large for his shrunken frame. We did not have English until the third period and I wondered if he would even make it that far. He was certainly the sickest child I had ever seen.

Heath and the rest of the boys were waiting for him long before the first period bell rang.

'Hey, Kelvin, awesome to see you, man.'

'Yeah. It's so good having you here.'

'Welcome back.'

He smiled, shook hands, accepted hugs and pats on the beanie. 'Thanks. How are The Spuds?'

'The Spuds are great.' Heath led the way towards the Year 8 locker area. 'We actually had a game in your honour.'

'What do you mean?'

'Check it out.'

He took out his phone and held up a photograph. It was of the team on court, blazing potatoes adorning their shirts, each of them with socks hitched almost to their knees.

'Gotta hand it to you, Kelvin,' Heath grinned, 'your socks are gravity-defying.'

They laughed as the crowd grew and locker doors squealed. Kelvin had been afraid that they would tiptoe around his perceived fragility; this early jibe was a relief. Heath would be the same old Heath and he would be the same old Kelvin. There would be no grace period for re-integration. He was in the real world again.

Still, waiting in that line as the bell tolled, he couldn't help but feel the other children watching him. Some would glance away the moment he turned, while others (usually students he didn't know) stared unashamedly from across the courtyard, their expressions a mix of pity, horror and dark fascination. He could almost hear what they wanted to ask but never would: Can you take off your beanie? Can I touch your head? What does chemo feel like? Are you still sick? Are you going to *die*?

Oh my *God*, he imagined girls whispering as they waited for their teachers. Did you see *Kelvin Lloyd*?

While some students stared, others in his own class seemed to have decided that not looking at all was the best solution. They sat rigid, eyes to the front, perhaps forewarned by well-meaning parents not to let their curiosity get the better of them. Kelvin decided that he would not begrudge any of his classmates. He had felt that way himself sometimes, especially during his early days on the ward when he saw the sickest children being wheeled through the corridors. They were strange and frightening and it was hard not to look. To judge his peers would have been to judge himself.

By the time he arrived at English, things had thawed. The class, I thought, felt very much the same as it always did. The talkers talked, the listeners listened, and everybody got on with their work. My approach was to keep things as normal as possible, not just for Kelvin but for the rest of the students as well. Though the Spuds boys had kept in touch with their friend and understood the seriousness of his condition, I knew there were other children who had probably thought little of Kelvin since writing their letters. I kept an eye on them all. For some, this would be their first confrontation with serious illness, certainly in a person so young. For others, Kelvin's presence could act as a reminder of a sick or dying grandparent, parent, even sibling.

I checked in on Kelvin towards the end of the lesson and asked him how his day was going.

'Yeah, good, sir.' Smiling up from beneath that beanie I thought his eyes looked very black, as though the pupils had swallowed the irises. 'I'm having a fun day, actually.'

'Fantastic. It's great having you back in class.'

The bell went and 8G headed to their next session before lunch: Physical Education.

They met at the stadium and had their names marked off, then walked across The School to the oval. It was an overcast day, cold, a gusty wind making strange swirling patterns in the uncut grass. Spread at intervals all around the perimeter of the oval were orange witches' hats.

'Boys and girls – let's start with some stretches.' Their PE teacher was young, her hair pulled back in a tight braid and a stopwatch strung around her neck. She was a relief teacher who did not ordinarily work at The School. 'First up, a supine leg stretch. Lie on your backs. The ground is nice and dry.'

Kelvin did as he was asked, feeling the first cramps of anxiety as he looked left and right at the rest of his class. Six months ago he was perhaps the strongest PE student in 8G, but now he felt uncertain, vulnerable. He pushed the feelings down and stared into the bright silver of the sky.

They did their stretches then assembled at the first witch's hat. The PE teacher needed to raise her voice over the wind.

'This is the twelve-minute run,' she shouted. 'What we're assessing is how far you can get in twelve minutes. We count it in laps and witches' hats. So, you might do one lap and three witches' hats, or three laps and one witch's hat. The hats are thirty metres apart.'

Kelvin looked at her and then across to the other side of the oval, where those hats shone a lurid orange against the damp grey of a beaten-down fence. It seemed an impossible distance away. His heart began to pound.

'I'll be timing,' she shouted.

Everyone began lining up at the first hat, the fittest students in front and the rest congregating behind. Kelvin hesitated, waiting for the teacher to say something, then mingled into the crowd. He was frightened, knew he should not be running, but stayed silent. Perhaps she had not been informed, he thought, or did not realise the seriousness of his condition. But how could she not see? He wore a beanie and had not a trace of eyebrows or lashes.

'Three . . . two . . . one . . .'

It was the final opportunity to speak but he did not.

Kelvin's fear ignited into a dull, obstinate anger. Suddenly – for reasons he didn't fully understand – he felt that he had a point to prove. To exactly *who* he wasn't sure; perhaps himself, perhaps his classmates, perhaps the universe that had conspired to put him in this absurd position.

There was a shout and he began to run.

One witch's hat passed, two, and already he was exhausted. Heath and the other boys jogged away. He watched Jen, the girl with whom he most liked to compete, recede into the distance. Even some of the slowest students began passing him. Kelvin pushed. The grass swished and swished as he went, tugging at his sneakers. Cockatoos screamed. He passed still more witches' hats. Nausea rose but he ignored it, putting one foot in front of the other. His chest began to ache. The margins of his vision buzzed with descending insects and he realised he was covered in sweat, utterly drenched so that his shirt clung to the corrugations of his ribcage. Impossibly, he looked up and realised he was close to completing one lap, the PE teacher standing by with the stopwatch in her hand.

He passed her and kept going.

I should stop, he thought. But he did not. His feet kept moving, one in front of the other in front of the other. Two forces warred within him: a fear that told him to rest, that he could be killing himself, and an anger that made him keep going. He did not understand that anger but he respected its strength. His bald head hung down and his arms flopped, rubbery, but he ran on. The nausea rose still further, the pain. More witches' hats passed. It was only a twelve-minute run. If he couldn't hold out for such a short amount of time, what good was he for anything?

The world began to bend and swim. He had no idea how many of those twelve minutes remained, and knew only that another witch's hat glowed ahead like a beacon. The grass felt longer with each step. Now it was at his knees; now his waist; now over his head, so that he ran blindly through a hissing gloom illuminated only by the next hat, and the next, and the next. Everything hurt.

Kelvin knew that he should stop, that he should never have come this far, should never have run in the first place. But he pushed on.

*

Ana and I sat in the office discussing the upcoming Year 12 examinations as though nothing in the world was more important.

'When's the Literature exam?' Ana had her plush Philosophy die and tossed it to me as she asked the question. It hit my palm.

'Next week.' I threw it back. 'When's English?'

'Only a couple of days now.'

I caught the die again. It went back and forth as we chatted.

'How do you think they'll go?'

'They'll get the results they deserve,' she said. 'Don't they say that's what usually happens?'

Just then came a series of quiet knocks. A Year 7 boy I did not recognise peered around the edge of the door. He had dreadlocks and each of his fingernails was coloured black with texta. Ana smiled.

'Well, well, well, Adrian. What can we do for you?'

'I need some sticky tape.'

'May I have some sticky tape *please* Ms Nikolic?'

'Can I please have some tape, Miss Nik?'

Ana looked at me. 'What do you think, Mr Murray? Should we allow this young man access to our precious sticky tape? Or should there be some cost?'

'A small cost, surely.'

'I agree.' She handed him her die. 'We make all the kids do this. Throw the die.'

He looked at me and I nodded. 'Yep. Hard as you can. You won't break anything.'

The boy thought for a moment, shrugged, then sent the die bouncing around the little office. It struck one wall, then another, knocked over a cup of pens then came to rest alongside my foot. We all looked down.

'*Who?*' I read in the most dramatic voice I could muster. 'It's all yours, Miss Nik.'

She looked at him. 'Here's how this works, Adrian. We ask you a question. You have to answer it honestly. Then I'll roll the die and you can ask me a question so it's fair. *Then* you get your sticky tape.'

He was smiling faintly now, as almost all students did when we played this game. 'Sure.'

'*Who*,' Ana asked, 'do you look up to more than anyone else?'

He touched his chin, stared at the die. 'Me nan.'

'Why?'

'Because she, like, works hard and that. And she never complains about nothing. And she's nice to me and me brothers.'

'A beautiful answer,' Ana said. 'Mr Murray, pass me the die.'

I did, and the moment it was in her hand she tossed it at the boy. He ducked, grinning broadly now. It struck the door behind him and rebounded off his dreadlocks.

'Ick.' I made a face. 'We're going to have to disinfect it now.'

'Fair go, sir!'

Ana pointed to the die then looked at Adrian and raised her eyebrows.

'It's *Why*,' he said.

'There you have it.' I sat back and waited. 'The die has spoken.'

He picked it up and thought. 'Why are you a teacher here, Miss Nik? Like, at The School?'

'Because the kids are nice. And the teachers care and have real passion. And each morning when I drive to work I get to look at the sea.'

'Good answer, Miss.'

'Thanks. Now make sure this tape comes back at lunchtime.'

He left and we kept tossing that die back and forwards.

'My biggest worry about the Year 12 Literature exam is Claire,' I said. 'It's been a hard road for her. Pretty much since Year 7. And now all this pressure . . . It isn't *good* for her, you know?'

'I know. But you've done everything *you* can.'

I caught the die, threw it back again. 'I just hope she's happy at the end of all this. Screw the results.'

'Yeah. Screw the results and the rankings and the ATAR scores. Let's just turn them all into Adrian's grandma. She sounds like a legend.'

'Totally.'

She threw the die and it bounced off my hand, ricocheting across the room to pose some new question to the universe.

*

The twelve minutes ended. A faint voice screamed over the wind.

'That's it! Count your laps and the witches' hats you've passed from the first!'

Kelvin stopped on the far side of the oval, bent at the waist, hands on his knees. He was sick and sore and exhausted. Now that he was still, he feared that if he tried to move again he would collapse. Blood roared in his ears. He waited, and slowly the world came back into focus: the green of the grass, his sneakers, his shins thin and pale as poured milk.

'I'll write your results!'

There was a moment when he thought he would cry. What if he had done something to himself in those last twelve minutes, set everything back – or worse? He pinched his eyes closed, then snapped them open again to escape the strange colours swirling there. No; he would not cry. He would stand up straight, march across the oval and have his distance recorded along with everyone else.

The PE teacher stood in the distance holding her clipboard with a queue of students before her. For a moment Kelvin worried that somebody would notice him all alone and away from the group, but then he saw other students too, some straggling and some skylarking. One boy marched along the oval's perimeter holding a branch twice the length of his body.

Kelvin hobbled back, focused on not passing out, then had his distance recorded.

He spent the rest of the day dragging himself from class to class. He was utterly spent. It was the most tired he had felt since the chemotherapy itself. As much as he had wanted to come to school (had dreamt about it, in fact, waking disappointed to the reality of the hospital) he was now desperate to get home. His friends did not seem to notice, joking with him in voices he could sometimes hear and sometimes not. The classroom clocks with their slow-moving hands reminded him of the ward, and the sight of them made him want to cry once more. They seemed accusatory, almost. He felt guilty.

When at last the final bell tolled, he made it to his mother's car and all but fell into her arms.

9

I know you can hear me

THE DAY OF the Literature exam I drove to school early. The bay was dark but the waves were gilded with the first coppery light of dawn. The examination was at eleven forty-five, but I knew students would come in well before that and I wanted to be there for them.

For the most part I worried about Claire. I knew what today meant to her. Paradoxically, her love of Literature was in danger of making this her most difficult examination. She was a passionate writer and reader, and as such her sense of self was threatened by the possibility of a bad result. It did not matter how many times I reminded her of Peter Carey's confessed insecurity, or insisted that examinations were unnatural environments that largely assessed an individual's ability to cope with stress. Nothing about today would be easy for her.

When I arrived I went straight to the Year 12 Study Centre. Mya, Tim and a handful of others appeared soon afterwards.

'Mr Murray?' Mya was in full uniform, a clear ziplock bag of pens clutched in one hand. 'I have a feeling "The Chance" will be on the exam. Do you think I should spend the morning reading it again?'

A teacher's job on exam day is to reassure the students and keep them calm. 'How many times have you read it?'

'I don't know. Heaps. Over and over.'

'Then I don't think you need to read it again.'

Tim smiled and nodded. 'Yeah. You'll smash it, Mya. Know what I did before I got here, Doc?'

'Went surfing?'

'Bingo.'

We all joked, chatted about the books, brushed up on essay-writing strategies. When eleven o'clock came and the nervous energy began to build, I suggested a walk. Claire still had not arrived.

We made our slow way around the perimeter of The School, studying the landscape that had hemmed in the last six years of their lives. There is always a sense of nostalgia around the end of Year 12, and it began to manifest. They told stories of Year 7, of students who had dropped out years before, of teachers loved and loathed. It was a good distraction.

'Remember,' I said when we got back to the Study Centre. 'You've done this a hundred times before. This time you just have to do it in the hall with some nice old ladies keeping an eye on you.'

I am always half-sick with worry on exam day, something that is partly rational and partly absurd. I worry that an error on the paper will destabilise my students (one year, a laser-wielding robot was accidentally included alongside socialist revolutionaries on a History exam); I worry that I have taught the wrong course (completely irrational, but I ponder this every year); I worry that I have got my ranking wrong; I worry in a general sense for the wellbeing of my students. I want more than anything for them to be happy, and fear that, at the end of the day, some may not be. I worry that I have not done enough.

'It's eleven-thirty.' Mya stood, resolute. 'I think we should head to the hall.'

We stood outside in the sun, squinting at a board that showed where everybody would be sitting. The stragglers started to appear. The very last was Claire. She stayed back from the crowd, sitting on a lonely bench across the asphalt. I was about to approach her when the hall door opened and one of the supervisors appeared, a woman of perhaps seventy with a kind, tired face.

'Year 12 Literature? Everyone make sure you have your student cards ready. No labels on drink bottles. Pens and pencils in clear bags only.'

I wished all the students well as they disappeared into the hall. Claire was the last. I put a hand on her shoulder and smiled.

'Good luck, Claire. You've got this.'

She turned to me but seemed only to half register that I was there. The door clicked shut and for the first time that year they were truly on their own. I had no choice but to let them go.

That day, though, something made me stay. I lingered in the quiet sunshine, not wanting to return to my office and the rest of the day's work. A warm spring wind blew. The cockatoos were in that elm tree again, riding the slender branches and fanning their crests. I watched them for a while and then checked my watch. It was ten to twelve; that meant the students were five minutes into 'reading time'. At midday, their two hours of writing would commence.

Then the hall door slammed open.

I turned, knowing already who it would be. Claire came stumbling out, choking, crying, almost vomiting. She managed only the two or three steps to me before collapsing at my feet.

I knelt, told her that it was going to be okay.

*

Sitting on that bench outside the hall in the minutes before the exam, Claire had suddenly been struck by a sense that she was not prepared.

It did not matter that she was a poet, so passionate about language that she sometimes dreamt in words; it did not matter that she had read the Literature texts more times than she could count; it did not matter that she had written practice essay after practice essay; it did not matter that she had spent hours listening to my optional Literature podcasts. None of it mattered. The exam wasn't really an assessment of competence but a ranking against the rest of the state. In that context, how could she *ever* be prepared?

In five years it won't matter. The thought calmed her, but just for a moment. She repeated it to herself over and over. *In five years it won't matter. In five years it won't matter.*

Then, in the distance, the hall door whined open and the rest of the students started walking inside. It was real. The countdown had ended.

She knew how the system worked. If she screwed up the exam, the marks she had achieved throughout the year would be downgraded on the assumption she had been marked too kindly. Her final Literature result was supposed to be determined through a fifty-fifty split of classwork and the exam, but she knew what really mattered. The external assessment was the only thing the bureaucrats and their algorithms trusted.

Never mind that the people marking the exams were overworked and (rumour had it) correcting so many papers they could spend only a few minutes on each one.

As she walked across the asphalt a new voice spoke: *It's a competition. You have to win.*

The darkness of the hall closed over her. High on the brown walls, pennants celebrated netball wins from decades ago. Steel cages protected the windows. The place smelt of dust and was cold despite the warmth of the morning. The tables were separated.

Claire sat down. A square of folded paper under one leg of her chair stopped it from wobbling.

The supervisor announced something, her voice echoing. Then came the bird-wing flutter of paper and Claire realised reading time had commenced. A new silence descended on the hall. Her throat tightened and she opened the exam booklet.

Something was wrong. The pages were unreadable. Snails had crawled over them in the dark, chewing at the letters so the whole thing was reduced to cipher.

Time lunged forward then slowed again. Her hands went cold and started to tingle. She squinted at the unreadable examination. What she was seeing wasn't real, she knew. The pages were fine. The text was about the same books she had studied all year, the books she had sweated over, deconstructed, loved. And that was the worst of it. For an instant the words came into focus but then they were gone again, swept away in an appalling surge of hot adrenaline that crushed the air from her lungs as surely as if the roof had slammed flatly down upon her.

Claire's throat seized, she was choking, but she couldn't speak. *Someone*, she thought, *someone, please notice me and let me out.* She thought the fear might recede but it did not, doubling and doubling in a feedback loop that shrieked through her head. She realised she was gasping. *Someone, save me. I know you can hear me.*

The supervisor was at her shoulder, huge glasses and sickly soap scents. 'What's wrong, sweetheart?'

But she did not know what was wrong. Choking, dying, she ran.

*

I crouched beside Claire as she gasped, coughed and cried. 'It's alright,' I whispered. 'You'll be okay. It doesn't matter.'

The supervisor appeared at the door, peering down at this crying girl with the same sad, tired face I had seen earlier.

'I'll look after her,' I said.

After some coaxing, Claire was able to get off the ground and hobble with me back to the bench she had sat on earlier. After a few minutes she was able to speak.

'Mr Murray.' Her eyes were filled with tears. 'Why can't I do it? Why can't I?'

I knelt in front of her. 'It doesn't matter, Claire. The exam is just a hoop they want you to jump through. This has got *nothing* to do with you as a Literature student. You've been amazing all year. You're an amazing writer.'

By chance, a teacher named Eleanor passed by. Like me, she had known Claire for years. She reiterated my words, telling her how well she had done just making it this far.

We stayed at that bench for some time with Claire bent over, her head cradled in her hands. I realised younger students were watching us from the window of a nearby portable and turned to Eleanor.

'I'll take her back to my office,' I said. 'Can you ask the Head of the Senior School to come over?'

Dozens of students' eyes followed us as we crossed the patchwork asphalt, which bulged in places where the roots of trees proved their strength against the thin surfaces of The School.

As soon as we got inside, Claire sat on the couch and closed her eyes, holding herself. When she spoke, her voice was barely audible. 'They're going to make me go back in.'

'Nobody's going to make you do anything. Just do what's right for you. I'll support you either way.'

She looked at me, uncertain, and then I began to speak. I knew that the student–teacher barrier divided us, but I also knew that now was a time for honesty. I told her that I understood how she felt. I told her about my own panic attacks, the times I had gone to hospital thinking I was dying, the days when even getting out of bed felt impossible. I told her of the months of school I missed as a little boy, and of the university courses I had pulled out of again and again, not really understanding why. But I told her, too, that I was now happy, and that whatever she was feeling in that horrible moment, she would be happy again, too.

The Head of the Senior School was a gently spoken PE teacher about my age. When she arrived, she explained that she had already telephoned the VCAA and told them what had happened.

'They said you are allowed to go back in and sit the exam,' she said, 'even in a separate room by yourself. We can use the office beside the sick bay. You'll need to be supervised by somebody other than Mr Murray – a non-Literature teacher. But you have to decide in the next few minutes. I'll leave you to think for a bit then come back.'

By that stage Claire's breathing had calmed and she had stopped crying. 'What do you think I should do, Mr Murray?'

'I think you need to look into yourself and do what feels right,' I said. 'You shouldn't be pressured. Not by me, or the VCAA, or anyone else.'

'There's a part of me that really wants to do it.'

I nodded, considered for a moment. 'They won't let me into the room. But there's nothing stopping me waiting outside. If you go in and then need to come straight back out, I'll be there. I'll sit there for the whole thing.'

She wore no make-up and the tears had dried cleanly on her pale face. 'You sure?'

'Definitely. And you won't have lost anything. In fact –' and here I remembered Connor and his persuasive profanity, '– if you go in and then come out again, who really gives a shit?'

She thought for a moment, eyes downcast, then looked at me and nodded. 'I want to do it.'

Together we walked to the small office beside the sick bay at the front of the school. The Head of the Senior School was there with Eleanor, who had agreed to supervise.

'Thanks, Mr Murray.' Claire's voice now was completely level. She smiled and disappeared into that little room.

Hers was one of the greatest acts of resilience and fortitude that I had seen at The School. No results from the VCAA assessors could ever measure the magnitude of her accomplishment. Any data would be powerless in the face of her courage.

In my first interview for a teaching position, I said that teaching is a career of the heart and mind in equal measure. It has taken me a decade to realise how wrong I was.

After an hour and a half of sitting outside that door like a security guard, I realised two things: first, that Claire was not going to have another panic attack; and second, that the rest of the class was about to finish the exam.

I jogged across The School and reached the hall just as the doors were opening and the others were spilling out into the sunlight. When they saw me they gathered around in a laughing, chattering mob. I knew they had gone well.

'Now, before I say anything, I want to talk about Claire – I know you'll be really worried about her.' They nodded, their giggling relief suppressed for a moment. 'She's fine. The VCAA let her finish the exam and she's doing it right now in a spare office. You'll be able to catch her when she gets out in about half an hour.'

When I returned to the office Claire still had some time left. I waited, watching the clock, then at last the door opened. She was smiling.

'How did it go?'

Her eyes shone. 'I think it went pretty well, Mr Murray.'

We walked up the corridor and I stopped where it forked, one passage leading towards the Study Centre and the other back towards my office. 'Now go catch up with your friends. And have a study-free afternoon.'

'I will. And thanks, Mr Murray. For looking after me.'

I told her it was a privilege.

*

Claire's very human moment of courage was to be tainted by a flavour of bureaucratic interference. The exam supervisor filled out an 'incident report'. Of particular note was the insistence that no other students had been affected by what happened (not that they were asked). The system moved quickly and reflexively to defend itself from future claims of disadvantage.

This is often a mantra amongst bureaucrats when things go wrong on examinations, from major, traumatic interruptions to the accidental teaching of incorrect courses: *No student has been disadvantaged.*

And perhaps that's true. But there is always an impact, and often one that cannot be numerically quantified.

Mya had been sitting two tables across from Claire that day. When the timer started she had opened her exam paper and begun to read, tingling with a kind of terrified excitement that she knew would soon abate. She was a good student. She was suited to exams. Before long, her pen would be dancing.

Then she heard shallow, rasping breaths somewhere to her right.

Turning from the exam she saw tears spilling down Claire's face. It sounded as if she was going to throw up. The exam supervisor came to her side and the next moment she was running from the hall, feet slamming on the lacquered boards as she sobbed.

In that moment, Mya had only one desire: to go after her friend and comfort her. She had known Claire for years and knew that she had not always been happy, that things had sometimes been hard for her in ways that nobody would ever fully understand. Mya half-turned, rising from her chair but then stopped. A voice that was only partially her own spoke: *Don't focus on Claire now. This is more important.*

So she turned back to her paper and got to work.

After the exam was over, when I had met the class and reassured them all that Claire was fine, Mya had been stricken with a combination of guilt and shame. In the fleeting instant when her friend had run from the hall, Mya felt she had prioritised the examination over compassion. She thought about this for a long time. Had she turned her back on Claire because she knew somebody else would be there for her? No. She had no idea what lay out in the empty schoolyard. Mya had simply decided that the examination was more important than caring for her friend.

She felt that the Year 12 system had stolen one of the better parts of herself.

10

Just another fight

EACH TIME CHARLIE stepped into the ring he knew that, in a sense, he was there alone – or, at least, not *quite* facing whichever opponent was trying to knock him down. The jabs, crosses, hooks and uppercuts (whether dealt or received) concealed a more complex reality: he was in the ring with his past and his possible future, and that was why he would always win.

Or so he hoped. The title fight would be like no other bout of his amateur career. Garvey's record was as impressive as his own and there wasn't a chance that the belt would come easy. And if the fight was something more than a fight, then a loss would be something more than a loss. Charlie didn't like to think about that.

On the flight to Sydney his coach had gone over the basics for perhaps the tenth time.

'There's gonna be thirty matches on the night, mate – first amateurs, then the pros.' They were crammed into economy, surrounded for the most part by bored men and women in business attire. 'You'll be the very last of the amateurs. So there's gonna be a bit of a wait.'

Charlie stretched his legs into the aisle, tried to get comfortable. 'That's cool. I'll watch some of the fights.'

'No. Do what you usually do. Read one of your books.'

'Why?'

His coach half-glared at him, a look enhanced by the oily ponytail, sloping nose and coin-slot mouth. 'Because it's just another bloody fight.'

That was the mantra Charlie had been hearing for weeks. Sometimes he even started to believe it.

'The belt is up for grabs,' his coach continued. 'Fine. But there's also a prize for the "fighter of the night". That's a crowd favourite. There'll be a whole lot of hoo-ha, but remember – it really is just another fight. None of the bullshit going on outside the ring counts for shit.'

The first nerves came the day before the bout when Charlie met his opponent for the weigh-in. It was Garvey's coach he saw first, a scrawny man with deep lines in his cheeks and a neck so dark with tattoos that his face hovered above it with a strange pallor.

Charlie was wearing nothing but his jocks and a gold crucifix. He leaned over to his own coach. 'Creepy dude.'

'You don't need to worry about fighting him.'

Garvey was almost half a head taller than Charlie, tattooed, with short bleached hair gelled into spikes. He had a reputation as a show-boater, but that day he didn't utter a word. In fact, Charlie noticed, he barely even made eye contact with him. They were weighed then photographed together, each holding one end of the championship belt.

That night Charlie lay on top of the covers of his motel bed. The room was dominated by exposed brick and smelt of old carpet and deodoriser. Motorbikes roared from the highway as a muted television showed disasters both local and foreign.

Closing his eyes, he thought of home.

What would Tia be doing at that moment? Xavier? Rachel? Mr Murray and Miss Khatri and the librarians with whom he often laughed and joked for the whole of lunchtime? A part of him wished they could be there for the bout, but another part (elusive, troubling) recoiled from the thought. The more he tried to make sense of that feeling, the more it evaded him. As he drifted to sleep he wondered if he was afraid of showing them a part of himself of which he was not entirely proud.

*

Before coming to Sydney, all Charlie's fights had taken place in gymnasiums and town halls. As he walked into the hotel the following evening, he was confronted by an atmosphere unlike anything he had experienced.

His coach put an arm around him and patted his shoulder. 'Remember, mate. It's just another fight.'

The ring had been set up in the centre of a room that dwarfed even the largest town halls in which he had fought. Spot-lamps shone from a vertiginous roof, and all around the space were tables – hundreds, perhaps – crammed with people talking, shouting, drinking. Already there was the smell of beer and cigarettes, and a sound system eliminated almost any chance of conversation. Every now and then a commentator stepped into the bright white of the ring, his voice a crackling boom. Names rattled out, including Garvey's and his own. Then Charlie saw some of the professional kickboxers in the crowd.

'Hey, coach! Check it out.'

'I know. You can grovel for autographs later. For now it's just another –'

'Yeah.' Charlie rolled his neck. 'I get it.'

The amateur fights started, and Charlie had no intention of reading the book he had in his gym bag. He watched, studying the punches and the kicks and sometimes raising his hands above his head and clapping along with the crowd. This was a moment like no other and he was intent on experiencing it. His coach's mindset might help him win, but it could make him miss the moment, too. Currents of energy seemed to hum through that huge noisy space, generated by the crowd, the music, the occasion. From time to time one of those currents would surge through him, making the hair on his arms stand on end. At such moments fear was impossible. This is the *Australian Title*, he almost whispered to himself. Everything had led to this moment.

When his own fight drew close, Charlie and his coach retreated into a small room guarded by a pair of skin-headed bouncers.

'Don't worry about the height difference.' His coach knelt before him as he sat in a hard plastic chair. 'You've got Garvey. You've got him on speed and cardio. You've trained harder than any of these fuckers. Just ignore all this bullshit pomp and ceremony and get out there and do what you do.'

'And it's just another fight, right?'

'Nothin' more. That belt isn't even good for keeping your bloody pants up.'

Charlie walked out into the blinding darkness and he let it come: the anger. From where exactly he wasn't sure, but it first trickled, then welled and then drove him with a leap into the ring itself. Garvey was there, and the referee with his neat bow tie. All around them the crowd was like some great drunk wave that never stopped breaking. He pushed his mouthguard in with his thumb and tried to block it out. His coach's voice came from somewhere below and behind.

'You've got him, Charlie.'

Then the first round started and Garvey attacked. Charlie felt the punches thudding into him and knew instantly that his opponent was stronger than he was, capable of throwing strikes that he could not. He grimaced, raised his arms and felt the elasticity of the ropes at his back as those gloves smacked into his arms and shoulders. Charlie threw some punches of his own, swung through air, was pushed back once more. Garvey's strategy was clear: he had no intention of a points victory and wanted only to knock Charlie unconscious as soon as possible.

Just as he thought this, Charlie took his first hit to the face, a glancing blow that snapped his head back and had him off balance for an instant. He paused, took stock and again Garvey was belting into him, aiming low now to draw his guard down. Charlie saw the uppercut coming and stepped back, anger faltering. He could hear his coach yelling but couldn't make out any of the words.

Okay. He spoke to himself frankly. *If it's all going to be like this, I'm in trouble.*

Charlie punched, missed again, took still more hits. He was able to block a few but Garvey's reach complicated things, the slight downslope of his blows forcing Charlie into awkward defensive postures.

The bell rang and the first round was over.

Charlie retreated to his corner and flopped down, his coach squirting water into his mouth but then taking him by the chin and directing his gaze towards Garvey. 'Look at him, Charlie!'

'He's good.'

'Yeah, he's good, but look at his *breathing*. You've got him like a fucken steam train.'

He saw it. In his wild determination to end the bout with a quick knockout, Garvey had exhausted himself. His lungs were heaving, his face contorted. Charlie felt a flair of excitement, then the anger returned. He wasn't breathless in the slightest and knew he would still be going strong even if they went all the way to five rounds.

The second round was completely unlike the first. Garvey played for time, trying to get his breath back, but Charlie would not let him. He kept advancing, head lowered and gloves raised, and was soon giving his opponent the same thrashing he had endured himself in the first round.

The bell rang.

'That's it, Charlie! He's buggered. You keep doing that and he doesn't have a hope.'

Charlie fought, advancing and swinging and never tiring, a hot wind of anger at his back. When he threw kicks his legs felt almost weightless, yet when they struck Garvey's ribs his opponent winced and staggered and tried to regroup. But Charlie would not let him. He pushed him into the ropes, they clinched, then the moment the referee separated them he forced him back again. Once he hit him hard enough that he thought Garvey would go down, but when he didn't he was almost pleased: it meant he could keep fighting, keep letting out the anger that pulsed inside him like an overcharged battery. It all started to click. The crowd faded, then his coach's voice, then the ring, then eventually Garvey himself. Charlie was alone, beating back some undefined force that he knew couldn't ever really be defeated (not in the ring, anyhow); after this victorious night it would recede for a while but then gather its strength again, reforming, reshaping, lurking on the periphery of everything Charlie did until he had no choice but to fight it once more, hoping that one day it might stay down forever.

The fifth round ended and Charlie came back. He and Garvey patted one another on the back. There was a lull, a checking of the score, then the two fighters were in the centre of the ring with the referee between them. The PA crackled.

'*The winner of the A-Class Australian Title, by unanimous verdict –*'

Charlie felt his arm being raised, then the belt on his shoulder, then his coach hugging him and lifting him from his feet. What came next was a euphoric dream: a thousand handshakes from the crowd, offerings of phone numbers from promoters, congratulations from professional fighters he had watched on television and who were now insisting that he was ready to go pro.

Once his adrenaline dropped and he had finished his warm-down, Charlie turned to his coach. 'I'll be back. Give me five mins.'

Getting back-slapped and hair-ruffled the entire way, he pushed through the crowd to the bar. When he arrived the crowd parted, men and women looking at him with a respect he had never experienced before. The congratulations kept coming and he lost count of the number of times he had said thank you, thank you, thank you. Finally he ordered a beer, though he had never drunk a drop of alcohol in his life. Careful not to spill any, he went searching for Garvey.

The crowd was loud and drunk and chaotic. As he moved

from table to table, people patted and grasped at him, sending the beer running sticky down his arm. His smile had become a grimace. Nobody seemed to know where Garvey had gone. After what felt like a very long time Charlie finally spotted the pallid face and tattooed neck of his opponent's coach. The man congratulated Charlie and told him that Garvey had gone outside for some air.

Compared to the hot raucousness of the hotel, the carpark was cold and still. Charlie looked at the beer and swore. More than half of it was gone. He was considering going back for a replacement when he saw his opponent squatting in a garden beyond the glow of the streetlights. He had not seen Charlie.

Garvey's hands were planted on the cigarette-strewn tan bark and his head was lowered. All at once he was sick, coughing and spitting and snorting. Charlie took a step towards him then hesitated, tipped out the beer and went back inside.

When he told his coach what he had seen, he just laughed. 'Leave him to himself. Let him have some dignity in defeat.'

Charlie did as he was told, and spent the next hours watching the professional bouts. Those currents of energy persisted, but now there was a flatness beneath it all, a strange and niggling discomfort. He thought of his father, of his coach's laugh which he had no desire to share. He thought of that beer he had bought, every last drop of it either spilled on the floorboards or tipped onto the garden.

But he had won. He had trained, he had worked and he had achieved his goal. He would allow himself this moment.

When the night grew late and the last fight ended, the judges were ready to announce their choice for the best bout of the evening. Charlie stood waiting, fingers drumming on the great gold plate fronting his belt.

'*When the fight is announced, make sure to fill out your voting slip.*' The voice through the speakers had an almost ringleader quality. '*You choose your fighter. Could be for an impressive win or a noble loss. Crowd favourite.*'

Charlie almost couldn't believe it when the speakers boomed the answer: the *A-Class Australian Title, Blanco versus Garvey.* He gaped at his coach.

'Don't get your hopes up,' he said as they prepared for the announcement. 'Garvey's the local boy. And he did fight well.'

But the crowd had seen something in Charlie, perhaps in his comeback following the first round, perhaps in his athleticism, perhaps in the rumour that the first thing he did after his victory was buy Garvey a beer. Whatever the case, it became Charlie's night.

Later though, on the flight home, his mind kept returning to the image of his opponent vomiting in that lonely carpark, defeated, doubled over, broken by Charlie's own hands.

11

Parting ways

STEVE DIED SOMETIME after Kelvin's agonising twelve-minute run around The School's oval. He did not know precisely when. It had been a while since he was a regular on the ward, and despite the intensity of the boys' brief closeness they had never exchanged numbers. In some strange way, though, Kelvin felt that he had known, as though his subconscious had sensed his friend's new and final absence.

Shortly after his trial day back at school, Heath had invited him to a Saturday night party. Despite feeling ill, he had been determined to go, and to enjoy himself. Beanie pulled down close to his eyes, he had rung the doorbell and lingered nervously on the step, shooing away his mother, who still waited with the engine idling. He needn't have felt self-conscious. One of the first people he saw when he walked through to the backyard was Margaret.

'Hey, Kelvin – lookin' good!' Like him she wore a beanie despite the improving weather, and her forehead was smooth and white where her brows should have been. 'But are you *feeling* good?'

'Better. Still shitty, but better. The doctors say the treatment is working.'

She hugged him and they sat talking as the evening settled in and more children arrived. Music played and a barbecue sizzled. Kelvin watched as a few members of The Spuds took turns shooting three-pointers at a backyard ring.

'Did you hear about Steve?'

As soon as Margaret asked the question Kelvin felt a weary sadness descend over him. He knew what she was going to say and felt little surprise. It had been a long time since he had seen Steve or even heard his name mentioned, whether by his mother, his doctor or the staff during the few times he had been back to the hospital. Watching his friends throwing that ball through the fading light, he let Margaret tell him that he had lost his battle a little while ago, and that the ward wasn't the same now that he was gone.

'Funny,' Kelvin said, realising he had deceived himself for months about how sick Steve really was. 'He was so *quiet*. Or calm maybe.'

'Yeah. He was a presence, though. Guess I talked enough for everyone.'

Kelvin would never forget what Steve had done for him simply through his openness to friendship with a younger patient. Often he thought of those hours they spent playing video games together. In later years he would occasionally see kids playing *FIFA* on an old Xbox and remember. For them and so many others it was just a video game, but for him it was a window back to that brief period when he and a friend had used it as a distraction before parting ways.

That night at the party, Kelvin's sadness was tempered with gratitude.

*

On the final day of Term Four, we ended the last period early to allow students time to clear out their lockers. Next year they would move to another part of The School and be allocated new ones. At each year level, coordinators filled locker areas with recycle bins and asked teachers to help with supervision.

I stood in the sun in the middle of the Year 8 locker area as the bell went and students poured from the classrooms. Laughing, screaming kids were soon wrenching armloads of books and worksheets from their lockers. Papers blew across the asphalt. A few forgotten sandwiches appeared, mouldering beneath bloated cling wrap.

A boy whose name I did not know approached the bin beside me and dumped an entire Mathematics textbook inside. I reached in and retrieved it.

'Why are you throwing this out, mate?'

'Going inta Year 9. Don't need it.'

'Couldn't your parents try to sell it?'

But he was gone, running through air already warm with summer and the imagined chords of the carnival. There was no point going after him so I set the book aside for donation to the Wellbeing Department. Next year there would be plenty of families in Seadale who lacked the money to buy all the textbooks their children would need.

Ana wandered by on her way to another part of The School. 'Another lot gone?'

'Yep.'

'You coming to the Year 12 graduation tonight?'

'Of course.'

The lockers were dented and grey, with vents on the doors and thick steel rings for padlocks. A few had rust on the hinges. I supposed they could have been thirty or forty years old. Just then a memory leapt at me: I was perhaps fourteen, and at the end of a summer day I had stood too quickly without looking and hit my head on the underside of an open locker door. Decades later and I winced, almost felt it. Once again I had a sense that the past was so close I could reach out and touch it. I walked across the courtyard to look over the students' shoulders into the lockers. Many had insides scratched with graffiti and plastered with faded stickers. They were cartoon characters, surf logos, bands to which these students' parents had once listened.

'Hi, Mr Murray.'

I looked down and it was Grace. She was scooping the last crumpled scraps of paper from her locker. I took them from her so she could move out into the centre of the courtyard. The pages, I saw, were four terms of incomplete, disorganised work tasks, from Mathematics to English to Humanities. One was a map of Europe with Italy highlighted, and I held this up to her. 'I can speak some Italian,' I said.

'No you can't!'

'Pizza. Spaghetti. Ferrari.'

She smirked. 'Oh, Mr *Murr*ay.'

I pointed to the art portfolio under her arm. 'Going to do a lot of drawing over the summer?'

'I'm getting pencils for Christmas.'

'That's perfect. I'm proud of what you've done this year. Have a lovely holiday, Grace.'

'You too. Thank you.'

I watched her leave. If this were a novel, I would tell you that Grace's strengths eclipsed her weaknesses in the adult world, that she found her place. If I wanted to push it further, risk the reader's suspension of disbelief, I might even describe some future art exhibition or painting sale. None of this, of course, would be true. Grace was a wonderful illustrator, but what she really needed was the aide that she never received because she did not qualify for funding. The School did the best we could in the following years, by hook or by crook: we put her in classes with funded students so the aides could be shared; we gave her all the class time we could spare; we gifted resources to her family; and, of course, we retreated to the time-worn teacher strategy of working for free, tutoring Grace during lunchtimes and recesses and for long hours after school. Our work gave her a protective standard of literacy, but it was not the standard she deserved or what her parents' tax dollars should have provided. Wherever she is now, I can only apologise on behalf of a system that let her down.

The Year 8s cleared out quickly, so I headed across The School to the Year 9 area. I soon found Teagan and Jada preparing to leave. Both were wearing all their make-up again. It saddened me, but there had been that moment, at least, when they were just two kids watching *Shrek*. And who was I to say? What would I ever truly understand of their lives and experiences? My views, I thought, were probably far more superficial than that make-up. It was a ritual for them, an armour perhaps, and we all need our rituals and our armour. I made no mention of it.

'What are you doing over the summer, sir?' Teagan removed the last of the books from her locker. 'A heap of partying?'

'Ha! If you count reading a heap of books as partying.'

'That's cool. Whatever makes you happy, sir.'

We chatted for a few minutes before being interrupted by a shout from across the yard. Connor ran over, his backpack so heavy he was almost bent over at the waist.

'*Sir!*' His face glistened with sweat under the lank red hair. 'I was looking for you.'

Before I could say anything he had slapped something into my hand and was gone. When I looked, it was a piece of lined paper, folded over about eight times to the size of a matchbox. Written on the front in biro was *Mr Murry*. I showed it to the girls.

'A year of teaching this kid. You'd think he could have learnt how to spell my name.'

Teagan smiled. 'Yeah. I think he's grown up a lot this year, though.'

'I agree.'

'I remember when he apologised about that cake-face thing. I mean, he really meant it. Like, *really* meant it. He felt bad. You could tell.'

I put the note in my pocket. 'I saw him change a lot. I think he's going to be a pretty decent young guy before too long. Sounds cheesy, but he has a heart.'

'Yeah. That's probably why the other guys give him a hard time.'

'What do you mean?'

She hefted her bag onto her back. 'They're his friends. Well, sort of. But he's just . . . Different from them. He isn't like the other boys. So he's always kind of on the outside. Like when they play basketball. He's always the one just sitting and watching. I'm not saying they bully him, but . . . I dunno.'

'I've never noticed.'

'It is what it is. Have a nice summer, sir. Thanks for letting us watch *Shrek*.'

I was genuinely stunned by Teagan's revelation about Connor. I never saw a hint that he was an outsider and in fact saw plenty of evidence suggesting the opposite. He was the ringleader, the class clown, even if that had reduced somewhat since the beginning of the year. In that moment I was reminded of how little we often know of the lives of the children for whom we care, sometimes even the children we raise.

I forgot about that scrap of paper until later that night when I was getting ready for the Year 12 graduation. It narrowly avoided disappearing into the wash. Unfolding it and flattening it on the table, I read Connor's scrawled pencil note:

Thank you for being supportive of me in English. Before this year i had a conpletly diffrent view of the subject, but i'm glad it changed and that is because of you. If I did'nt have you this year im pretty sure I would still hate English. You were easily the best teacher this year. Thank you for putting up with my crap because I know I wasnt the best student (especially at the start of the year). I wish I could of bought you a gift but I did'nt have the money sorry. I hope you understand. Anyway because of you my best work was in English and I can truthfully say I was trying my hardest in English. But this is where I stop writting and this is where I say thank you. I really hope Im in your class again someday.

I've kept that note and always will. It helps sometimes, on the difficult days. It also reminds me that no child is ever quite what they appear, especially those who can be the most frustrating. When I have a new class now and a student challenges me in Term One, I tell myself that they could be another Connor. He said it best, with the simple honesty that comes so naturally to children but from which adults often shy: It's hard to argue that people don't deserve a second chance.

12

Goodbye and good luck

THE YEAR 12 graduation ceremony was held in an expansive auditorium owned by a local church, though The School and the event were entirely secular. Students and their families were spread across hundreds of tables before a stage complete with projector screen and sound system. Ana and I sat with Wambui's family. The students were backstage, waiting to be presented with their certificates.

'I saw a lot of them outside in the carpark.' Ana kept craning her neck to scan the crowd, searching for her own students. 'Every single one of them was happy. Scores, apprenticeships, gap years, whatever. How did the Literature kids go?'

'I'm proud of them,' I said. 'There were some awesome scores, especially Mya's.'

That was true. Still, I felt that it was Claire who had really achieved something on the day of the exam, even if it would never be reflected in her final ranking. I thought of the students at the very top of that rank, the tiny number of young people around the country awarded ATARs of 99.95 for their academic performance. How many of them had experienced the struggles of children like Claire, or Wambui, or Charlie?

Some, I thought. I had to believe that the system was fair.

One by one, the Year 12 coordinator began calling out the names of the graduating class. There is a tradition at The School that, as each student walks onto the stage, their Year 7 photograph is beamed onto the projector. Laughter and applause filled the auditorium as confident young men and women were reduced to wild pigtails, braces, ridiculously squinted grins.

'Oh my *God*!' It looked as though Ana might cry. 'My *heart*.'

Eventually it was Wambui's turn. I looked at her parents, thinking of all they had been through and all the lessons I had learnt from their daughter's writing. They beamed. For how long had they dreamt of this moment? At least since Wambui had been born, I thought, and perhaps in an abstract way long before that. They had given her a good life, and that was all they had ever wanted – was the only reason, really, that Jacob had risked his life on the security patrol night after night. After that thief was killed the burglaries and attacks in Kaandiki had stopped. The people of the village raised funds to install two new police posts, and made sure they were manned by officers who could be trusted. They knew that through hard work and sacrifice things could be made better, and that was a value their graduating daughter would carry out into the world.

As we looked up onto that stage more faces passed: Charlie, Tim, Mya, Claire, the rest of my Literature students for whom I cared just as deeply.

The first to visit our table after the presentation were Mya and Tim, resplendent in gold formal gown and tuxedo respectively. I do not believe in asking students their scores, so only asked if they were happy; the question was superfluous.

'You know what my highlight was, Doc?' I loved Tim for his intrinsic understanding that almost every moment in life has a punchline. 'Getting an A+ on my Art exam. My teacher said I was going to fail. Must have been those writing skills I picked up in Lit. Peter Carey saves the day again.'

Years before, while helping raise her little brother as her mother slaved away in a bakery, Mya had made a choice. There was a world beyond Seadale, a world of wonder where pyramids thrust up from ancient sands and voices four thousand years old whispered into the present. The only way to access that world was through learning. And she had made sacrifices: the sport unplayed, the parties unattended, the movies unwatched and the concerts unheard. Now, on this glittering night, it had all been validated. Mya's score was higher than even she had anticipated. She had cried when she saw it. What really mattered, though, was that she would be getting an offer from Melbourne University to undertake a double major in History and Ancient World Studies.

'I called Mum at work as soon as I saw the score,' she said. 'You should have heard her telling all her co-workers. I don't think she actually knew what it meant, though. I had to explain it to her.'

Mya's achievements would only continue. Before long, the girl from Seadale who had once worn a uniform far too big for her would be at Cambridge University, and undertaking conservation field work at the sites of archaeological digs.

When they had gone I told Ana there were a couple of students I needed to go and find.

Moving through the crowd, I was afflicted with the strange nostalgia that always haunts these events. Everywhere students waved, shook my hand, in some cases asked their parents to photograph us together. Again and again I asked it: 'Are you happy?' Almost invariably the answer was yes, even if a few shrugged, smiled and said that their result was what they had expected. Regardless of ATARs, the future was now theirs. I felt privileged to have played a part in this turning point in their lives. For them, The School now belonged to the past. But did it? Not entirely, for in some ways they *were* The School. To reduce the place to its bricks and buildings and asphalt was an oversimplification. Any school is in a constant state of flux. It is made up of its students, teachers and staff, and in that sense none of us ever leave it behind, but depart as fragments of the mosaic that once was. At reunions we strive to reconstruct its past magic but know we will never quite succeed.

I was beginning to think that Claire had gone home when I heard her voice. 'Hey, Murray.'

She was sitting at a table with her mother. I joined them, chatting for a while before getting to the point.

'Look, I don't want to sound cheesy, Claire, but I was blown away by your courage on the day of the exam. I won't go on and on about it. But it really moved me.'

'Thanks, Murray. *And* for putting up with me for the last few years.'

'Don't be silly. It was a pleasure. And stay in touch. You know where I am.'

There is a danger in a narrative such as this of overlooking the role of students' broader support networks. I congratulated Claire's mother as I left, and knew that my contribution paled in comparison to hers. She would help Claire through the next stage of her life, one that took her into the joys of creative freedom found in poetry and filmmaking. Today I continue to be amazed by Claire's work.

The crowd had thinned somewhat when I found Charlie standing with a glass of water by the bar. He had removed his tie and slung it over his shoulder. We shook hands and it occurred to me that we hadn't spoken since he had won his title.

'It was a great night,' he said, leaning back on that bar and watching as his classmates and their families slowly filed out of the building. 'The first round was tough, let me tell you. I thought I had no hope.'

'Well, you've always had the resilience part covered.'

'Thanks, sir.'

'So when's the next one?' I nudged him in the shoulder. 'I suppose you'll be running twenty kays tonight before bed?'

'I'm actually quitting fighting. For a while, anyway.'

'Yeah?'

He seemed to think for a moment, then nodded. 'Yeah. Other things to focus on. I might go back to it – one day. But I'm leaving it alone for now.'

'Fair enough, Charlie.' I thought again of how empty The School would feel with him gone. 'You've got to do what's right for you.'

'Hey, sir – I had a funny conversation with Mr Sansom earlier. He coordinated me way back in Year 7.'

'What did he say?'

Charlie laughed. 'He congratulated me for graduating. Said, "You were a terror in Year 7 but you came good."'

'That's a funny way of putting it.'

'That's what I thought. But I thanked him. I wanted to say more but I couldn't.'

'What did you want to say?'

'I just wanted to tell him that I wasn't like that because I was a bad kid.'

We walked out together and I wished him well, knowing that he would not need luck. A car pulled up with Tia waving furiously from the driver's seat. Charlie shook my hand for the final time, climbed inside and I watched them drive away.

'Murray! Going home?' I turned and it was Ana.

'Yep. Bedtime for me.'

'Check your pigeonhole first thing tomorrow.'

'Why?'

She called over her shoulder as she kept walking. 'Next year's class lists have gone out.'

'No way!' I shouted after her. 'I'm not ready to think about that yet!'

But I was there first thing, before I had even put my lunch in the fridge. For the moment they were just names, but soon they would be students, and eventually, as I got to know them, human beings who would briefly fill a special place in my own life. And how do I convey what these young people mean to me? How do I explain that, years later, those past students appear in my mind at unexpected times, and I find myself wondering not what they are doing, not where they are, but simply if they are happy? I fear that even this book does not feel like enough.

So all I can do is never take this job for granted. For me, it's the best there is.

Epilogue

Summer's return

THERE HAVE BEEN two principals at The School since David Carver retired. Years have passed and things have changed. There are new buildings and facilities, and much of the brickwork of my childhood has been painted over, modernised. The current principal is young for a school leader, her short hair often streaked with garish colours and an Australian terrier trotting at her heels.

'If you want attention from CJ,' she will tell the students, 'you need to get down to his level.' In response, a hulking Year 12 boy might spread himself out on the asphalt and let the dog clamber over him, its tail flapping and its tongue dripping.

Whenever any decision needs to be made at The School, she always begins by asking: Will this be good for the kids?

This is an important question for any of us, whether we be teachers, parents or simply those wanting to leave the world a better place than we found it.

*

We ring bells to signify important moments, whether they be beginnings or endings. More often than not they conclude things: school lessons and days, boxing matches, even lives in the ancient European tradition of the churchyard. For some cancer patients, a bell is rung to signify the end of the disease and the journey into remission.

For Kelvin there was no bell, just a measured, reasonable conversation with his doctor months after he had learnt of Steve's death. The end of his disease shared similarities with the beginning. There were blood tests, CAT scans, anxious waits. Still, he had suspected the disease was beaten for a long time. All the specialists had insisted that the treatments were working and the tumours shrinking. When he first hinted at the 'R word' with his mother, however, she had pinched her eyes shut and waved him away, superstitious. She didn't want him to jinx it.

Though he was euphoric at the official news, there was no formal celebration. It seemed wrong, somehow, with Steve gone and all those other children still suffering on the ward. Kelvin's way of celebrating was simply being with his friends and getting back into training.

Years passed. He and Jen (his greatest childhood competitor) fell in love. Kelvin was eventually voted The School's vice-captain, and at his own graduation there was a special guest: Margaret. It had been a longer journey for her, but, like her friend, she had escaped the ward. She would survive.

After finishing Year 12, Kelvin and Jen travelled the world together.

'My experience of cancer and all the reflections I had – in primary school as well as high school – made me who I am today,' he said recently. 'They particularly affected how I interact with others. I like to think I'm more grateful. I wouldn't wish cancer on anybody, but I think hardship in some form is important for young people. It helped me realise that the world doesn't revolve around me and that there are always more important things going on.

'It has given me a lot of strength, too. When I first got back on the sporting field, there was no way I was going to let anybody beat me. I'd look at my opponents and think, *You've got no idea how hard I worked to get back here.* And that would drive me.

'My body isn't entirely recovered. Take my immune system – it's compromised. So I'm very cautious, but not scared. People sometimes ask me if I worry that the cancer could come back. I know it could, but I don't dwell on that. There isn't any point.'

He nodded, a young man with kind eyes and a warm smile who, so long ago, had stood on a primary school footy oval and argued that everybody deserved a chance to play.

'What will be will be.'

*

While writing this book, I looked up Tessa on social media. What I saw was a young woman who I barely recognised. She was tall and carried herself with confidence in those pictures. Her hair was long and the large glasses were no longer so large. I wondered if she still read Lewis Carroll from time to time. I considered sending her a message, but then decided that sometimes the past belongs in the past.

What I did notice was that there were beagles in many of her pictures. I did not know if any of them were Gonzo but supposed it was possible. He would be an old dog now.

I am neither the teacher nor the person I was back then. Like my students, I have learnt and grown. Charlie would be pleased; Greta and I are married now. As I write this, we are expecting our first child.

I hope I will be a good father.

I hope I have been a good teacher, and will continue to be.

One day, when our child is old enough, I know I will take them to the Seadale Carnival. We'll play the games, ride the rides, eat the fairy floss. I'll take them onto the Ferris wheel and point to the lights of the city across the bay, then look back inland at the gloom where The School waits for the first bells of Term One to sound. Childhood passes with flashbulb suddenness but I will do everything I can to ensure our child has the best early years I can offer.

At some point that son or daughter will face their own struggles. I hope, when that day comes, he or she will feel safe enough and loved enough to come to me, perhaps even ask for some advice. Knowing the limits of my own experience, I will sit him or her down, hold them close and say, Let me tell you about a student I once knew.

Acknowledgements

THIS BOOK WOULD not have been possible without the openness, honesty and patience of the many former students and their families who agreed to participate. I was extraordinarily appreciative of the time they spent sharing their stories, answering my questions and, later, helping me get the manuscript as true to their experiences as possible. I have used false names to protect their privacy. People such as Kelvin, Wambui, Charlie, Claire, Teagan and others are the heart and soul of this book. Knowing them and hearing their stories has taught me a great deal and, I hope, made me a better person.

There were also a large number of teachers (from various schools) who shared their thoughts with me but chose to remain anonymous. These people offered memories, opinions and feedback, some of which ended up in the final manuscript. Again, I am extremely grateful for the help they provided.

Some people should be thanked directly for their assistance with the manuscript, in some cases because they contributed ideas and expertise, in other cases because they offered feedback on draft manuscripts. These people are Deb Fisher, Tiffany Greenhill, Lisa Holt, Chris Holton, Bianca Lobo, Kim Murrie, Amra Pajalic, Jovana Rapajic, Megan Seymour, Laura Sykes and Andy Wain.

I would like to acknowledge Regine Abos for her evocative cover design, and Ian McDonald of Simpsons Solicitors for his work on the manuscript. Vanessa Lanaway and Brianne Collins both provided invaluable support through their considerable editing expertise.

Special mention must go to Mathilda Imlah of Picador Australia. Without her, *The School* would not have been written, and her encouragement, support and dedication are things for which I will be forever grateful. I look forward to a lot more coffee and conversation.

Lastly, I would like to acknowledge my wife, another of the most passionate and hard-working teachers I know. What can I say? Charlie, of course, was right.